The Spirit of Things

Cornell University

Julius Bautista, editor

The Spirit of Things

Materiality and Religious Diversity in Southeast Asia

SOUTHEAST ASIA PROGRAM PUBLICATIONS
Southeast Asia Program
Cornell University
Ithaca, New York
2012

Cornell Southeast Asia Program Publications
640 Stewart Avenue, Ithaca, NY 14850-3857

Studies on Southeast Asia No. 58

Printed in the United States of America

ISBN: hc   978-0-87727-788-0
ISBN: pb   978-0-87727-758-3

Cover: designed by Kat Dalton
Cover image: Vietnamese spirit medium in a temple from which the statues were removed during an anti-superstition campaign. Photograph by Laurel Kendall, reprinted with permission.

TABLE OF CONTENTS

Preface:
Motion, Devotion, and Materiality in Southeast Asia

Julius Bautista

The chapters in this volume are based on invited papers delivered during a conference entitled "New Directions in the Study of Material Religion in Southeast Asia," which was held at the National University of Singapore in August 2008. We acknowledge the generous assistance and participation of Professor Bryan S. Turner and Professor Lily Kong, as well as the administrative staff of the Asia Research Institute who facilitated the smooth running of the event. The conference featured Southeast Asianists from universities and museums in the United States, Europe, and the region itself. Collectively, the contributors spoke about the diverse ways in which materiality is crucial to the crafting of personhood and belonging, particularly in the context of religiously diverse states where the demands of citizenship and nationalism often place great strain on religious belief and practice.

The gathering was inspired by the time and place in which it was held, as much as it was by the central problematic that compelled it. Our gathering coincided with the Hungry Ghost Festival in Singapore, when the spirits who wander through the gates of Hell are appeased by burning material objects like paper money or joss sticks throughout the seventh month of the lunar year. In Daoism, burnings performed at one's home altars are an essential part of lifting up petitions to the ancestors and deities. As Tong Chee Kiong and Lily Kong put it, "the bigger the joss sticks, the greater the lift."[1] More recently, however, this ritual has become subjected to increasing governmental control. In March 1998, new regulations, punishable by fines, mandated town councils to provide public bins to contain all burnings. The measures were taken in response to complaints about unsightly ash spots on public spaces, as well as to prevent fire and environmental hazards. But, more significantly, the regulations were consistent with the state's approach to inter-religious relations, which seeks to uphold the ideological commitment to religious co-existence, even if it means imposing penalties to mitigate potential flashpoints of contestation.

While the use of the government bins for discarding burned material has gained some acceptance, a significant number of people still choose to disregard them. After

---

[1] Tong Chee Kiong and Lily Kong, "Religion and Modernity: Ritual Transformations and the Reconstruction of Space and Time," unpublished manuscript, p. 14.

all, as one practitioner put it, how would individual ancestors know which offering is for them if all burnt objects are "mixed up"? Many Singaporeans use their own bins to perform the burnings, and draw a circle of chalk or tea around ritual objects so that the deities can recognize their respective offerings.[2] What is interesting is that such new and recalcitrant engagements with religious materiality have arisen in reaction to modern day, state-driven managerialism. While religious institutions offer formal compliance with government norms, this is often accompanied by a variety of calculated subaltern agencies that material things make possible in a religiously plural landscape. It is with these kinds of agencies that the papers in this volume are concerned.

What the papers in this volume collectively reiterate is that religious materials are embedded in a whole host of embodied practices that enable the faithful to negotiate the often tumultuous experience of living amidst other believers, and the overarching authorities that seek to regulate the conditions under which they do so. In Southeast Asia, this is evident even where the vicissitudes of nationhood and religious pluralism call for the management or even restriction of the possession, display, or use of religious materials. What we see in many cases, however, is that the call for plurality actually renders religious objects more important, as they are often the means by which the distinctiveness of a particular faith is reiterated and (in this case, literally) "ring fenced" in a field of competing religious discourses.

In our group, the discussion of these themes pivoted around the concept of *motion*, of which there are three distinct permutations. The first concerns the locomotion of objects themselves, in the process of ritual or procession. What happens to people's faith in the process of the object's movement? How does the movement of religious objects provide the conditions for the enactment of religious piety? The change in the physical location of objects, either through the agency of the faithful or through the perception of an object's own agency, is a crucial part of the internal subjectivities of those around the object. When objects move, people's emotions and sensibilities are likewise placed in motion, forming the basis for specific kinds of social relationships. The examples from Buddhist Laos and the Catholic Philippines stand out in demonstrating that piety is enacted by what I describe as an object's locomotive sociality, or the actual movement of an object of veneration in a social and public capacity.

Secondly, motion can be thought of in terms of the actual objects that circulate in the process of commerce and exchange, legally or illegally, in market places and what could be thought of as *pious economies*. How does the traffic in and of objects exert an impact upon their spiritual value and efficacy? Do the objects diminish in potency or significance when they are bought, sold, or traded? One of the most immediately striking aspects of religious objects traded in the market is the effect of mass production and multiplication on the spiritual meanings of things. In Singapore, as described by one of the panelists in the conference, sociologist Vineeta Sinha, many painted and sculpted stone, clay, or bronze statues, paintings, and photographs of Sanskritic and folk Hindu deities are bought and sold in a frenetically dynamic marketplace. In Cebu City, where I have conducted my own ethnographic research, replicas of the Christ Child Santo Niño—an icon that is thought to be four hundred years old—are often bought by devotees who bypass the

---

[2] Tong Chee Kiong and Lily Kong, "Religion and Modernity: Ritual Transformations and the Reconstruction of Space and Time," *Social & Cultural Geography* 1,1 (2000): 29–44.

official Church store in favor of mercantile chaos generated by the replica stalls around the Basilica.[3]

If one looked only on the surface, one might assume that multitudes of cheaply produced images can hardly match the value of each, respective original on which they are modeled. Yet the value of the replicas is crafted in the context of a market in which the "end user" forges a personal relationship with his or her purchase, an action that, in turn, facilitates a highly individualized connection with deities and the divine. Unlike the original model, replicas are not generally expected to have an exalted place in a grand altar of communal worship. Rather, they are held close to one's body, placed in one's bag, and displayed on car dashboards, personal bookshelves, bedside tables, kitchen cupboards, and computer desks—places that are typically associated with the pursuit of life's toils. Thus, for the buyer, commerce facilitates religious piety. When objects circulate in transactory and reciprocal processes, notions of belief and peity are, in turn, crafted and reconfigured.

The objects that move in "locomotive sociality" or are circulated in a "pious economy" are easily transportable. But not all religious objects can traverse physical space so freely and readily. Sheer size or weight, for example, can preclude the object's movement from one location to the next. This does not mean, however, that relatively immobile religious materials do not have a significant impact upon the lives of the faithful. Many other objects are highly regarded because of their embeddedness to one location. The spiritual potency that is ascribed to these relatively large or heavy religious things is not a function of their capacity to change location. Rather, it is the way they inspire a kinetic energy in those around them that is significant. This is demonstrated, for example, by the "awe" worshippers experience in the presence of enshrined statues or sacred architectures. In this respect, faith is defined by one's being "moved" or inspired by religious materials even if those materials themselves remain static and immobile. This was the third type of motion that we considered. What kind of dynamism did immovable objects inspire and encourage, or, conversely, impede and inhibit?

Certain motionless objects, such as large statues or visual displays, are thought to motivate the energies of the deities and spirits around them, infusing spaces and things with spiritual potency. Others may affect how the human body itself moves, as in ritual performance, trance, spirit possession, and a wide variety of kinesthetic engagements with representations of the divine. Aside from individual movement, static religious materials also affect the movement of collective bodies, such as in religious pilgrimages or migrations across borders. In this context, religious objects influence people's movement within hegemonic state authority, often evoking the larger political and cultural milieu in which the faithful in Southeast Asia are entwined. What had been highlighted in our gathering was not simply the nature, direction, and frequency of an object's actual movement, but how kinetic energies are generated in and around objects that stay put. These energies, in turn, animate bodies, whether individual and communal, as well as the spirits themselves.

The various contributors' concerns are quite similar to each other in that they trace the ways in which religious materiality make it possible for the faithful to negotiate the challenges of citizenship or nationhood. These three permutations of motion and devotion—each of them facilitated through objects, spaces, architecture,

---

[3] Julius Bautista, *"Figuring Catholicism: An Ethnography of the Santo Niño de Cebu"* (Quezon City: Ateneo de Manila University Press, 2010), pp. 34–37.

and images—provided the canvas on which we depicted how the challenge of religious diversity is being met in different places in Southeast Asia. This constituted our attempt to encourage a *thinking beyond belief* in understanding religious traditions, getting into the spirit of things by considering materiality as a meaningful heuristic in the understanding of faith communities.

Julius Bautista
Singapore, September 2011

Introduction: Materiality in a Problematically Plural Southeast Asia

Julius Bautista and Anthony Reid

Tensions ran high in August 2010 when a group of Indonesian clerics under the banner of the Indonesia Ulema Forum (Forum Ulema Indonesia, FUI) protested outside the district government office in Purwakarta, West Java. They demanded that the district head immediately demolish a huge statue of Bima, which had just been erected near the highway between Bandung and Jakarta. Bima is one of the heroic brothers of the Indian epic Mahabharata, who embodies the virtues of strength and loyalty, and who has long been a central figure in Javanese and Sundanese puppet theater. The Purwakarta Regent had the statue erected there to inspire these positive values in the citizenry, and also as a testament to Java's diverse cultural and religious heritage.[1]

The protesters insisted, however, that Bima had a negative impact on the public's economic and religious interests. Their spokesman declared that Bima only exists in people's "superstitious beliefs," and that only "Islamic figures" should be erected in Purwakarta's public spaces. Rallied by hardline clerics, students wielding hammers and blunt objects defied riot police and inflicted significant damage to the statue. Such acts of iconoclasm were vehemently defended as expressions of the need to uphold a distinctive Islamic religious identity, which had been endangered even in what the protestors held to be the "*Santri* City" of Purwakarta. A little over one year later, by September 2011, three other Wayang statues had been burned or vandalized by further attacks, prompting many around Indonesia to call for the government to take action against the "Taliban-minded" perpetrators.[2]

In the chapters that follow, we discuss the various ways in which materiality is crucial to the very formation, enactment, and maintenance of religious belief in Southeast Asia. The vibrant, if contested, pluralism in the region ensures that

---

[1] Antara News Agency, "Indonesian Muslim Clerics in West Java Protest 'Un-Islamic' Bima Statue," *The Jakarta Globe*, August 7, 2010.

[2] "Hardliners Vandalize, Set Alight Wayang Statues in Purwakarta," *The Jakarta Post*, September 18, 2011; and Tami Koestomo, "Letter: Wayang's Destruction," *The Jakarta Post Readers Forum*, September 24, 2011.

materiality is demonstrated in a myriad of ways, some indicative of more recent trends towards religious exclusivism and decontextualized orthodoxies. While global patterns of homogeneity have created new tensions and sporadic violence in Southeast Asia, it is our view that they are also tempered and even subverted by the many instances in which religious materials manifest the creative and edifying engagement with the divine world. Aside from statues of deities, there are a host of ephemeral objects of offering, amulets, relics, artworks, sacred sites, and buildings in the region—all of which reflect the everyday engagement with the divine, and the way beliefs and actions are, in turn, shaped by the interactions with *things*.

Religious pluralism, particularly in the material realm, has long historical roots in Southeast Asia. Its cities were inherently cosmopolitan to a degree unknown in Europe, the more so after the Europeans added their churches to the mix of temples, mosques, and *viharas* (Buddhist monasteries). In the Siamese capital of Ayutthaya, for example, European visitors noted the "great multitude of strangers of different nations ... settled there with the liberty of living according to their own customs, and of publicly exercising their several ways of worship."[3] The Siamese King Narai famously told the Jesuits who sought his conversion that God Himself appeared to prefer being worshipped in a great variety of material forms, since he had created such diversity among his people. In queen-ruled Patani, the Dutch similarly noticed how Malays, Siamese, and Chinese each had distinct religious systems, while even among the last-named they were "not of one mind but of various sects."[4] Even more fundamental than this urban cosmopolitanism, indeed, was the way in which both Indian and Chinese religious systems were more concerned with sacred places, times, objects, and rituals than with doctrines and boundaries. There were, therefore, fundamental realities in Southeast Asia ensuring a richer diversity of religious belief than in Europe.

In the new nation-states of Asia, however, the quest for tighter national integration has placed great strains on this pluralistic pattern. The accessibility of alternative religious views, and their association with ethno-nationalism, have encouraged faith communities to "ring-fence" the distinctiveness of their traditions with the view towards maintaining and enhancing their memberships.[5] It is often in the material realm that this act of defense is most prominently deployed. Since about 1970, for example, Malaysia, Indonesia, and Brunei have built numerous spectacular mosques with state funds, greatly strengthening an official version of what Islam is. The teaching of Islam in state schools produced a lowest common denominator version of belief. A new unification of Islam had developed in Indonesia under Soeharto largely through the Ministry of Religion, and in Malaysia under Dr. Mahathir. This state patronage of Islam, while helping to resolve some internal tensions, has served to stress the boundaries of Islam and what all Muslims must have in common. Just as materiality was a testament to the Southeast Asian acceptance of diversity, so, too, has it been the medium through which tendencies towards exclusivism has been given vociferous expression.

---

[3] Simon de la Loubère, *A New Historical Relation of the Kingdom of Siam* (Kuala Lumpur and New York, NY: Oxford University Press, 1969 [1693]), p. 112.

[4] J. van Neck, in *De Vierde Schipvaart der Nederlanders naar Oost-Indië onder Jacob Wilkens van Neck (1599–1604)*, Vol. I, ed. H. A. van Foreest and A. de Booy (The Hague: Nijhoff for Linschoten-Vereeniging, 1980), p. 223.

[5] Maznah Mohamad, "Making Majority, Undoing Family: Law, Religion and the Islamization of the State in Malaysia," *Economy and Society* 39,3 (2010): 360–84.

In the multi-religious, multi-ethnic environments of Southeast Asia, the public engagement with and through religious materials reveals greater fissures in the liberal ideal of secular disenchantment, according to which religion is reduced to a matter of *belief* that ought be kept out of civic space.[6] Religious pluralism remains a challenge because faith is not simply interiorized belief that demands privatized assent. Faiths have social, public lives that are lived in and through the believer's engagement with tangible things and spaces. This is a point well articulated by an anthropologist of Southeast Asia, Webb Keane, who has pointed out that "Religions may not always demand beliefs, but they will always involve material forms. It is in materiality that they are part of experience and provoke responses, that they have public lives and enter into ongoing chains of causes and consequences."[7]

An analysis of the terrain of religious pluralism, therefore, can certainly not neglect a consideration of how *things* are crucial in a person's realization of ontological, moral, and ethical possibilities. Whether Muslims and Christians are protecting or building one another's sacred places or burning them, or sharing a meal or a handshake or refusing to do so, it is in material things that the plural is realized. Our title indicates that we seek to consider "the spirit of things," by which we do not merely suggest that there is a spiritual element to materials, and that things are often the central focal point of religious activity in the region. The phrase resonates with a tone of intellectual inquiry, which brought together contributors from a rich array of intellectual and disciplinary backgrounds. This work is an endeavor to consider the social, political, and economic outcomes that tangible religious materials make possible or preclude, and, indeed, to examine what pursuing and achieving these outcomes might mean for a person's sense of herself or himself amidst the challenges of a religiously diverse environment.

MANY BUT ONE: CONTESTED RELIGIOUS PLURALISM IN SOUTHEAST ASIA

The humid tropics, including Southeast Asia, was and is peculiarly resistant to homogenizing political structures of any kind. More than elsewhere in Eurasia, these high-rainfall areas have permitted the survival of stateless, animist hunter-gatherers and swidden farmers in the hills, even while peasant rice-farmers, as well as modern cosmopolitan cities, flourish on the plains. Consequently, we find in the region an extraordinary abundance of languages, modes of production, cultures, and belief patterns continuing to coexist in close proximity, in contrast with the relative uniformity that strong states, print media, and modern media generally have established in China, Japan, Europe, and Russia. Fieldworkers continue to report "the enormous religious diversity" of the Mainland uplands, and the "profound religious heterogeneity" of Indonesia.[8]

This has been a fertile field in which a host of religious traditions has taken root. Indigenous religious traditions remain in scattered parts of almost all countries of the

---

[6] José Casanova, *Public Religions in the Modern World* (Chicago, IL: University of Chicago Press, 1994).

[7] Webb Keane, "The Evidence of the Senses and the Materiality of Religion," *Journal of the Royal Anthropological Institute* 14 (2008): s110–s127.

[8] James C. Scott, *The Art of Not Being Governed: An Anarchist History of Upland Southeast Asia* (New Haven, CT: Yale University Press, 2009), p. 156; and Anne Schiller, "An 'Old' Religion in 'New Order' Indonesia: Notes on Ethnicity and Religious Affiliation," *Sociology of Religion* 57,4 (1996): 409.

region, often practiced in addition to or alongside "foreign" faiths. Communities in northern Myanmar, northern Laos, and the interiors of the large Philippine and Indonesian islands overtly practice their indigenous faith traditions and rituals in spite of their minority status and pressures from more powerful ethnic and religious groups. In their dealings with material things, like the offerings placed on old trees and in places of death or sacred remembrance, nominally mainstream believers of Java, the Philippines, and Thailand also honor more ancient traditions. In addition to the varieties of indigenous belief, and the majority of scriptural or world religions, Bali maintains an intensely local religious system under the name of Hinduism; Chinese popular religion (officially Daoist, though often mixed with Buddhism and spiritism) continues to be vibrant particularly in Malaysia, Singapore, and Vietnam; and new Pentecostal groups are making inroads in many other places throughout Southeast Asia. Meanwhile, New Religious Movements (NRMs) within and outside of the mainstream religions add greatly to the diversity of material religion in Southeast Asia. Reform and Prophet-based movements in Burma, Thailand, and Vietnam have arisen in reaction to the influence and spread of Buddhism and Christianity. In Indonesia, messianic and apocalyptic movements have drawn from Javanese mysticism to offer alternatives to both indigenous and institutional religious networks.[9] In the Philippines, millenarian and syncretistic *Colorum* sects present varying interpretations of the Christian message, often in terms that intersect with precolonial *anitismo* beliefs even while expressed through the veneration of Christian icons.[10]

Yet this is not the whole story. A more exclusivist character tempers religious plurality in Southeast Asia. Consider that overwhelming majorities of the populations of Indonesia (86 percent), the Philippines (80 percent), Thailand (94 percent), Burma (89 percent), and Cambodia (92 percent) today formally subscribe not just to a single religion, but to a single school of that religion: Sunni Islam of the Shafi'i legal school (*mazhab*) in Indonesia, Roman Catholic Christianity of the Latin rite in the Philippines, and Buddhism of the Theravada School in the Mainland countries.[11] Although Malaysia looks statistically more diverse, it is the least tolerant of any state towards its majority population, legally allowing no Malay at all to be other than a Sunni Muslim. Church-burnings directed at minorities outside the *"Umma,"* and violence towards those within it who have been deemed to act in a deviant way (Ahmadis most recently), have made a very public impact even though carried out by tiny minorities.[12]

In comparison with the situation in older centers of competitive Abrahamic (or revealed) religion, religious fault lines in Southeast Asia remain weakly institutionalized, perhaps just because of the "frontier" character of the scriptural

---

[9] Merle C. Ricklefs, *Mystic Synthesis in Java: A History of Islamization from the Fourteenth to Early Nineteenth Centuries* (Norwalk, CT: Eastbridge, 2006).

[10] See Julius Bautista, *Figuring Catholicism: An Ethnohistory of the Santo Niño de Cebu* (Quezon City: Ateneo de Manila University Press, 2010); and Reynaldo Clemeña Ileto, *Pasyon and Revolution: Popular Movements in the Philippines, 1840–1910* (Manila: Ateneo de Manila University Press, 1979).

[11] For statistical information on the religious profile of Southeast Asia, see Gary Bouma, Rod Ling, and Douglas Pratt, eds., *Religious Diversity in Southeast Asia and the Pacific National Case Studies* (Dordrecht and London: Springer, 2010), part 2.

[12] "Religious Persecution in Indonesia: Murder in God's name," *The Economist*, February 8, 2011.

religions there. Where old beliefs survive in the private domain, they do so as "women's business," and in Indonesia as ill-defined *adat* (custom). Although Islam and Buddhism cover a huge variety of beliefs and practices on the ground, not even such relatively coherent sub-cultures as the *waktu telu* (a variant of Islam) of Lombok are recognized by the modern and official sector. In the Philippines, *espiritistas* (spirit mediums), *albularyos* (shamans), and *mangagamots* (faith healers) continue to be consulted by a large cross-section of rural and urban folk, even while their informal networks and ad-hoc associations are vigorously denounced as "illicit" by Church authorities.[13]

What could account for such homogenizing tendencies, seemingly in conflict with a fundamental acceptance of diversity? There are at least two aspects specific to Southeast Asia's political and social history that are relevant to this question. Firstly, the periods of expansion of precolonial states have consistently ridden on the back of homogenization in the religious field. Precolonial kings, especially those rendered newly wealthy through the "Age of Commerce," had a habit of embracing externally validated orthodoxy or orthopraxy. This was a way in which they could arm themselves with a new kind of legitimacy that could undercut the local legitimacies of every lineage and sacred place. We may think of the example of Tai and Mon kings in the fifteenth century who sent missions of monks to Sri Lanka to bring back Mahavihara rites of ordination, which they then insisted were the only legitimate ones, thereby turning the new *sangha* into an instrument of unification they could control.[14]

Secondly, anti-imperial nationalism in the twentieth century had the effect of homogenizing religious identity. In Southeast Asia, the dominant form of nationalism was one that sought the unity of what Sukarno called the *kaum sini* ("us here") against the *kaum sana* ("them there").[15] *Sarekat Islam* in Indonesia and the Young Men's Buddhist Association in Burma, for example, mobilized people around the majority religion before the idea of secular nationalism was understood. In general, however, anti-imperial nationalism made efforts in the 1930s to embrace Christian and other minorities in the broadest possible front. Only in Thailand, where anti-imperial nationalism was not a persuasive option, did the religious element become a necessary central feature of the nationalist triad—king, nation/race, and religion. In Thai nationalism's most extreme form during the 1940s, Phibun Songkhram encouraged moves against Christian, Muslim, and Chinese minorities with a ferocity not usually associated with the "land of smiles."[16]

Southeast Asia's traditional openness to religious diversity, therefore, has been challenged by both premodern and anticolonial efforts to commandeer avenues towards spiritual transcendence, often in ways that have complemented specific visions of citizenship and authority. These examples may suggest that the celebrated

---

[13] See Robert Love, *The Samahan of Papa God: Tradition and Conversion in a Tagalog Peasant Religious Movement* (Manila: Anvil, 2004).

[14] Anthony Reid, *Southeast Asia in the Age of Commerce, 1450–1680, Volume One: The Lands below the Winds* (New Haven, CT: Yale University Press, 1988), p. 195; Victor B. Lieberman, *Strange Parallels: Southeast Asia in Global Context, c. 800–1830, Volume 1: Integration on the Mainland* (Cambridge: Cambridge University Press, 2003), pp. 43–44, 430–31.

[15] Anthony Reid, *Imperial Alchemy: Nationalism and Political Identity in Southeast Asia* (Cambridge and New York, NY: Cambridge University Press, 2010), pp. 8–10, 28–30.

[16] Shane Strate, "An Uncivil State of Affairs: Fascism and Anti-Catholicism in Thailand, 1940–1944," *Journal of Southeast Asian Studies* 42,1 (2011): 59–87.

tolerance of Southeast Asian countries is no better able to resist nationalism and religious exclusivity in modern guise than are countries elsewhere. The question that needs to be addressed is whether or not the fundamental sources of religious tolerance in Southeast Asia's more distant past have been completely expunged by the modern factors that make for homogeneity.

The essays in this volume suggest otherwise. While the state-defined versions of pluralism are manifested through the regulation, and at times cooption, of religious materiality, the persistent and continued use of materials in ways that defy the state testifies to what Keane has called an "anxious transcendance."[17] In this volume, we think of religious materiality as an ensemble of practices in which the crafting of individual religious subjectivity becomes coterminous with assertions of group distinctiveness. More than acting merely as paraphernalia or the tangible manifestation of interiorized belief, materials facilitate platforms from which alternative claims to pluralism can be upheld, even to the extent of provoking regimes that seek to regulate religious diversity and unchecked public demonstrations of religious vitality.

THE MATERIALITY OF BELIEF

In this volume, "religious materials" is a term that collectively refers to objects and things as well as places and structures, and it is used in a way that is expansive enough to accommodate a diversity of form, size, age, number, construction, and craftsmanship. To be sure, the chapters that follow discuss things that one would intuitively think of as "religious," such as statues, icons, monuments, relics, and buildings that bear the likeness and representational register of religious symbol and personality. But it is also important to think about (as authors in this volume do) the things that may not immediately evoke religious ideas—like money, cars, theater props, and water—to underscore the diverse ways that, as Daniel Miller has put it, "objects make selves" in religiously plural Southeast Asia. There have been some significant scholarly attempts to situate the material as a central concern in the humanities and social sciences.[18] In 1986, Arjun Appadurai described in *The Social Life of Things: Commodities in Cultural Perspective* how commodities lead social lives and have "cultural biographies" as they circulate across different regimes of value. Seminal as that work is, much has changed since the mid-1980s.[19] The end of the Cold War, globalization, the rise and fall of the market, and the global war on terror have altered the intellectual and social terrain considerably. These developments may encourage the claim that, while religion and terrorism have "taken over" from ideology as the master "problem" of the twenty-first century, environmental degradation, such as climate change, is rapidly shaping up as the predominant challenge humans face on a global scale. What remains constant in all of these scenarios is that they each evoke the significance of *things* as the locus of human engagement with the social world, whether as commodities that manifest the

---

[17] Webb Keane, "Epilogue: Anxious Transcendence," in *The Anthropology of Christianity*, ed. Fenella Cannell (Durham, NC: Duke University Press, 2006), pp. 308–25.

[18] Daniel Miller, "Materiality: An Introduction," in *Materiality*, ed. Daniel Miller (Durham, NC: Duke University Press, 2005), pp. 1–50.

[19] Arjun Appadurai, *The Social Life of Things: Commodities in Cultural Perspective* (Cambridge: Cambridge University Press, 1986).

ideological commitment to liberal free markets, or as the stuff of the pervasive hyper-consumption that must be curbed in the name of environmental sustainability. Given that things lead social, political, economic, and ecological lives, it is important to investigate the kinds of religious lives they lead as they move through different regimes of devotion and piety.

The foremost thinkers who are taking up this challenge show some complementarities in their ideas about materiality as central to the crafting of people's beliefs.[20] In *Materiality*, Daniel Miller calls for a "republic of mutual respect," which is a mentality that acknowledges that the faithful and the materials they engage with are embedded in processes of individual self-construction and renewal. Miller calls for ethnographic practice in particular to " ... focus upon how precisely our sense of ourselves as subjects [is] created ... In short, we need to show how the things that people make, make people."[21]

David Morgan's call to "materialize belief," meanwhile, encourages a rethinking of the concept of religion as an ensemble of assertions that demand and proclaim ascent (the ideal of disenchantment in a religiously plural society), towards considering (1) the material properties of things, and (2) the sensory experiences that things elicit in the process of their use in ritual. In his volume entitled *Religion and Material Culture: The Matter of Belief*, Morgan focuses on the "use of things, the sensation of things, the cultivation of feeling that objects, spaces, and performances induce and are in turn colored by."[22] Materializing belief, therefore, means attending to a broad spectrum of sensory experience, "a matrix in which belief happens as touching, seeing, hearing and tasting, feeling and emotion, as will and action, as imagination and intuition."[23] Materiality, rather than being peripheral to and secondary to belief, invites us to expand our very definition of religious belief itself. Belief is not simply a matter of doctrinal, theological, or scriptural transmission, privatized and internalized in the name of securing religious harmony amid diversity. It is crafted, rather, from a topography of underlying assumptions, which are conditioned by tangible things that are "out there" in the public sphere.

Webb Keane's work on Sumba, Indonesia, offers a contextually relevant framework from which we can pursue a study of materiality in Southeast Asia.[24] The approach to material things cannot be based upon an analysis of language or texts alone, he argues, but rather should stem from an emphasis on the historically specific background assumptions that undergird these things and their significance. These "semiotic ideologies" are shared ideas about words and things that condition commonsense understandings of concepts such as "freedom," "agency," and, I would suggest, "diversity." The valuable contribution that Keane's work brings to

---

[20] Over the past decade, several academic gatherings have taken this discussion further. Conferences such as "Thinking through Things: Theorizing Artifacts in Ethnographic Perspective" at the University of Cambridge in October 2004, and "Things: Material Religion and the Topography of Divine Spaces" at the University of Amsterdam in June 2007 encourage us to question, if not abandon altogether, the conventional dichotomies of concept/object, idea/thing, and representation/stuff.

[21] Miller, "Materiality: An Introduction," pp. 27–28.

[22] David Morgan, *Religion and Material Culture: The Matter of Belief* (Oxford and New York, NY: Routledge, 2010), p. xiii.

[23] Ibid.

[24] Webb Keane, *Christian Moderns: Freedom and Fetish in the Mission Encounter* (Berkeley and Los Angeles, CA: University of California Press, 2007).

the discussion is a nuanced account of the relationship between thought, speech, action, and materiality. His is a dialectical approach to the process of objectification, in which varieties of belief (not just religious) are linked to the public, external materiality of words, objects, and practices. In this way, Keane provides a framework for an approach to material religion that problematizes the primacy that is typically placed on interiorized, "sincere" thought.

SYNOPSIS AND OVERVIEW OF THE STRUCTURE

The approaches to materiality above encourage us to seek out those tacit assumptions that condition and produce engagements with material forms in the region. In response to this, the contributors discuss the multifaceted settings in which materials craft spiritual life amid the challenges posed by religious plurality. The chapters are divided into four sections, arranged not so much according to the kind of religious materials they discuss, or the places in which these materials are located, but according to the economic, political, cultural, and performative contexts in which these objects are embedded. Taken together, the chapters enable us to reflect comparatively across a rich tapestry of cultural, linguistic, and historical family resemblances in Southeast Asia.

In the section entitled "Commodification, Consumption, and Exchange," Laurel Kendall, Vu Thy Thanh Tâm, and Nguyễn Thị Thu Hương, (chapter 1), and Johan Fischer (chapter 2) consider religious materials when they are caught up in the frenetic circulatory forces of market exchange. Ho Chi Minh City and Kuala Lumpur exemplify principles that are gaining increasing currency in Southeast Asian urban spaces. Economic prosperity is an ideal citizens aspire to, and pragmatism is the mindset with which to achieve it. Both essays trace the significance of religious materials in the often creative negotiation between piety and commercial pragmatism. Kendall, Vu, and Nguyễn ask whether religious objects in Vietnam "can still be agents" amid contrasting forces that, on the one hand, inscribe a monetary value on their circulation and, on the other, subjects them to a state-sponsored iconoclasm in which their value is diminished. Johan Fischer's essay on Islamized Proton cars in Malaysia encourages us to inquire into the same interplay of market consumption and religious piety, given that these cars are not simply indicators of class status but also indexical of the modes of consumer behavior that bear social and religious capital in a rapidly rising economic sphere, such as urban Malaysia.

In the second section, "Ethnicity and Nationalism," Janet Hoskins (chapter 3), Klemens Karlsson (chapter 4), Yeoh Seng Guan (chapter 5), and Alexandra de Mersan (chapter 6) discuss how crucial themes of state-formation, ethnic conflict, and nationalism are embedded in and through the reverence for spaces and devotion to objects. The engagement with religious materials is particularly crucial in regimes that have highly regulated, managerial (or in some respects repressive) policies on religion, as in the cases of Vietnam, Malaysia, Singapore, and Myanmar. In these places, the religious lives of citizens are made to conform to a state-defined vision of community and nation, often resonating with the ideal of religious exclusivism that is, at times, hostile to the inherent principle of heterogeneity in the region. Even where states formally encode religious and ethnic diversity as part of civic life, as is the case in Malaysia, the vehement insistence by public officials that they must be subordinated to a narrowly defined national identity ironically renders ethnic and religious harmony increasingly fragile and elusive.

In these kinds of tension-ridden political environments, it is interesting to juxtapose the Grand Temple of Caodai in Vietnam and the Bukit Mertajam shrine in Malaysia, both of which, as described by Hoskins and Yeoh, respectively, are ecumenical structures that facilitate the dissolution of those tensions. On the other hand, Buddha images are tangible signifiers of recalcitrance to the military regime in Burma. As Karlsson and de Mersan describe regarding two states in Myanmar, religious materials remain relevant in crafting identities that are either strategically complicit with or resistant to state attempts at suppression and regulation. It is in these examples that we see most prominently the central theme we highlight—that engagement with materiality has the capacity to temper often repressive exclusivist tendencies.

The third section, on "Power, Potency, and Agency," contains essays that take as their starting point the inherent power of objects. In his book *Art and Agency*, Alfred Gell argues that agency can and is "abducted" by viewers, such that art works are considered the equivalents of persons, and are, in that respect, social agents themselves.[25] This process is evident among believers and adherents in Southeast Asia for whom religious objects derive their potency precisely because they have, as it were, a "life of their own." Amulets, for example, are the source of protective potency for Thai volunteers in the Vietnam–American War, as discussed by Richard Ruth (chapter 8), who argues that soldiers were emboldened by an arcane power that is potent regardless of whether the bearers were Buddhists. Kenneth Sillander (chapter 9), meanwhile, traces how permanent household altars called *longan* are sources of reproductive potency among the Bentian of Indonesian Borneo, exerting a volition that is beyond the control even of those who conjure them. For both Thai Buddhists and Bentian animists, the inherent potency of religious objects is only one aspect of their importance. The two chapters draw our attention to those social dynamics among coevals—whether fellow villagers, or fellow conscripts in war— that are forged by the interaction with religious materials. Both the essays ask not only what kinds of potencies are inherent in objects themselves, but also how they empower and inspire the people who engage with them. They inquire into how materials exert an impact upon the vertical and horizontal relationships within faith communities in Southeast Asia, as the faithful negotiate their duties to nation or village. In this sense, materials are, as Keane observes, "crucial media for the self-objectification by which human subjects *know themselves and make themselves recognizable to others.*"[26]

The essays above demonstrate how tangible objects have the power to enable living people to be aware of and interact with beings and powers that are otherwise not perceptible to the human senses. But what happens when materiality is conspicuous in its absence? In Sarawak, "empty" Christian crosses become a problem for Bidayuh Christians, argues Liana Chua (chapter 7), particularly amid the pressures exerted by a Borneo Evangelical Church "unmediated by the physical protocol" of religious materials. Evoking parallels to Matthew Engelke's work on the "problem of presence" among Friday Apostolics in Zimbabwe,[27] Chua's study

---

[25] Alfred Gell, *Art and Agency: An Anthropological Theory* (Oxford and New York, NY: Clarendon Press, 1998).

[26] Keane, *Anxious Transcendence*, pp. 309–10; emphasis added.

[27] Matthew Engelke, *A Problem of Presence: Beyond Scripture in an African Church* (Berkeley, CA: University of California Press, 2007).

discusses the tensions that arise in the process in which religious authority, meaning, and authenticity are invested in certain actions, words, and objects. She demonstrates the ways in which Bidayuhs craft "a set of object- and protocol-centered practices and discourses," through which they "generate effects through things: instead of being ends in themselves." But rather than thinking of Bidayuh Christians as simply fetishists or materialists, Chua focuses on the "futuricity" of their material forms, on the actions and beliefs that empty crosses make possible, and on the memberships that these objects testify to or preclude in a context where religious pluralism often results in a competition for adherents.

In the section entitled "The Spirit in and of Things," three chapters trace the importance of religious objects in the context of rituals, performances, and pilgrimages. Catholics in the Philippines resemble Theravada Buddhists in Northeastern Thailand and Laos in the way they grant importance to the public parading and display of religious materiality. Sandra Cate and H. Leedom Lefferts, Jr. (chapter 10) and Cecilia De La Paz (chapter 11) describe how religious materials craft personal religious petitions into the public sphere through procession. Similarly, as discussed in Margaret Chan's essay (chapter 12), the reverence shown towards anthropomorphic images of Chinese ancestors in Singapore situates the individual's personal, familial obligations in a wider social context of community and kin. In these cases, we can observe the public nature of religious piety in a collective effervescent spirit of *communitas*, whether it is among Buddhists seeking to make merit, Catholics fulfilling their spiritual vows, or those seeking to ensure the welfare of the spirits of ancestors who have passed on. These essays problematize the secular ideal of private, internalized (and ostensibly unintrusive) belief. They demonstrate that religious piety can and must be public, even demonstrative, in order to be meaningfully enacted in a context that remains vibrant, though problematically plural.

CHAPTER 1

ICON, ICONOCLASM, ART COMMODITY: ARE OBJECTS STILL AGENTS IN VIETNAM?

Laurel Kendall, Vũ Thị Thanh Tâm, and Nguyễn Thị Thu Hương

THE INCIDENT

It happened in a village on the southern periphery of greater metropolitan Hanoi in a family shrine honoring the historic General Trần Hưng Đạo, who repelled the thirteenth-century Mongol invasions. Today, Saint Trần's votive tablet, elevated on a ritual chair, sits in state on a well-fitted antique altar, freshly refinished in sparkling red and gold lacquer. Three sticks of incense burn in front of the altar, and there are offerings of cakes and bananas, vases of roses, and a bottle of champagne. The family has honored Trần Hưng Đạo for over a century, from the time of the elderly shrine-keeper's grandfather, and produced succeeding generations of spirit mediums who embodied the saint's formidable exorcistic powers. The shrine-keeper's retired cousin shares vivid childhood memories of an uncle who, in the saint's persona, thrust skewers into his own neck, ingested and expelled fire from the mouth, and slashed his own tongue to empower paper amulets with the gushing blood; the shrine-keeper's cousin tells us that he has not seen anything like it since. The present medium, our host's wife, manifests Trần Hưng Đạo as well as the saint's warrior daughter and other popular religious figures, but does not perform such wondrous feats. In her study of Trần Hưng Đạo, Pham Quyen Phuong makes a contrast between the graceful dances performed by spirit mediums as followers of the Mother Goddess and the violent exorcistic activities of Saint Trần's traditionally male mediums.[1] She also reports a number of women among the saint's mediums today, a phenomenon she attributes to women's recent experiences in socially significant positions.[2]

---

[1] Pham Quynh Phuong, "Tran Hung Dao and the Mother Goddess Religion," in *Possessed by the Spirits: Mediumship in Contemporary Vietnamese Communities*, ed. Karen Fjelstad and Nguyen Thi Hien (Ithaca, NY: Cornell Southeast Asia Program Publications, 2006), pp. 31–54.

[2] Pham Quynh Phuong, "Empowerment and Innovation among Saint Tran's Female Mediums," in *Modernity and Re-enchantment: Religion in Post-revolutionary Vietnam*, ed. Philip Taylor (Singapore: Institute for Southeast Asian Studies, 2007).

In St. Tran's shrine. Photograph by Laurel Kendall

The shrine-keeper proudly describes nearly all of the shrine fittings as more than one hundred years old, and we ask how these things were protected during the anti-superstition campaigns that swept through this and other villages in the Red River Delta during periods of resistance and high socialism (1945 to 1986). We have heard of other shrines in this same village where the statues were cast down, burned, or tossed into the village pond. The shrine-keeper and his cousin lock eyes and laugh. One day in the late 1950s, our host returned home to find a delegation from the Greater Hanoi Bureau of Culture and Information and a commune representative waiting for him with an official order to take down Trần Hưng Đạo's shine. He nodded, burned incense, and told them, "This isn't a matter of just setting things on the floor." His grandfather and father had tended this same shrine; his mother maintained it after his father left for the war. The shrine-keeper claimed that it would be a breach of filial piety for him to take down his family's altar to Saint Trần. He would agree to do this only if the members of the delegation took down the altars dedicated to their own ancestors. Alternatively, he would stand aside and let them take down Saint Trần's shrine themselves, "You are the ones who will have to disassemble it and carry it away with you." The delegation balked at approaching the altar, desisted, and went away.

Even during subsequent anti-superstition campaigns, when other shrines in this same village were destroyed, the family continued to burn incense to Trần Hưng Đạo. In the shrine-keeper's telling, there were multiple reasons for their relative immunity. Trần Hưng Đạo is, after all, Trần Hưng Đạo, a national hero as much as an empowered popular religious figure, and the shrine-keeper and his family also have impeccable patriotic credentials. The shrine-keeper had followed his father into the resistance, returned home wounded, and thereafter worked for the commune administration as a party member. His doubled identity, as a patriotic socialist and an adherent of popular religion, bridges and so confounds de Certeau's "cleavage that organizes modernity" as a contrast between rationality and folklore, between village popular religion and progressive state projects.[3] The would-be iconoclasts who shrank from touching empowered objects in the shrine, the source of the knowing chuckle shared between the shrine-keeper and his cousin decades later, betrayed their own ambivalence, their own ambiguous posture in the shrine. And they are not unique; recent writing on popular religion in Vietnam sometimes compounds the expectations of type by describing party members, civil servants, and former revolutionary fighters who double as spirit mediums and ritual masters.[4]

In this chapter, we approach the topic of sacred objects in contemporary Vietnam with a concern for the ambiguities of enchantment, magic, and materialist rationality (the ideological position that things are "just things"). Specifically, we consider the multiple and complex agency of statues and other ritually empowered objects—like Saint Trần's altar, chair, and tablet. We will consider how the objects' claims to such enchantment have fared in the face of revolutionary iconoclasm in the recent past and their commodification as marketable art and curios in the present. We will argue that the disenchantment of sacred objects is a necessarily incomplete project, and that the reasons for this have something to do with contemporary Vietnamese understandings of recent Vietnamese history, an explicit working of the frictions Latour identified in the problematic relationship between modern people and the material world.[5]

THE POWER OF THINGS

In his provocative rethinking of the anthropology of art, Alfred Gell offers the radical suggestion that people commonly abduct agency to things, that not just pre-modern "animists" but all of us tend sometimes to "see things [including cars and computers] as initiating causal sequences of a particular type, that is, events caused by acts of mind or will or intention rather than the mere concatenation of physical events."[6] Gell invokes the philosophical notion of "abduction," the common mental operation whereby the subject imputes causation without immediate proof (I see smoke; I abduct fire as the cause). He thus moves the idea of object agency from associations with, and imputations of, "primitive thought" into the domain of sociological process; people enter into relationships with things, and these relationships can be examined in the manner that anthropologists examine the rights and obligations that obtain in other relationships. This is a complement to and also a more radically object-centered position than Arjun Appadurai's seminal observation

---

[3] Michel de Certeau, *The Practice of Everyday Life* (Berkeley, CA: University of California Press, 1984), p. 6.

[4] Nguyễn Văn Huy and Phạm Lan Hương, "The One-eyed God at the Vietnam Museum of Ethnology: The Story of a Village Conflict," *Asian Ethnology* 67,2 (2008): 201–18; Vũ Hồng Thuật, "Amulets and the Marketplace," *Asian Ethnology* 67,2 (2008): 237–56; and Q. P. Pham, "Empowerment and Innovation."

[5] Bruno Latour, *We Have Never Been Modern* (Cambridge, MA: Harvard University Press, 1993).

[6] Alfred Gell, *Art and Agency: An Anthropological Theory* (Oxford: Clarendon Press, 1998), pp. 16, 13–18.

that things have "social lives," that they move between different domains of social construction and different regimes of value that are best apprehended through a focus on the peregrination of the things themselves.[7] Following Appadurai, Richard Davis describes Hindu images as "fundamentally social beings whose identities are … repeatedly made and remade through interactions with humans."[8] In Gell's scheme, however, the object is not so much puppet as provocateur, inspiring devotion, fear, awe, or even vandalism. Art historian David Freedberg anticipates the notion of object agency in his provocative *The Power of Images*, considering "the active, outwardly remarkable responses of beholders as well as the beliefs (insofar as they are capable of being rerecorded) that motivate them to specific actions and behavior. But such a view of responses is predicated on the efficacy and effectiveness (imputed or otherwise) of images."[9] Considering the human form in Western representational traditions, and with a nod to "primitive art" in museum displays, Freedberg makes a speculative and ultimately essentialist appeal to universal human emotions that might account for the sometimes uncanny responses provoked by images—both profound devotion and impassioned acts of destruction. In contrast, Gell posits "abducted agency" as a generalized process rather than as specific content, thus permitting a broad and varied exploration of relationships between people and things—including, but not restricted to, figurative images—in diverse settings that admits the possibility of different reactions to common events—a critical point in our discussion.

Abducted agency, in multiple guises, is at play in the story of the reluctant iconoclasts at Trần Hưng Đạo's shrine. The shrine-keeper described his reluctance to take down the shrine as an obligation to his parents and ancestors, mediated through the shrine, which functioned as a material and sacred site. He drew equivalence to similar mediations that might take place in relation to ancestral altars in every village home. The policies that the members of the delegation were meant to uphold also abducted the objects in the shrine as agentive, but in a negative sense. This agency was thought to foster false, irrational, superstitious beliefs that ran counter to the objectives of a modern socialist society, so that the iconoclasts were opposing, in effect, the agency of false agency, the sacred object as a counter-revolutionary agent. In this sense, the things in the shrine "provoked" an iconoclastic response, a phenomenon we will return to below.[10] At the same time, at odds with the policy they were sent to enforce and distinct from the Confucian pieties expressed by the shrine-keeper, all parties to this incident shared in the tacit understanding that the objects in the shrine had been empowered by a ritual master. It would be, or could be, dangerous to remove them without taking proper ritual precautions. In effect, this is an instance of what Latour calls "iconoclash," "when one does not know, one hesitates, one is troubled by an action for which there is no way to know, without further inquiry, whether it is destructive or constructive."[11]

---

[7] Arjun Appadurai, ed., *The Social Life of Things: Commodities in Cultural Perspective* (Cambridge: Cambridge University Press, 1986).

[8] Richard H. Davis, *Lives of Indian Images* (Princeton, NJ: Princeton University Press, 1997), p. 8.

[9] David Freedberg, *The Power of Images: Studies in the History and Theory of Response* (Chicago, IL: University of Chicago Press, 1989), p. xxix.

[10] See Gell, *Art and Agency*, pp. 63–64; and Freedberg, *The Power of Images*, chapter 14.

[11] Bruno Latour, "What is Iconoclash? Or is there a World beyond the Image Wars?" in *Iconoclash: Beyond the Image Wars in Science, Religion, and Art*, ed. Bruno Latour and Peter Weibel (London: MIT Press, 2002), p. 2.

In this same community, villagers describe how, during an anti-superstition campaign in the 1970s, statues were removed from shrines protecting the banks of the Red River, cast into the village pond, or burned. They abduct subsequent illness and misfortune to the agency of violated statues. In a widely circulated story, the wife of the man who drowned the statues went mad, or one of the policemen who carried the statues out of a small family temple that protected the riverbank saw his own son carried away in a flood and died himself within a few months, or, in another version, the policeman drowned and his father died a month later. Another policeman gave a small statue to his son who kicked and abused it, and grew up to become a drug addict. The woman who rescued the statue has a good life, with children living abroad who send her money.[12] The villagers consider the pond an inauspicious place and use the adjacent land as residences for schoolteachers who come from outside the community because no one familiar with the story of the statues would dare to live there.

In their study of another Red River Delta village, Nguyễn and Phạm describe how the statue of a tutelary god was improperly inducted into the communal house in place of a tablet.[13] Tablets direct supplications toward a deity that has been animated in a statue in a distant temple, something in the manner of a spiritual cell phone, while a statue is a more immediate presence. While the sponsoring family described the induction as an act of religious devotion and community philanthropy, others saw it as a means of transforming the communal house (*đình*) into a temple (*đền*) where worshippers' donations would line the pockets of the management committee. When the statue was ritually deanimated and removed from the communal house, the original donor's daughter-in-law called out a curse on the opposing faction, claiming that the wrath of the tutelary god would fall upon them. A decade later, villagers speculated that, to the contrary, the tutelary had exacted punishment on the donor's immediate family through the death of his senior daughter-in-law and the debilitating illness of his son. Shaun Malarney similarly describes afflictions and punishments cast by tutelary deities on those who "have treated the communal houses in an inappropriate or offensive manner" or on a man who "threw a statue of the Buddha down the well."[14]

During the years when the authorities converted temples and communal houses to secular uses, statues dedicated to the Mother Goddesses and their retinues were sometimes stored in a temple's forbidden room, the backmost chamber closed to all but the shrine-keeper. We heard repeatedly that these statues survived intact as much because potential thieves were afraid of retribution from the Mother Goddess as owing to the absence of a market.[15] A spirit medium described how in 1983 or 1984, a man from another place passed by this medium's temple, which was not being maintained at the time, and stole two small god images, thinking that he would take them home and venerate them. The thief put the statues into his bag, but

---

[12] Laurel Kendall, Vũ Thị Thanh Tâm, and Nguyễn Thị Thu Hương, "Beautiful and Efficacious Statues: Magic and Materialism in Vietnamese Popular Religion," *Material Religion: The Journal of Objects, Art and Belief* 6,1 (2010): 60–85.

[13] Nguyen and Pham, "The One-eyed God at the Vietnam Museum of Ethnology."

[14] Shaun K. Malarney, *Culture, Ritual, and Revolution in Vietnam* (New York, NY: Routledge Curzon, 2002), pp. 93–94.

[15] One major Hanoi spirit medium temple remained completely intact even when everyone fled the site for several days during heavy bombing.

for some mysterious reason, he could not move beyond the temple gate. He stood frozen at the threshold until some villagers saw and apprehended him. At the People's Committee Office, the chief of police made a report and then locked the statues inside his cabinet, neglecting to return them to the temple. Two nights later, the guards observed that whenever they turned out the light, mysterious noises emanated from the cabinet but ceased once they turned on the light. They reported this to their chief whose mother promptly brought bananas and other fruit to make offerings and apologize to the deities.[16]

MAKING SACRED

Viet popular religion recognizes statues as particularly potent sites of object agency. As elsewhere in the Buddhist world,[17] in Chinese popular religion,[18] and as with the Hindu "idols" described by Gell and others,[19] a temple statue in Vietnam is ritually animated with the active presence of the deity. It becomes "a locus for person-to-person encounters with divinities ... [and] obeys the social rules laid down for idols as co-present others (gods) in idol-form."[20] To bring the statue to this state, a ritual specialist fills a cavity in the statue body with amulets and other appropriate matter, making, in Gell's terms, a "mind-homunculus" that becomes ritually animated with the active, conscious presence of the god or Buddha. In a ritual of *hô thần nhập tượng*, or "calling the god into the statue," the ritual master inducts the deity into the statue body and awakens its senses. Like a spirit medium during the act of incarnation, the animated statue *is* the deity.[21]

The study of different Asian traditions reveals that the empowerment of things is accomplished both through subsidiary material (such as animation packets) and non-material acts (the recitation of texts and accompanying ritual acts), and that statues in

---

[16] Kendall, Vũ, and Nguyễn, "Beautiful and Efficacious Statues."

[17] Paul Groner, "Icons and Relics in Eison's Religious Activities," in *Living Images: Japanese Buddhist Icons in Context*, ed. Robert H. Sharf and Elizabeth Horton Sharf (Stanford, CA: Stanford University Press, 2001); Donald K. Swearer, "Presencing the Buddha in Northern Thailand: Perspectives from Ritual and Narrative," in *Buddhist Legacies in Mainland Southeast Asia*, ed. François Lagirarde and Paritta Chalermpow Koanantakool (Paris: Publications de l'École française d'Extrême-Orient, 2006); Chandra L. Reedy, "The Opening of Consecrated Tibetan Bronzes with Interior Contents: Scholarly, Conservation, and Ethical Considerations," *Journal of the American Institute for Conservation* 30,1 (1991): 13–34; Chandra L. Reedy, "Religious and Ethical Issues in the Study and Conservation of Tibetan Sculpture," *Journal of the American Institute for Conservation* 31,1 (1992): 41–50.

[18] James Robison, *Inside Asian Images: An Exhibition of Religions Statuary from the Artasia Gallery Collection* (Ann Arbor, MI: Institute for the Humanities, University of Michigan, 2007); and Margaret Chan, "Bodies for the Gods: Image Worship in Chinese Popular Religion," in this volume.

[19] Gell, *Art and Agency*, pp. 130–35; Davis, *Lives of Indian Images*; and Diana L. Eck, *Darsan, Seeing the Divine Image in India*, 3rd ed. (New York, NY: Columbia University Press, 1998), pp. 51–55.

[20] Gell, *Art and Agency*, pp. 125, 128.

[21] Strictly speaking, *Hô thần nhập tương* sacralizes all of the statues in the temple. When statues are added sequentially, a smaller temporary incarnation might be held. See Kendall, Vũ, and Nguyễn, "Beautiful and Efficacious Statues"; Nguyễn and Phạn, "The One-eyed God"; Gell, *Art and Agency*, p. 125; and Chan, "Bodies for the Gods."

human form are not the only objects so empowered.[22] In Vietnam, animation locates statues in a more potent locus of worship than other objects of devotion found on or near Vietnamese altars, such as incense burners, pictures, photographs, tablets, spirit chairs, and blocks for printing amulets. Even so, altars and their significant contents are activated through appropriate ritual procedures and become objects of abducted agency. The terms and protocols of an agentive relationship govern the care, use, and placement of objects related to an altar, as well as their removal from an altar and possible disposal. Before the keeper of Trần Hưng Đạo's shrine could initiate his project of re-gilding the shrine fittings, he asked Saint Trần's permission to do so with a toss of coins, a necessary protocol that also precedes a statue's removal from a shrine. And as in the case of statues, before taking the chair and tablet down from the altar, the shrine-keeper summoned a high-ranking ritual master to perform the elaborate ritual that would deactivate these objects. Otherwise, "no one would dare to touch them." Nguyễn Thị Hiền has described how the infelicitous turning of an incense bowl, without asking permission of the deity to whom it was dedicated, became the putative cause of a young man's mental instability.[23] Not paying scrupulous attention to the ritual master's instructions when installing or carrying an amulet can also be abducted as the source of illness and misfortune.[24]

While ritual masters perform the ritual work of calling a deity into a statue and of activating altars, altar fittings, and amulets, these acts have been preceded by processes of artisanal production that combine technologies of magic and craft in a manner reminiscent of Trobriand canoe building and gardening.[25] Elsewhere, we have described the procedures of self-consciously traditional statue carvers and bronze casters in the Red River Delta of Vietnam who observe a variety of taboos and precautions in their workshops.[26] A series of small rituals punctuates the process of statue-making; these span the act of receiving the initial commission to initiating carving to the client's acceptance of the completed statue. These acts are described both as making the statue a more beautiful, pure, and efficacious container for the deity and as ensuring an auspicious outcome for the workshop itself. Mr. Nguyễn Bá Hạ, a master carver, describes his craft as a quasi-religious act, "doing the gods' work," for which the carver must have a strong moral sense. A carver who is dishonest about his products' quality and price will soon become jobless, either owing to dissatisfied customers or through divine retribution, even as the gods and Buddhas reward a carver who performs well. A well-made statue is pleasing to the gods and, consequently, auspicious for all who have dealings with it.[27]

---

[22] These concerns are addressed in the contributions by Daniella Berti, Robert M. Gimello, and others to Phllis Granoff and Koichi Shinohara, eds., *Images in Asian Religions: Texts and Contexts* (Vancouver: University of British Columbia Press, 2004); and, outside Buddhist and Hindu practice, in Liana Chua, "The Problem with 'Empty Crosses': Thinking through Materiality in Bidayuh Religious Practices," in this volume.

[23] Nguyễn Thị Hiền, "Yin Illness," *Asian Ethnology* 67,2 (2008): 305–22.

[24] Vũ, "Amulets and the Marketplace."

[25] Bronislaw Malinowski, *Magic, Science, and Religion and other Essays by Bronislaw Malinowski* (Garden City, NY: Doubleday Anchor Books, 1954).

[26] Kendall, Vũ, and Nguyễn, "Beautiful and Efficacious Statues."

[27] A carver's integrity and experience comes into play when he selects wood for the statues. Carvers use jackfruit (*mít*), said to repel insects with its bitter taste, for religious statues. The material must be core wood that is not infested with woodworm and does not have knots, and the base of the tree must form the base of the statue. Ông Đồng Đức, a prominent spirit

A similarly complex process attends the carving of a woodblock for printing amulets. The carver first seeks the deity's permission to undertake the task, then purchases the wood only on an auspicious day, and conducts an appropriate ritual on an auspicious day to initiate the carving.[28] The proportions of statues and altars are talismanic, coinciding with auspicious measures on a traditional Chinese-derived carpenter's ruler, and the different materials of production have relative efficacy in the Chinese five-element theory (*wu xing*), which construes wood as dominant over clay and metal over wood. In sum, the abduction of agency to objects in Viet popular religion is not, in any sense, a simplistic animistic imputation of spirits or souls to things but is the consequence of a multi-faceted work of cultural production involving the artisan who produced the object, the ritual master who empowered it, and the devotee who maintains it over time. This web of belief and practice, and the role of compensated specialists in effecting it, became the target of anti-superstition campaigns such as the one that threatened the Trần Hưng Đạo shrine and caused statues from village shrines to be burned or cast into the village pond, as described above.

ICONOCLASM AND COUNTER-REVOLUTIONARY AGENCY

The term iconoclasm, from the Greek "image-breaking," emerged from eighth- and ninth-century Christian debates over whether the representation of Christ in human form constituted idolatry—the mistaken and sinful worship of "graven images"—or divinely inspired devotion. As a legacy of the sixteenth-century Protestant Reformation, iconoclasm versus iconicity marked a critical and abiding divide between Protestant and Catholic religious worlds.[29] The iconoclasm and anti-ritualism of the Reformation gained a modernist gloss in Enlightenment understandings of utilitarianism and a disenchanted material world. Webb Keane describes how Calvinist converts on Sumba in Indonesia define themselves through the rejection of material practices of devotion and custom, and, as a consequence, see themselves as more "modern" than their Catholic or unconverted neighbors.[30] In the history of modern East Asia, the identification of iconoclasm with "anti-superstition" transcended missionary activity and Christian conversion to became the work of modern nationalist and religious reformers well in advance of explicitly revolutionary projects such as the mass destruction perpetrated by China's Red Guard during the Cultural Revolution.[31]

---

medium, recalled beautiful statues that were consumed by woodworms within a few years of their manufacture. Before carving, a conscientious carver also soaks the wood in white limewater as a further precaution against woodworms. See Laurel Kendall, Vũ Thị Thanh Tâm, and Nguyễn Thị Thu Hương, "Three Goddesses in and out of Their Shrine," *Asian Ethnology* 67,2: (2008), pp. 219–36.

[28] Vũ, "Amulets and the Marketplace."

[29] Freedberg, *The Power of Images*, pp. 29, 386–88; Graham Howes, *The Art of the Sacred: An Introduction to the Aesthetics of Art and Belief* (London: I. B. Tauris, 2007), pp. 8–10; and Victor Turner and Edith Turner, *Image and Pilgrimage in Christian Culture* (New York, NY: Columbia University, 1978), pp. 140–43.

[30] Webb Keane, *Christian Moderns: Freedom and Fetish in the Mission Encounter* (Berkeley and Los Angeles, CA, and London: University of California Press, 2007).

[31] For China, see Myron L. Cohen, "Being Chinese: The Peripheralization of Traditional Identity," *Deadalus* 122,2 (1991): 113–33; Prasenjit Duara, *Rescuing History from the Nation: Questioning Narratives of Modern China* (Chicago, IL: University of Chicago Press, 1995);

In Vietnam, early twentieth-century reformers similarly attacked superstition in the name of science, taking aim at many popular religious practices.[32] This logic would also fuel attacks on popular religion in the period of revolutionary struggle and under high socialism and become a source of continuing discomfort amid popular religious revival in Vietnam today. Widespread destruction of sacred sites, including temples and shrines and the sacred objects housed inside them, occurred during successive waves of revolutionary fervor: the August Revolution in 1945,[33] the defeat of the French in 1954 and the establishment of the Socialist Republic of Vietnam, and the First Five Year Plan for socialist industrialization (1960 to 1965). In the French war, many communal houses in the north of Vietnam were destroyed, explicitly to deny billets to the French but also as an act of retaliation against the physical embodiments of the local elites that had dominated these gathering places.[34] Shaun Malarney's conversations with the residents of a Red River Delta village who lived through periods of revolution and high socialism offer a close-focused portrait of the fate of sacred sites and objects over the course of this history, "Zealous villagers tore down many of the symbols of the old order ... Sacred items, such as altar pieces, were broken into pieces. Several prized statues were either destroyed or thrown down wells. And what was not smashed was often stolen and later kept or sold."[35] During the land reform, which began in this community in 1955, temples were dismantled or consolidated, the surviving temples and lineage halls turned to secular uses, and the shrines associated with spirit mediums either vandalized or destroyed. In similar conversations in other places, we also heard of the destruction of divination books and other ritual manuals important in the work of consecrating sites, paraphernalia, and statues.

In Malarney's words, "Party officials regarded superstitions as one of the greatest obstacles to the development of the new society," signifying, in effect, that they abducted counter-revolutionary agency to the temples, communal houses, statues, and divination books.[36] As in the anti-superstition campaigns of Republican

---

Prasenjit Duara, "Knowledge and Power in the Discourse of Modernity: The Campaign against Popular Religion in Early Twentieth-Century China," *Journal of Asian Studies* 50,1 (1991): 67–83; and Vincent Goossaert, "1898: The Beginning of the End for Chinese Religion?" *The Journal of Asian Studies* 65,2 (2006): 307–36. For Korea, see Boudewijn Walraven, "Shamans and Popular Religion around 1900," in *Religions in Traditional Korea*, ed. Henrik Hjort Sorensen, Proceedings of the 1992 AKSE/SBS Symposium, SBS Monographs Number 3, 1995; Boudewijn Walraven, "Interpretations and Reinterpretations of Popular Religion in the last Decades of the Chosŏn Dynasty," in *Korean Shamanism: Revivals, Survivals, and Change*, ed. Keith Howard (Seoul: Royal Asiatic Society, 1998); Laurel Kendall, *Shamans, Nostalgias, and the IMF: South Korean Popular Religion in Motion* (Honolulu, HI: University of Hawaii Press, 2009); and Laurel Kendall, "The Cultural Politics of 'Superstition' in the Korean Shaman World: Modernity Constructs its Other," in *Healing Powers and Modernity: Traditional Medicine, Shamanism, and Science in Asian Societies*, ed. Linda Connor and Geoffrey Samuel (London: Bergin and Garvey, 2001). For Japan, see Allan G. Grapard, "Japan's Ignored Cultural Revolution: The Separation of Shinto and Buddhist Divinities in Meiji (*shimbutusu bunri*) and A Case Study," *History of Religions* 23,3 (1984): 240–65.

[32] David Marr, *Vietnamese Tradition on Trial, 1920–1945* (Berkeley, CA: University of California Press, 1981), pp. 344–45.

[33] These acts persisted despite a directive signed by Ho Chi Minh against the destruction of national heritage. Personal communication, Nguyễn Văn Huy, September 29, 2007.

[34] Malarney, *Culture, Ritual, and Revolution in Vietnam*, p. 45.

[35] Ibid., p. 46.

[36] Ibid., pp. 81–82.

China, acts of iconoclasm would destroy the agency of sacred objects by revealing them to be no more than "useless bits of mud or wood" whose desecration provoked no consequence. And like the Rokeby Venus that provoked "Slasher Mary" to an act of vandalism, and the Lenin, Marcos, or Saddam Hussein images decisively smashed when worlds changed,[37] or the lace handkerchiefs that tempted otherwise respectable matrons to commit petty theft, the presence of the object provoked and "made them do it."[38]

LEGACIES OF VIOLATION

In 2000, reflecting on the resurgence of popular religion and the refurbishment of sacred sites, a friend related how "people say" that, as a consequence of having torn down the shrines and temples in a period of revolutionary fervor, the Vietnamese people suffered the bitter poverty of the subsidy period (1975 to 1986). More than a decade into the market economy, they still lagged far behind the more successful economies of China, Malaysia, and Thailand. The speaker thus abducted (or claimed that others abducted) present circumstance to acts of iconoclasm in decades past, to the gods and Buddhas who had been so violated. Võ Văn Trực's autobiographical novel, *Cọng Rêu Dưới Đáy Ao* (Pond Scum), presents this logic in the intimate context of his boyhood village in the revolutionary base area of Nghệ An Province in Central Vietnam.[39] Following a party directive to destroy the sites of superstitious worship, Hiền, a young activist in the novel, mobilizes the village youths for a month's rampage that will obliterate most material traces of the village's six-hundred-year history. They tear down the Buddhist temple, the ancestral tutelary's shrine, and the shrines to other local deities. They cut down the dozen venerable banyan trees, one of them five-hundred-years old, that surround the cemetery as harborages for wandering souls. They desecrate the ancestral graveyard and dump the remains in a common burial pit. When one of his comrades is injured during the destruction of a temple, Hiền suggests in jest that this is a punishment from the deities who should be placated, and earns an official reprimand, an ironic foreshadowing of what is to follow. Although some villagers oppose the desecration, most are willing participants in these events, the victims of a recent famine who embrace the Revolution in the hope of a better life. Mr. Võ's own boyhood memories of that period are of a buoyant, even festive atmosphere.[40]

The remainder of the novel charts Hiền's subsequent miserable life. His attempts to better himself and his community repeatedly run afoul of the authorities; he becomes the object of slander and loses his ability to work. Reduced to living in poverty, he becomes ill and dies. The revolutionary-era party leader has been similarly cursed, with all of his children dying young and in unfortunate

---

[37] Freedberg provides Gell with the much-cited image of "Slasher Mary" defaming the Rokeby Venus, interpreting this act as a magical protest against the incarceration of the suffragette, Emmeline Pankhurst (see Freedberg, *The Power of Images*, pp. 409–10), an exercise of "magic" in Freedberg's terms, interpreted as "volt sorcery" in Gell's analysis.

[38] Adela Pinch, "Stealing Happiness: Shoplifting in Early Nineteenth-Century England," in *Border Fetishisms: Material Objects in Unstable Spaces*, ed. Patricia Spyer (New York, NY: Routledge, 1998).

[39] Võ Văn Trực, *Cọngê Rêu Dươi Đáy Ao* [Pond Scum] (Hanoi: Nhà Xuất Bn Hội Nhà Văn, 2007).

[40] Võ Văn Trực interview, Hanoi, Socialist Republic of Vietnam, September 29, 2007.

circumstances. By the time of Hiền's funeral, the villagers recognize that their own misfortunes and the pervasive poverty of their village are a consequence of their past destruction of temples and graveyards. The ghosts that once settled in the aged banyan trees haunt their dreams, driving one dreamer insane. But they cannot restore the mixed and scattered bones of their ancestors to proper graves, they are too poor to rebuild the ruined temples, and the moral community they once shared, under the sway of tutelary gods and ancestors, has been shattered.

Võ describes his novel as 90 percent true, and is proud that his childhood neighbors regard it as a work of local history. He also relates that, since its publication, many readers have responded with accounts of similar histories in their own villages. Like his subjects, Võ abducts agency to the objects of iconoclasm, but he adds a layer of meaning to the phenomenon he describes: in destroying the material and spiritual basis of their history, the villagers destroyed the source of their collective morality, the village customs and compacts that were enforced to acknowledge and guard against divine or ancestral retribution.[41] One hears variations of this sentiment in Vietnam today in the claim that atheism has failed to provide a basis of communal morality. In such contexts, the robust presence of popular religious phenomena, from soul-calling to the elaborate refurbishment of temples, takes on a positive gloss against the seeming amorality of the market economy. Võ's literary project navigates between agentive popular religious expression and the case made by folklorist Ngô Đúc Thinh and his colleagues that the restoration of popular religious practices is socially beneficial, strengthening local communities and restoring and perpetuating an important national heritage.[42]

The work of Malarney and others, such as Nguyễn Thị Hiền, and our own interviews reveal that a great deal of popular religious practice went on quietly even in periods when it was strongly sanctioned against.[43] Popular religion has gained visibility since the "renovation" (*đổi mới*) of 1986 heralded a new era of market economics and relative tolerance of a variety of social practices, including religion. The refurbishment of temples, shrines, and sacred sites and the return to visibility of all manner of ritual life could be discerned in the 1990s, and the revival, elaboration, and continuous improvisation of popular religion has been a marked feature of Vietnamese life in the new millennium.[44] The newly refurbished shrine to Trần Hưng Đạo, described in the opening passages of this chapter, is of a piece with activities

---

[41] Ibid.

[42] Michael DiGregorio, and Oscar Salemink, "Living with the Dead: The Politics of Ritual and Remembrance in Contemporary Vietnam," *Journal of Southeast Asian Studies* 38,3 (2007): 8; Olga Dror, *Cult, Culture, and Authority: Princess Lieu Hanh in Vietnamese History* (Honolulu, HI: University of Hawaii Press, 2007); *Vietnamese Studies*, "Special: The Cult of Holy Mothers in Vietnam," *Vietnamese Studies* 131,1 (1999, special issue).

[43] Malarney, *Culture, Ritual, and Revolution in Vietnam*, pp. 47, 51; and Hiền Thị Nguyễn, "The Religion of the Four Palaces: Mediumship and Therapy in Viet Culture" (PhD dissertation, Indiana University, Bloomington, IN, 2002).

[44] DiGregorio and Salemink, "Living with the Dead"; and Fjelstad and Nguyen, eds., *Possessed by the Spirits*; Shaun K. Malarney, *Culture, Ritual, and Revolution in Vietnam*, pp. 103, 106, 219; Shaun K. Malarney, "Return to the Past? The Dynamics of Contemporary Religious and Ritual Transformation," in *Postwar Vietnam: Dynamics of a Transforming Society*, ed. Hy V. Luong (Singapore: ISEAS, 2003); Phillip Taylor, *Goddess on the Rise: Pilgrimage and Popular Religion in Vietnam* (Honolulu, HI: University of Hawaii Press, 2004); Phillip Taylor, "Modernity and Re-enchantment in Post-revolutionary Vietnam," in *Modernity and Re-enchantment: Religion in Post-revolutionary Vietnam*, ed. Philip Taylor (Singapore: Institute of Southeast Asian Studies, 2007).

carried out in temples and private shrines all over Vietnam. The production of goods for specifically ritual purposes, from altar tables to statues in spirit medium shrines, and the elaboration of village rituals and personal devotions testify to an enthusiastic linkage between things material and spiritual in contemporary Vietnamese popular religious life.[45] At the same time, much of the writing on contemporary religious life in Vietnam describes a continuing tension between popular devotion and an official ideology that explicitly denies the existence of gods and ghosts, much less the possibility of their speaking through spirit mediums, receiving offerings of burnt votive paper, or inhabiting statues.[46] A work like Võ Văn Trực's *Cọng Rêu Dưới Đáy Ao* reminds us that, while the tenacity of popular religion made disenchantment an incomplete project, the ideological force and experience of iconoclasm was not without abiding moral consequence. In the final section of this chapter, we discuss what some would describe as the diminished agency of sacred objects in the contemporary market economy of Vietnam.

THE SACRED OBJECT AND THE COMMODITY FETISH

When our interview subjects spoke of statues that had remained unscathed in abandoned temples in the not-so-distant past, statues commanding fear and awe sufficient to freeze a potential thief in his tracks, they would sometimes make unhappy comparisons with the present, where the market in antiquities encourages temple larceny. The tellers demonstrate a wry awareness that before the radical revision of economic policies in 1986, there was little or no market for stolen antiquities, but they also asserted that, in the past, such theft would have been unthinkable. The traffic in temple statues suggests both a lack of respect for the potential agency of divine images as "deities" and their revaluation as "art." In contrast to its prior identity as the material incarnation of a potentially punitive deity, the statue is abducted as a site of desire for possession or monetary exchange.[47] We have seen temple statues in the hands of private collectors; some of these statues reveal empty cavities suggesting they have been properly deanimated, but others appear to have more dubious origins. One dealer told us that he only handles statues that come to him with the temple's documents authorizing the sale of a properly deanimated statue, but we have also seen divine images, their cavities still intact, purchased by a collector from this same dealer. In the home of another private collector, we examined a beautiful old statue he had recently purchased in an

---

[45] Nguyen Thi Hien, "'A Bit of a Spirit Favor is Equal to a Load of Mundane Gifts': Votive Paper Offerings of *Len Dong* Rituals in Post-Renovation Vietnam," in *Possessed by the Spirits*, pp. 127–42.

[46] DiGregorio and Salemink, *Living with the Dead*, pp. 433–35; Fjelstad and Nguyen, "Introduction," in *Possessed by the Spirits*, p. 15; Malarney, *Culture, Ritual, and Revolution in Vietnam*, pp. 103, 106, 219; Malarney, "Return to the Past?"; and Taylor, *Modernity and Re-enchantment: Religion in Post-revolutionary Vietnam*, pp. 6–9.

[47] Janet Hoskins, "Agency, Biography, and Objects," in *Handbook of Material Culture*, ed. Christopher Tilley, Webb Keane, Susanne Kuechler-Fogden, Mike Rowlands, and Patricia Spyer (London: Sage Publications, 2006), p. 77.

Spirit medium in a now-active temple from which the statues had been removed during an anti-superstition campaign. Photograph by Laurel Kendall

antique shop with its cavity intact. The collector described himself as a practicing Buddhist and therefore a "good person" who did not fear punishment from the deity resident in the statue; he seemed untroubled by the possibility that the little statue was stolen. His attitude is akin to that of the dealer who described herself as a serious Buddhist who visits the temple twice a month but for whom placing the statues at a respectful height above the floor is a sufficient gesture of respect; she claims to make no distinction between statues with their amulets still inside them and empty statues. When an ambitious collector experienced a family tragedy, acquaintances thought of the still-potent images in his home. Others told us of a notorious theft from a Buddhist temple, during which the thieves killed a monk but were subsequently apprehended at the border, an act of divine retribution. Punishing gods persist as a shadow presence, haunting an art market that would belie the commanding presence of animated statues in newly refurbished temples. Meanwhile, temple-keepers who can afford heavy bronze statues install them as a precaution against theft. In sum, the traffic in antiquities—the abducted appeal of filthy lucre and beautiful, collectable art—can override fear of the statues' own punitive agency, but not completely, as demonstrated when tales of retribution make some dealers and some potential buyers uneasy. This, too, is an example of iconoclash.

Old statue in a private collection. Photograph by Laurel Kendall

If the government's official encouragement of market activities since 1986 had the unintended consequence of fostering a market in stolen antiquities, it was also indirectly responsible for the production of new objects in a climate that tolerated the revival of popular religious activities that had been muted under high socialism. All of these developments have complicated the identity of sacred objects in an accelerated market economy. In another place, we have described how, with rising demands for religious goods, some family workshops in the wood-carving village of Sơn Đồng, near Hanoi, are turning out ready-made statues of dubious quality for sale off the shelves of their own workshops or in the shops on Hanoi's Hàng Quạt Street.[48] These statues are more likely to be made of less durable branches, rather than from the core wood of the tree trunk, and so may be infested with woodworm. Cheap and readily accessible statues appeal to those mediums who regard the unanimated statue as "just a piece of wood," and the animation ritual, in and of itself, as sufficient to transform the statue into a god. Other mediums and temple-keepers continue to commission statues from reputable carvers, despite the expense, because poor quality statues will deteriorate quickly and because, in the words of

[48] Kendall, Vũ, and Nguyễn, "Beautiful and Efficacious Statues."

another prominent Hanoi spirit medium and temple-keeper, "ready-made statues often bring bad luck."

Vũ Hồng Thuật describes a similar rationalization expressed by mediums regarding the production of amulets.[49] Drawing on long relationships with several ritual masters within and outside Hanoi, Vũ was able to gain esoteric knowledge of how these masters produce and subsequently empower amulets. The most precious and powerful amulets were drawn by the ritual master in a state of bodily purity and with a clear and focused mind, while chanting appropriate incantations. The act of striking a printed amulet from a woodblock made to conform to a ritual master's original was similarly ritualized, and the woodblock itself was produced in a manner that recalled the taboos and precautions that attend the carving of statues in traditional workshops. In contemporary Vietnam, as the demand for amulets swells, cheap, stenciled amulets are widely used, struck off in bundles with no accompanying ritual. Vũ found that ritual masters are also less scrupulous about personal prohibitions and purifications when they prepare to empower these mass-manufactured amulets. These changes and the ritual masters' sense of a descending index of power that measures of relative efficacy of hand-drawn to wood-blocked to mass-produced amulets recall Benjamin's notion of the "aura" that surrounds sacred objects produced in ritual settings, but that diminishes in the age of mechanical reproduction.[50] The continued and widespread use of amulets, and the powers abducted to them, suggest, as in the case of statues, that the "aura" is a relative and not an absolute condition of production.

CONCLUSION

In his study of religion, modernity, and materiality in Sumba, Indonesia, Webb Keane offers a reflection on the impossibility of a fully abstract, transcendent, amaterial religious expression: "the human subject cannot free itself from objectification. It retains a body, depends on objects, and speaks by means of publicly known, material forms of speech. People cannot free themselves from the practices by which they are embedded in the world of other persons."[51] This brief account of the use, efficacy, and production of some sacred objects in the popular religious experience of contemporary Vietnam suggests that these artifacts of the material world are deeply embedded in significant and tenacious social relationships with gods, ancestors, and ghosts, and in notions of auspicious and malevolent fates that gain social recognition through the stories people tell. At the same time, it cannot be denied that the social embeddedness of sacred things has been shaken by contradictory forces in the recent history of Vietnam. Modernity discourse and revolutionary campaigns and propaganda challenged the agency of sacred objects, even as the skeptics were themselves challenged by tenacious tales of retributive agency. In more recent times, the market demonstrated competing agency by offering alluring cash for stolen statues and other antiquities, and by highlighting the seductive power of these objects themselves as collectable art. Heightened demand and commoditized production have compromised the quasi-ritualistic process of

---

[49] Vu, "Amulets and the Marketplace."

[50] Walter Benjamin, "The Work of Art in the Age of Mechanical Reproduction," in *Illuminations: Essays and Reflections*, ed. Hannah Arendt (New York, NY: Schocken, 1969).

[51] Keane, *Christian Moderns*, p. 81.

making efficacious things and the sense of moral purpose expected of those who engage in this work. But if some Vietnamese have cause to regard both anti-superstition and commodification as having threatened patterns of social morality mediated in and through sacred objects, the process is more a dialectic than teleology. In contemporary Vietnam, popular religion offers a means of auspicious engagement with a risky and uncertain market, as manifested in the new production and consecration of agentive things. It also suggests the perpetuation of a moral order that transcends naked market forces but, at the same time, trades in sacred objects that are produced in and through the market. The final image, then, is not of a disenchanted world, but of a complex and contradictory one, as internally contradictory as the responses of the local bureaucrats to the prospect of taking down Trần Hưng Đạo's shrine. Philip Taylor reminds us that popular religion in Vietnam must necessarily be understood as an innovative and changing process, the sum of all its history.[52] Negotiations and renegotiations with sacred objects are a part of this process.

---

[52] Taylor, "Modernity and Re-enchantment in Post-revolutionary Vietnam."

CHAPTER 2

OF PROTON, MERCEDES, AND MPVS: CAR CULTURE AMONG MIDDLE-CLASS MALAYS IN SUBURBAN MALAYSIA

Johan Fischer

INTRODUCTION

On November 11, 2007, the BBC (British Broadcasting Company) reported that the Malaysian state-owned carmaker, Proton, was planning to develop an "Islamic car" designed for "Muslim motorists."[1] This car would fill "a huge gap in the market." Proton's plan was to team up with manufacturers in Iran and Turkey to create a "unique vehicle" that would "boast special features, like a compass pointing to Mecca and a dedicated space to keep a copy of the Koran and a headscarf." The vision to produce a Muslim car in Malay-Muslim-dominated Malaysia is inseparable from Islamic revivalism, economic growth, and the emergence of a Malay-Muslim middle class over the last three decades.

In May 1983, the Malaysian government had established the car manufacturer Proton, also called the National Automobile Enterprise, and this brand dominates the Malaysian automobile market. Proton is the most common car in the streets of Malaysia, but the company is experiencing difficulties, as the Malaysian government has allowed more foreign cars to be imported, abolishing its prior Approved Permit (AP) system. At the time of my anthropological fieldwork in urban Malaysia (2001–02), Proton cars were exempted from the high import duties that are placed on other cars, and the government was able to offer these cars at a price that undercut the total price of imported vehicles, which are taxed at between 140 percent and 300 percent. As could be expected, this type of protectionism strengthened Proton's position in the Malaysian car market.

Over the last three decades, Malaysia has witnessed rapid economic growth and rising incomes among urban middle-class groups, and these developments are driving forces behind car ownership. The rapidly expanding car market in and around Kuala Lumpur is a product of this economic performance and "the huge

---

[1] Robin Brant, "Malaysia Firm's 'Muslim Car' Plan," BBC News, Kuala Lumpur, available at http://news.bbc.co.uk/2/hi/7089707.stm, accessed May 1, 2012.

economic role such areas play to the general development of Malaysia."[2] The state in Malaysia views "the auto industry as a strategic sector that needs real support and protection. Rising car sales are also an important sign of positive and strong consumer sentiment which the Malaysian economy needs badly."[3] Malaysia has sustained economic growth in the past three decades, and, in that period, the meaning of Islam has become evermore contested.

This paper explores how cars have emerged as one of the most significant markers of physical and social mobility among the Malay Muslim middle-class in Malaysia. The ethnographic focus of the paper is on a relatively affluent middle-class suburb, Taman Tun Dr. Ismail (or TTDI), outside Malaysia's capital, Kuala Lumpur. Building on ten months of fieldwork in suburban Malaysia, I have argued that the more cultures of consumption assert themselves, the more controversies over what Islam is, or ought to be, intensify.[4] As new consumer practices emerge, they give rise to new discursive fields within which the meaning of Islam and Islamic practice are being debated. One key effect of these transformations is the deepening and widening concern for *halal* (permissible according to Islamic law) commodities among Malay Muslims that I label *halalization*. Halalization signifies a major preoccupation with the proliferation of the concept of *halal* in a multitude of commodified forms. Out of halalization, new forms of Malay aesthetic communities have emerged based on the different taste preferences of various middle-class fractions. This proliferation of halalization in suburban Malaysia has incited a range of elaborate ideas concerning the boundaries and authenticity of *halal* purity versus *haram* (not permissible under Islamic law) impurity. An "Islamic car" is an example of a commodity that, due to the expansion of halalization, is being subjected to new types of religious requirements, standards, and contestations.

My informants in the suburban setting were selected to obtain a good representative sample. The initial selection was made on the basis of a survey covering 241 households in my suburban fieldwork site, a survey designed to specify and identify particular indicators such as family size, income, and consumer behavior, and to introduce the theme of consumption to informants in the wider resurgence of Islam in Malaysia. On the basis of survey data, Ten Malay families were then selected for interviews and participant observation on the basis of two criteria: first, their relative statistical weight in the survey, that is, did they resemble others taking the survey and thereby provide relatively equal distribution in relation to socioeconomic parameters such as gender, income, occupation, and education, and, second, what was their appearance, style of decoration of the house, cars, dress, and so forth, all details that I could observe when visiting families. More specifically, I looked for material markers of "Islam" such as the *kopiah* (skullcap) and *janggut* (beard) for men and *tudung* (headscarf) for women, but also objects such as stickers

---

[2] Jamilah Mohamad and Amin Tamale Kiggundu, "The Rise of the Private Car in Kuala Lumpur, Malaysia: Assessing the Policy Options," *IATSS Research* 31,1 (2007): 69–77, particularly p. 70.

[3] Ibid., p. 72.

[4] Johan Fischer, "Boycott or Buycott? Malay Middle-class Consumption Post-9/11," *Ethnos* 72,1 (2007): 29–50; Johan Fischer, *Proper Islamic Consumption: Shopping among the Malays in Modern Malaysia* (Copenhagen: Nordic Institute of Asian Studies Press, 2008); and Johan Fischer, "Nationalizing Rituals? The Ritual Economy in Malaysia," *Journal of Ritual Studies* 22,2 (2008): 13–22.

and plaques with Islamic calligraphy. Both informants who displayed and did not display these material markers of Islam were selected.

In the Malaysian population of 28.3 million persons, 67.4 percent are indigenous Malays (virtually all Muslims) and members of tribal groups, also labeled *bumiputera* (literally, "sons of the soil"); 24.6 percent are Chinese; 7.3 percent are Indians; and 0.7 percent are "Others." At the time of my fieldwork in 2001–02, Proton's suggestion to market an "Islamic car" had not yet surfaced, but, interestingly, this idea highlights a whole range of issues central to my focus on cars owned by middle-class Malays: the ever-expanding market for "proper Islamic consumption"; the consumption of locally produced cars as an example of what I call "shopping for the state" or "patriotic consumption," which contrasts with the excesses involved in the purchase of foreign luxury cars; the fact that middle-class Malays tend to be split in their decisions regarding positional commodities, that is, commodities that potentially can generate high social status, on the one hand, and commodities that reinforce the buyer's claims to demonstrate piety through consumption, on the other; and a consideration of cars as signifiers of a dualism between public and private consumption in the suburban setting. These themes will be explored on the basis of three brands or types of cars popular in middle-class suburbia: the Proton, the Mercedes, and the MPV (Multi-Purpose Vehicle). In the conclusion, I will discuss how these issues evoke some of the larger issues of this volume. I argue that Malay households, and houses, are crucial spheres in Malay middle-class formation in contemporary Malaysia, i.e., that styles of Islam and styles of consumption act as markers of one's class position. With specific reference to the understandings and practices of car consumption, I explore a field of contradictory Islamic visions, lifestyles, and debates articulating what Islam is or ought to be. These controversies frame the everyday organization and justification of consumer behavior within Malay middle-class households.

MALAY MUSLIM MIDDLE-CLASS MOBILITY

The Malays constitute the largest and fastest growing section of the middle class in Malaysia and are the focus of both commercial interests and current debates over the shape and meaning of Islam. In the 1970s, the state, dominated by United Malays National Organization (UMNO), the dominant political party in Malaysia since the country won independence from Britain in 1957, launched the NEP (New Economic Policy) to improve the economic and social situation of the Malays vis-à-vis the Chinese, in particular. The NEP conferred a number of benefits on the Malays and other indigenous groups, such as increased ownership of production and preferential Malay student quotas in the educational system.

The number and proportion of Malays engaged in secondary and tertiary sectors of the economy rose significantly as a result of these policies. Ideologically, the overall objective was to produce an educated, entrepreneurial, and shareholding Malay middle class, which the state's elite views as a necessary prerequisite for economic, national, and social cohesion. My Malay informants considered the NEP vital for the economic progress of the Malays, and told me that this legislation had a crucial impact on their social standing and emergence as modern consumers.

The NEP has, without question, actively drawn Islam into the economic sphere through the proliferation of a multitude of Islamic institutions starting in the 1980s. Simultaneously, the NEP transformed Malay dominance into Malay hegemony in this multiethnic society, so that Malay culture became synonymous with "national culture."[5] While the state may be a major ideological driving force behind the manufacturing of a Malay middle class, the influence of the market and capitalist relations of production should not be downplayed as factors in these developments.[6] In the 1990s, Kuala Lumpur and the urban region in which it is situated were exposed to "unprecedented attempts by federal authorities to discursively and materially reconstruct urban space and subjectivities in 'global' ways."[7] The government's fascination with and adoption of "global ways" has resulted in increased access to the electronic media, such as satellite television and the Internet, for Malaysia's urban residents, as well as the availability of a wide range of consumer goods due to expanding markets.

I explore how cars as objective parameters of status are involved in class performances among members of the emerging Malay middle class. Performances are highly formative of social relationships such as class. The consumption of cars as "fronts" or "expressive equipment," to use Erving Goffman's phrase,[8] works as the setting for such performances. Fronts function in general and fixed ways to define the specific situation for observers.

The increased influence of Islam in Malaysia has produced a range of competing visions of what Islam is or ought to be. For example, a number of divergent *dakwah* (literally "salvation") groups have emerged as part of the wider resurgence of Islam in Malaysia, a resurgence that started in the 1970s.[9] The state's attempt at molding a modern form of Malayness is intimately linked to these groups, which are challenging Islamic discourses, or *dakwah*, each having particular ideas and standards of how to combine consumption and Islamic practice. In order to preempt these confrontations, the state aggressively engages in a reconceptualization of consumption that envisions the amalgamation of Malay ethnicity, consumption practices, and Islam. This ongoing project, which started in the early 1970s, is intensifying in the context of economic growth and globalization. In the early 1970s, the state embarked on a wide range of measures symbolizing its dedication to Islamic values. The economy thus fused with a politics of ethnicity that, in itself, was defined in terms of religion.[10] More specifically, the state has institutionalized and

---

[5] Amri Baharuddin Shamsul, "Bureaucratic Management of Identity in a Modern State: 'Malayness' in Postwar Malaysia," in *Making Majorities: Constituting the Nation in Japan, Korea, China, Malaysia, Fiji, Turkey, and the United States,* ed. Dru Gladney (Stanford, CA: Stanford University Press, 1998), p. 146.

[6] Abdul Rahman Embong, "Social Transformation, the State, and the Middle Classes in Post-Independence Malaysia," in *Cultural Contestations. Mediating Identities in a Changing Malaysian Society,* ed. I. Zawawi (London: Asean Academic Press, 1998), p. 86.

[7] Tim Bunnell, *Malaysia, Modernity, and the Multimedia Super Corridor* (London and New York, NY: Routledge Curzon, 2003), p. 65.

[8] Erving Goffman, *The Presentation of Self in Everyday Life* (London: Penguin Books, 1971), p. 27.

[9] For broader perspectives on *dakwah* in Malaysia, see, e.g., Susan Ackerman and Raymond Lai-Ming Lee, *Sacred Tensions: Modernity and Religious Transformation in Malaysia* (Columbia, SC: University of South Carolina Press, 1997); Kwame Sundaram Jomo and Ahmad Shabery Cheek, "Malaysia's Islamic Movements," in *Fragmented Vision: Culture and Politics in Contemporary Malaysia,* ed. J. S. Kahn and F. Loh Kok Wah (North Sydney: Asian Studies Association of Australia, with Allen & Unwin, 1992), pp. 79–106; and Judith Nagata, *The Reflowering of Malaysian Islam: Modern Religious Radicals and Their Roots* (Vancouver: University of British Columbia Press, 1984).

[10] Shamsul Amri Baharuddin, "Consuming Islam and Containing the Crisis: Religion,

regulated Islamic banking, savings, insurance, and education, as well as implementing *halal* standardization and certification of local and international goods.

Abdullah Ahmad Badawi, Malaysia's prime minister from 2003 to 2009, has argued that:

> The Malays, UMNO, and Islam in this country cannot be separated. Together, the three elements form a distinct culture and identity. Through its words and actions, UMNO has the responsibility of building an Islamic culture that balances the needs of this world and the next, an Islam that balances *fardu kifayah* [the collective responsibility of providing the needs and well-being of Muslims in this world], and *fardu 'ain* [the individual Muslim's obligation to perform his religious duties towards Allah, such as the mandatory five daily prayers].[11]

Car consumption among middle-class Malays takes place in the interfaces between this-worldly performances of class mobility, privilege, and status, on the one hand, and performances orientated towards next-worldly piety and proper Islamic consumption, on the other.

PROTON, PIETY, AND PATRIOTISM

In Kuala Lumpur and its surrounding suburbs, the number of expensive and highly taxed luxury cars produced by BMW, Mercedes, and Volvo, for example, is impressive. In the context of the fieldwork, sample data showed that about 60 percent of middle-class respondents owned one car, 30 percent two, 6 percent three, and a small percentage owned more than three cars. The Malaysian-produced Proton was the most popular brand by far. Other popular brands were Honda, Toyota, Nissan, Mercedes, Ford, Volvo, and BMW, in that order. Cars in developing Malaysia have been studied as potent symbols of social status and identity:

> The cars for the rich and upper middle class are largely European made, such as Mercedes, BMW, and Volvo, or high-end Japanese brands. These different brands were further used to create differences among the high-end segment of the middle classes. Thus, businessmen favoured Mercedes, highly educated and younger professionals desired BMW, and the civil servants wanted the Volvo—in part because these were the cars given to them by the state as part of their remuneration. [...] Further down the line were locally produced "national" cars.[12]

It is relations between types of cars and social status, on the one hand, and claims for proper Islamic consumption, on the other, I explore. Unsurprisingly, men who responded to the survey were more explicit about car consumption compared to

Ethnicity, and the Economy in Malaysia," in *Southeast Asian-centered Economies or Economics?*, ed. Mason Hoadley (Copenhagen: Nordic Institute of Asian Studies, 1999), pp. 43–61.

[11] Abdullah Ahmad Badawi, *Islam Hadhari: A Model Approach for Development and Progress* (Petaling Jaya: MPH Publishing Sdn Bhd, 2006), pp. 6–7.

[12] Rokiah Talib, "Power Shifts and Consumption in Malaysia," in *Consumption in Asia: Lifestyles and Identities*, ed. Chua Beng-Huat (London and New York, NY: Routledge, 2000), p. 43.

women. It should also be noted that these informants' statements during the fieldwork surfaced at a time when the state's Approved Permit (AP) system allowed only up to 10 percent of vehicles in Malaysia to be imported, so owning a relatively scarce foreign vehicle automatically conveyed special status to the owner.

The informant Ahmad was a man in his late twenties, who had earned a degree in accounting in the United Kingdom and was now working as a business accountant. He was living with his sister, her husband, and children in their one-story terraced house. Ahmad, who owned a modest Proton, reasoned that a "prestige" car was the most effective way to show your friends that you are rich and have a high social standing. Ahmed explained to me that, typically, cars also modified the home of its owners, that is, a Proton car would signify that the car owner lived in a modest house with relatively common furnishings and decor. Besides this explicit concord between car and interior, for a bachelor such as Ahmad, there is an interest in the status of one's own car: "Even girls are looking for guys who are driving Mercedes and not looking for me because my type is a cheap Proton. This is the Asian attitude—wanting a big, expensive car, big house. Beautiful wife." Ahmad desperately desired a Mercedes or BMW. In this narrative, driving a Proton is premised on economic considerations rather than explicit claims for piety. In other cases, using a more religious perspective, informants would often evoke Proton cars as a form of proper or patriotic Islamic consumption. I shall return to this point later in this section.

A quite different narrative emerged with the informants Irfan and Murni, a couple in their forties who had lived in a two-story semidetached house with their four children since 1986. The husband, Irfan, had an education in mechanical engineering, and, when I spoke to her, Murni had retired from her work in accountancy to be with the children at home. Irfan was actively engaged in missionary work with the local mosque. The couple was alert to the moral perils of modern society, and, most of all, the complex relationship between Islam, class, and consumption in Malaysia. Irfan said: "What you can show to people is a car. Second is the house, because people don't visit it that often." Murni commented that when one sees somebody driving a Mercedes, one tends to reason that this person must be well off, "so, when you have this car, he's probably living in a big house. When he comes out, you do another assessment according to dressing. He's got a Rolex. Stuff like that." Cars, clothing, and brands are primary markers of identity, taste, and distinction, but among middle-class Malays, cars are also often seen to be the most reliable marker of moderation, piety, or excess. Irfan and Murni drove a Proton and were quite aware of the piety involved in this specific choice. They emphasized that even though they could easily afford a more luxurious car, it was a conscious decision on their part to drive a Proton. Their lack of desire for a Mercedes was determined by the proper pious attitude and lifestyle they had chosen in reaction against the excesses of upper-class Malaysians obsessed with brands "to maintain status." Murni cited automobiles as the most significant markers distinguishing middle-class from upper-class social strata in Malaysia. Driving a Proton signified a clear distinction between a pious middle-class lifestyle and a lifestyle driven by the quest for material status, typically adopted by members of the upper class indifferent to guidelines defining proper Islamic consumption. Compared to the narrative offered by Ahmad, Irfan and Murni's interpretation defined driving a Proton car in Malaysia as an action that was articulated and contested in a framework that divided excessive consumption from pious Islamic practices. Driving a Proton is considered the proper moral choice of the pious Malay, who typically perceives European luxury cars as excessive, unnecessary, and un-Islamic.

Izura and her husband, Yusof, are in their fifties. Their narrative is comparable to that of Irfan and Murni. In 2001, Izura and Yusof moved from their bungalow in TTDI to a newly built house in a prestigious estate outside Kuala Lumpur. Izura was educated as a teacher and Yusof as an electrical engineer. After earning his degree abroad, he returned to Malaysia and worked for a while before completing his master's degree in Australia. Yusof mentioned that a prestigious car, such as a Mercedes, was wasteful compared to a smaller Proton. Some time back, the couple had sold their Mercedes, and since then they have owned and driven three Protons and a Volkswagen. In essence, this is a performance of patriotic consumption.

Based on the tendencies shown in the two types of narratives about Protons, summarized above, I will discuss this form of modern car consumption. I consider how so many aspects of life in Malaysia have been Islamicized in recent years by purveyors and purchasers of consumer goods. Business in Islamic goods has grown and thrived. Such goods include everything from stickers, rugs, holiday cards, and plaques decorated with Islamic calligraphy, to items produced for celebrations of special types of holidays aimed at a Muslim audience, as well as wristwatches displaying prayer (*salat*) times and other features, ring tones and logos on mobile phones, and logos on clothes.[13] Joann D'Alisera explores in depth how and why Muslim Sierra Leoneans in Washington, DC, inscribe religious identity onto their cars by means of a variety of Islamic commodities, such as bumper stickers displaying Koranic verses in Arabic. This type of decoration "serves to reflect the ways they bridge the gap between various, sometimes competing modes of reference, and thus define their place in the community."[14]

In Kuala Lumpur and my suburban fieldwork site, it was common to see Islamic and other religious paraphernalia used as "labels" or "tags" on cars, and always on relatively smaller and inexpensive cars, such as Protons. I hypothesized that this type of branding in and on cars that were considered relatively low in status, and thus were not recognized as a "positional" commodity, effected some form of compensation or fulfilled a desire in their owners, enabling them to express a sort of patriotic piety through their ownership and display of a "national car." However, this type of branding of cars is not uncontested in Malaysia. While some middle-class Malays Islamicize cars, others argue that these sorts of practices are shallow displays of a kind of Islamic materialism that tells one little or nothing about the car owner's inner devotion.

Another aspect emerging from the fieldwork is what I have called "shopping for the state" and "patriotic consumption," as noted earlier.[15] The global economic downturn and insecurity following the attacks on the US World Trade Center on September 11, 2001, during the period when my fieldwork took place, moderated consumer sentiments in Malaysia. Consequently, the state launched a campaign in the media aimed at boosting the consumption of, especially, domestically produced goods such as cars. Under the title, "'Tis Season for Spending, Consumers Told," a

---

[13] Joann D'Alisera, "I Love Islam: Popular Religious Commodities, Sites of Inscription, and Transnational Sierra Leonean Identity," *Journal of Material Culture* 6,1 (2001), p. 97.

[14] Ibid., p. 100.

[15] Fischer, "Boycott or Buycott?"; and Fischer, *Proper Islamic Consumption*.

newspaper article encouraged patriotic shopping for the state. [16] Consumers were advised not to be "stingy about spending for the festive season as this will not help to stimulate the economy." Consequently, relatively expensive commodities, such as Proton cars, were resignified as the proper and patriotic choice for Malays. I call this network of overlapping and overspilling loyalties, compliances, and dependencies "shopping for the state," as these buying patterns demonstrate ways in which particular forms of consumption have come to represent novel modes of state reverence for Malays who are supported by the state.

Similarly, regarding South Korea, the phrase "consumer nationalism"[17] has been coined by Laura Nelson to describe a public movement to buy local products. Nelson explains that "as consumers encountered an increasingly complex market, they brought to this context their sense of identification with the nation. At a deeper level, consumers set themselves the larger task of making consumer choices that were in the best interest of the nation,"[18] and this patriotic inclination had a significant effect on a car market that was a product of state-directed industrial policies.[19] In Malaysia, state-owned car manufacturers were successful in expanding the domestic market for their product, and the state, in cooperation, ensured the urban development of roads, bridges, and parking facilities. My suburban fieldwork site is an example of a space that is entirely dependent on private transportation and urban infrastructure, and it is in this context my informants discussed and practiced car consumption.

In Malaysia, however, it was not only the car industry that was nationalized. From the 1970s onwards, the state was ethnicized to become a signifier of Malayness and unambiguous Malay identity. Hence, a state-controlled company such as Proton also came to symbolize this form of the Malay Muslim ethnicized state. It is these diverse forms of transformations that together constitute what I call the nationalization of Islam, i.e., the increased centrality of Islam as a national and ethnic signifier. The logic of this nationalization equates Islam with Malayness and identifies it as the naturalized core of the Malaysian nation. The nationalization of Islam in Malaysia has both produced and is in itself infused by a fascination with the morally proper Islamic way of life. This tendency embraces the consumption of specific goods, which may be seen to have a beneficial impact on domains such as the family, community, and nation. One could interpret a preference for certain locally produced goods, such as Proton cars, as an example of this tendency. Introducing the "Islamic car" is a sign of the latest expression of these tendencies.

MERCEDES: THE IMPORTATION OF EXCESS

The Mercedes brand of automobile has come to symbolize social status and excess in the eyes of my informants and the state in contemporary Malaysia. Some informants spread rumors about the way in which access to the state was an obvious avenue for acquiring expensive and foreign luxury cars, and Mercedes in particular,

---

[16] "'Tis Season for Spending, Consumers Told," *The Star*, November 13, 2001. *The Star* is a widely popular English-language newspaper generally considered to be relatively balanced in terms of political ideology in spite of government censorship.

[17] Laura Nelson, *Measured Excess: Status, Gender, and Consumer Nationalism in South Korea* (New York, NY: Columbia University Press, 2000).

[18] Ibid., p. 25.

[19] Ibid., p. 93.

in spite of the buyer's relatively moderate income. Yasir was a thirty-seven-year-old man working with IT development and a leading member of a local Islamic organization. He lived with his wife and young son in a condominium. The family moved into their flat in 1995. Yasir, for one, explained to me that:

> The government allows Malaysian students overseas to bring in one tax-free car. So, a lot of used car dealers use the students to bring in cars. The government and car dealers target students. The student gets paid about RM500 or RM1,000 [per December 7, 2008, one Malaysian Ringgit (RM) equalled US$ 0.27]. Students just have to give their name and sign a few documents, and the cars come in. In fact, lots of my friends buy Mercedes, and not from the real dealer, but imported ones at half price. You can get a Mercedes for the price of a new Proton. So, no big deal.

Obviously, informants such as Yasir were aware not only of these avenues for acquiring cars, but also of the value and status that might be ascribed to this commodity. He confided that a car is the item that people most often tend to use when judging one's status: "If you drive a Mercedes, even though it's not yours, they will look at you." This may be the quintessential performance—employing, "taking on," or handling a specific kind of expressive equipment to convey social messages to a large audience in public.

For this suburb, Yasir explained to me that:

> The upper class in the bungalows is the elite, really untouchable. When they come to the shop they walk like that ... [showing-off], then we know that, oh, this person is from up there. They drive Mercedes. You park your car wrongly, they horn like mad. Then there are people who live in the one-story terraced houses. They probably earn about RM3,000 to 4,000 a month.

The excesses of the "other" that guide informants and their families in classing their neighbors and fellow Malaysians are, to a large extent, dependent on the visible, even overt, consumption of cars.

Mascud and his wife are in their mid-forties. The family lived in a large bungalow. They moved from a *kampung* to Kuala Lumpur, and then to TTDI in 1986. Mascud held a bachelor's degree in economics and, after working in a bank, he had started his own business specializing in security printing. Mascud owned eight cars in all: a Volvo for himself, its price comparable to that of a Mercedes, and one car for each of his seven children. According to Mascud, one's car is a public measure of one's success that people actively recognize and display: "some have very moderate houses, but then a very big car." He added that "the car you can move everywhere whereas people have to come to your house." So the overtness and mobility of cars make them perfectly suited for display when the suburban audience is often unsure about the position or quality of the other's residence. From these narratives regarding luxury cars, two themes emerged. First, Mercedes ownership was often premised on access to the state and some sort of exploitation (of students, for example). Second, social status and sinful wastefulness cannot be separated from desiring or driving a Mercedes.

Obviously, the problem facing Malaysians whom I interviewed had to do with understanding and defining what are luxuries and what constitutes "excess" vis-à-vis Islamic piety, and then deciding how to achieve what informants often would call "balanced consumption." Nik Mohamad Affindi Bin Nik Yusuff, a former civil servant in the Malaysian government, has sought to identify and establish "the proper" and the "non-excessive" in Malay Muslim consumption. In his book, *Islam and Wealth: The Balanced Approach to Wealth Creation, Accumulation and Distribution,* Nik states that:

> Extravagance means exceeding the limits of what is beneficial in the use of what is allowed in Islam. The definition of goods considered overly luxurious depends on the overall standard of living in a country. In a very poor country, expensive sports cars can already be considered as too luxurious. In a very rich country, chartering a big aircraft to bring the whole family for shopping in London or Paris is obviously excessively luxurious.[20]

Yet the informants I interviewed perceived the purchase of a Mercedes automobile to be far more excessive than Nik, who adopts the perspective of the state, would judge it to be. The reasons for this difference in attitude are many, but in the eyes of my middle-class informants, the consumption of luxury cars is premised on licit (cars as part of remuneration) or illicit (exploitation of students, for example) access to the state. Thus, in the eyes of middle-class Malays, luxury cars are overt "state effects." The modern state can be seen to materialize out of "the powerful, apparently, metaphysical effect of practices,"[21] according to Timothy Mitchell, and my fieldwork shows that in the everyday lives of middle-class Malays, luxury cars often evoke the UMNO-driven[22] channeling of funds to some privileged Malay groups of cronies as a sort of party materialism. In effect, the state is implicated as contradicting its very own idealization of a pious Islamic identity through promoting Proton that is not meant to be excessive.

Slavoj Zizek writes that "We always impute to the 'other' an excessive enjoyment: he wants to steal our enjoyment (by ruining our way of life) and/or he has access to some secret, perverse enjoyment."[23] In other words, social and physical mobility as enjoyment tends to be premised on access to the ethnicized state. In many cases these forms of critiques among informants were articulated in "Islamic" terms as wastefulness and materialism.

MPV: GETTING THE CAR RIGHT

One last example stands out in this discussion of cars. Binsar and his wife, in their thirties, moved into their one-story terraced house in 1997. The couple have three children. Binsar originally moved to Kuala Lumpur to attend Maahad Tahfiz, an institute for Koran studies. He and his wife operated an Islamic school in their

---

[20] Nik Mohamad Affindi Bin Nik Yusuff, *Islam and Wealth: The Balanced Approach to Wealth Creation, Accumulation, and Distribution* (Kelana Jaya: Pelanduk Publications, 2001), p. 132.

[21] Timothy Mitchell, "Society, Economy, and the State Effect," in *State/Culture: New Approaches to the State after the Cultural Turn,* ed. George Steinmetz (New York, NY: Cornell University Press, 1999), p. 89.

[22] UMNO, United Malays National Organization, the dominant political party in Malaysia.

[23] Slavoj Zizek, *Tarrying with the Negative* (Durham, NC: Duke University Press, 1993), pp. 202–33.

terraced house. Binsar had purchased an expensive Nissan MPV. When we were discussing the advantages of this vehicle, Binsar was much more talkative and expansive than usual, and seemed eager to legitimize the purchase of this particular car. Before discussing Binsar's MPV in greater detail, it needs to be said that Binsar belongs to what I consider a particular Malay register of modern Islamic lifestyles. This register, or group, performs proper Islamic consumption as a localized form of behaving "purely"—these Malays oriented toward relatively orthodox "purity" are concerned about excessive and un-Islamic consumption, and they articulate a whole range of puritan ideals that tend to circle around the concept of "balanced consumption." This was Binsar's explanation when we discussed his purchase of the MPV one day:

> First of all, it's practical and functional. We need a Multi-Purpose Vehicle because sometimes we bring the children for a trip during the weekend, and also it's useful if we arrange activities like sports days and other activities. It's easy to bring all the things and equipment. Last time, we had to rent or borrow someone's van to bring all the things or equipment. In terms of design, I think it's okay. The price is not cheap and not too expensive. It's good value for money. I like the engine because I think it's better than a normal one. The difference between a Multi-Purpose Vehicle and a van is that the van engine is under the front seats. So, in time, the seat will get hot. But for this MPV, the engine is in front, like in a normal car.

As Binsar perceived the situation, everyday considerations regarding design, functionality, family, and the work in his Islamic school explained why he chose this particular car—it served multiple purposes, as it were. To Binsar, his preference ultimately seemed to signify balanced consumption. The MPV thus worked very satisfactorily as a piece of expressive equipment that helped shape a performance of perfectly moderate consumption. It has to be mentioned that, among the register of more purist, middle-class Malays, Binsar was the owner of the most luxurious car, and this might help explain his somewhat defensive attitude towards this particular and public type of consumption. The case of the MPV provides evidence that cars imply much more than personal ownership, for they also imply a broad range of related "externalities," that is "aggregate effects, landscapes of roadways, patterns of work, and patterns of leisure. In short a concern with externalities goes a long way in taking us from the car per se to the consideration of car culture."[24]

Cars and Dualism in Suburbia

In suburbia, where there is limited direct visual access to the intimate life that goes on inside bungalows, condominiums, and one- and two-story terraced houses, the front region of the house and visible, parked, family cars inevitably become signs of what life could be like in the private back region. Not surprisingly, cars were a favorite topic with male informants, in particular. The nature of the affluent Malaysian suburb is "deep" in the sense that it is intimately private. In many ways,

---

[24] Daniel Miller, "Driven Societies," in *Car Cultures*, ed. D. Miller (Oxford and New York, NY: Berg, 2001), p. 15.

the suburb I studied represents the idealized middle-class suburb, located at a safe distance from urban noise, crime, pleasures, excess, and crowds. A suburb like this is planned to be clean, constructed around family values, and focused on recreational facilities such as parks and playgrounds. This type of modern and affluent suburb monumentally symbolizes the progress of the Malaysian nation in a postcolonial context, the celebration of the growth of the middle class, and the ordering of space into manageable and exploitable forms.

In the suburban context, cars work as one of the most prominent examples of overt commodities that are seen to straddle and weave in and out of public and private domains. Consequently, among suburban Malays, the overtness of cars evokes speculation about the nature of the linkages between a family's visible, relatively public, property, on the one hand, and the make-up of the covert middle-class household, on the other. In other words, cars shape ideas and performances related to status, boundaries, and (social) mobility.

The car can signify a form of dualism, and embody distinct values that contribute to forming images of personhood and nationhood.[25] This dualism is what I refer to as the "convertibility" of cars, which I call "convertibles." In different ways, the three types of cars discussed above express complex relationships between individual car performances, that is, displays of cars by their owners in a particular national setting. Cars are capable of incorporating and expressing "the concept of the individual,"[26] and the most valuable insight in all this is that, while a public audience does notice performers' "aestheticization" of their own cars, the public rarely has an opportunity to observe the money and time invested in the interior of the house.[27] Thus, covering the upholstery of one's furniture with plastic, for example, suggests links to home furnishing and may evoke interiorization.[28] This example is similar to tagging or labelling a Proton car with a bumpersticker displaying Islamic calligraphy. Consequently, cars may be expressive of:

> a contradiction, a replication of the aesthetic of the interior which then has the potential for protecting the values of transcendence by maintaining them in the outside world. Equally, the car provides an ideal objectification of individualism and mobility, to be used in opposition to any association with the home.[29]

Inside the homes of middle-class Malays, one often finds an abundance of Islamic paraphernalia. While in the past most of these items would have been produced by craftsmen, now the majority of these religious commodities are mass produced.[30] These points reflect the domestication and individualization of Islam, and mark the

---

[25] Daniel Miller, *Modernity, An Ethnographic Approach: Dualism and Mass Consumption in Trinidad* (Oxford and New York, NY: Berg, 1994).

[26] Ibid., p. 237.

[27] Ibid., p. 239.

[28] Ibid., p. 243.

[29] Ibid., p. 244.

[30] Gregory Starrett, "The Political Economy of Religious Commodities in Cairo," *American Anthropologist* 97,1 (1995): 51–68.

widespread importation of Islamic paraphernalia, ideas, and practices into middle-class homes.

My fieldwork focused on and explored informants' ideas about status acquisition. It was in these discussions with informants that it became apparent that cars were expressive not only of ideas of status, but also dualism, confusion, and a spillover between the public and private domains and the way in which these were constantly charged and recharged with concerns about excess and frugality.

These points are reflected in the following narratives. Udzir and Nur are a couple in their thirties. They moved into their one-story terraced house in 1995, and they live there still with their two boys. Udzir was educated as an architect in both Malaysia and the United States, and has taught architecture. Nur held a degree in mass communication and worked as a public relations consultant. As was true of most informants, Udzir pinpointed the everyday difficulty involved in trying to assess the material or social status of others by judging from their interior decoration. Cars would supposedly, or rather hopefully, replicate, in style, the interior of the car owner's home, and indicate the everyday spending power of the household, as well as this household's strategies of display or concealment:

> You cannot see their items—it's more or less inside the house. But an expensive car means it's more expensive to maintain, high road tax, spare parts are expensive, the petrol it consumes. You don't know about status inside the house. We can't really see.

The car is much more overt than household furniture, and thus has the potential of inscribing the interior of the house with certain imaginary qualities in the eyes of outsiders. Interestingly, it is not so much the purchase price of cars that determines its value, but rather the everyday maintenance and costs, such as the expensive spare parts necessary for imported automobiles that are heavily taxed in Malaysia. Udzir and Nur drove a Peugeot they liked for its design, and a Proton that was far more economical to both purchase and maintain.

Another point reflecting the dualism of the car is the way in which suburban houses are all designed to protect, fence in, and encompass cars no matter how limited the space that might be available. The tendency is that as one moves upwards in class (one-story; two-story; semidetached; condominiums; bungalows), security of cars becomes more and more urgent, elaborate, and organized as a natural part of architectural design and aestheticization—domestication of cars as cherished objects that are part of middle-class households.

CONCLUSION

Cars are principal signifiers or modifiers expressive of status in and between public and private domains in urban Malaysia. Classifying the car consumption of others gives rise to charging and recharging these domains with tensions created by perceptions of others' pretences and frugality. In most cases, informants with whom I spoke did not regularly gain access to the interiors of the homes of members of their own or other class groups. Outward, public signs of a thrifty automobile purchase may mask excessive and irreverent practices taking place behind closed doors. Conversely, publicly displayed consumer goods that appear to be materialistic and extravagant may conceal a moderate lifestyle in the home, for some families with modest incomes choose to purchase expensive and conspicuous automobiles. Mostly, however, middle-class Malays believe that cars replicate the interior of the house occupied by that car's owners. The visible car, as the ultimate suburban status symbol, personalizes the house for the observant outsider or neighbor. Imported luxury cars may be "un-patriotic" compared to the locally produced Proton, but also function as essential "positional" commodities when displayed in public—either one's position as related to wealth or access to state privileges. Miller makes the case that "More than any other item of mass consumption, the car has become that classic instrument of modernity: the means of enabling contradiction without anxiety."[31]

I have shown how proper Malay middle-class consumption of cars in urban Malaysia is subjected to critique and distinctions that are equally political, religious, and social in orientation. To informants, Malaysia's capacity to match the quality of Western technologically advanced commodities aroused an element of national pride. Still, Western-produced cars, such as BMW and Mercedes, were seen to embody more status, and thus excess, compared to local brands, and those who chose to purchase or favor the Malaysian Proton effectively expressed this attitude. Compared to imported commodities, local ones were seen as inscribed with a national "surplus," i.e., a form of economic and symbolic devotion to the Malaysian nation.

Shortly after Proton's plan to develop an "Islamic car" designed for "Muslim motorists" was announced in 2007, this idea was critiqued by Dr. Syed Ali Tawfik Al-Attas,[32] Director General of the Malaysian Institute of Islamic Understanding Malaysia (IKIM). IKIM is an Islamic bureaucratic body set up by the state to address questions regarding proper Islamic thought and practice. The director critiqued "using the term 'Islamic' as an advertising tool purely for economic gain." In his opinion, the idea to promote an Islamic car was driven by "ambitious political entities" lacking "intellectual authority." He argued that "the term 'Islamic' betrays an activity [*amalan*], one which is derived from the fundamental elements of the worldview of Islam. As such, it necessarily requires an actor [*pengamal*]. [...] the term 'Islamic' refers to an activity or action and by necessity an actor, logically there must be a system of laws governing that action, namely the *shari'ah*." [33] This controversy raises several questions that also have a bearing on the broader themes in this volume.

Aldred Gell considers objects, and art objects in particular, "the equivalent of persons, or more precisely, social agents," because humans often treat them as such.[34] The central critique of the IKIM director, Dr. Al-Attas, is that a state-driven company such as Proton is imputing "Islamic" agency to a commodity. One major field of tension in contemporary Malaysia concerns such attempts to deepen and widen halalization to cover more and more types of commodities, ideas, and practices that can be classified as signs of proper, or improper, Islamic consumption. As we have seen in the accounts of the informants cited above, cars are often understood and purchased and displayed as much more than simply objects or commodities. Gell writes that:

---

[31] Miller, *Modernity*, p. 245.

[32] "Just What Is an Islamic Car," *The Star*, November 27, 2007.

[33] Ibid.

[34] Alfred Gell, *Art and Agency: An Anthropological Theory* (Oxford: Clarendon Press, 1998), p. 7.

It is in fact very difficult for a car owner not to regard a car as a body part, a prosthesis, something invested with his (or her) own social agency vis-à-vis other social agents ... Not only is the car a locus of the owner's agency, and a conduit through which the agency of others (bad drivers, vandals) may affect him—it is also the locus of an "autonomous" agency of its own.[35]

Cars in modern Malaysia can take on meanings as forms of prostheses or bodily extensions of their owners. In other words, many middle-class Malays perceive cars as powerful fronts performing a whole range of actions that are often articulated in Islamic or patriotic terms. Conversely, in other narratives, cars are simply positional goods that should not be Islamicized. The more cars are evoked as material extensions of persons, the more agency is attributed to them. In Gell's phrase, cars work as "indexes" of origin and modify their owners' intentions and actions in a particular cultural context, such as Malaysia.

"Motion" is intrinsic to ways in which cars are produced and exchanged between the state, the marketplace, and consumers in modern Malaysia. Motion, or "being moved" physically (transport and landscaping), socially (class formation), religiously (excessive or un-Islamic consumption), and nationally (shopping for the state or patriotic consumption) are significant to an understanding of car culture in modern Malaysia.

---

[35] Ibid., p. 18.

CHAPTER 3

A SPIRIT MEDIUM AS ARCHITECT: CAODAISM'S VISUAL THEOLOGY

Janet Hoskins

The eclectic architecture of the Caodai Great Temple in Tây Ninh, Vietnam, has attracted a great deal of attention from tourists and journalists, but relatively little from scholars. It was built from 1926 to 1954, based on instructions received in séances led by Phạm Công Tắc, a spirit medium who received messages in verse in both French and Vietnamese. The vibrant forms of the temple are themselves a form of religious teaching, a visual pedagogy that expresses certain concepts clearly and hints at others more obliquely. This paper argues that many points of Caodai theology were expressed first visually, and only later explained through commentary and narrative exegesis. This form of revelation emerged in the context of colonial surveillance, where the incorporation of French figures like Victor Hugo and Jeanne d'Arc was often seen as a "sly propaganda move"[1] on the part of anticolonial nationalists. I argue that the Great Temple and its administrative hierarchy anticipated the forms of an independent nation of Vietnam, and proved both inspirational and controversial because of this format.

While architecture would seem to be one of the more "static" forms of material religion, it does, in fact, participate in a kinetic form of motion and devotion. The hybrid modernism of the Caodai Temple is a magnet for religious pilgrimages (and, since 1990, the second most popular tourist destination in southern Vietnam, after the war museum in Saigon). The scale of the sacred city of Tây Ninh is immense, including more than sixty-five different buildings, and the Great Temple itself is larger than any European cathedral in Vietnam. Caodaists refer to Tây Ninh as "the Vatican of Caodaism," and see its construction as Phạm Công Tắc's greatest accomplishment.

The visual display of syncretistic teachings is said to move people to come together under one roof, and it also intrigues a large number of foreign visitors. Many conversion stories begin with a visit to Tây Ninh, where the visitor is overwhelmed by the beauty and complexity of Caodai architecture and then decides to begin to study its doctrine in order to be initiated. I will argue that the eclectic, hybrid architecture in Tây Ninh is strategically ambiguous, because it allows the

---

[1] Ralph B Smith, "An Introduction to Caodaism 1. Origins and Early History," *Bulletin of the School of Oriental and African Studies* 33,2 (1970): pp. 335–49.

disciples of Cao Dai to make their own selection of religious teachers, and thus display a certain agency while remaining submissive to the religious hierarchy.

WHAT IS A VISUAL THEOLOGY?

I define a visual theology as a set of religious ideas, doctrines, and practices that are expressed through images, statues, and architecture before the relationships among these various elements are specified in words. Such a theology has an inherently fluid, dynamic character, because it can be interpreted in a number of ways. It can be identified with what Ashis Nandy calls "religion-as-faith"—"religion as a way of life, a tradition which is definitionally non-monolithic, and operationally plural."[2] It can be opposed to "religion-as-ideology," which serves to identify populations seeking particular non-religious political or social goals. Visually, Caodaism is both syncretistic and multi-cultural, since it includes and celebrates many religious traditions. In the course of its history, and particularly its engagement in anticolonial struggle, it has assumed the characteristics of an ideology, become tied to certain texts that were seen as the purest form of the religion, and been associated with Vietnamese nationalism.

The key icon of Caodaism is the left eye of God (*Thiên Nhãn*) that appears at the top of every one of its altars, as well as on its flag, its publications, and the tall headdress worn by high-ranking ritual specialists in its major ceremonies. Sometimes pictured inside a triangle, with the rays of the sun projecting outward from all sides, it bears an uncanny resemblance to Freemason images of an "all seeing eye," and even the "Eye of Providence" on the US dollar bill (which was placed there in 1946, about the same time that Phạm Công Tắc performed a divination predicting that Caodaism would expand into the United States). In Caodai tradition, the eye appearing in the rising sun, with the moon and stars also visible, was a vision received by the ascetic mystic Ngô Văn Chiêu on the island of Phú Quốc in 1921. He was later contacted by a group of spiritists in Saigon, who received a series of messages from Cao Dai, the Supreme God, who revealed that he was the Jade Emperor who had sent Buddha, Confucius, and Lao Tzu, as well as his son, Jesus, to spread religious teachings on earth. Uniting Asian traditions under a new masculine monotheism, this movement attracted over a million followers within the first decade of its existence, inverting Orientalist ideas of Asian passivity by asserting that the left eye of God represented all that was dynamic, progressive, and positive in the world. Caodaism is now the third largest religion in Vietnam, having gathered about six million disciples over its eighty-year history.

The public, proselytizing side of Caodaism is called the "way of the eye" (*đạo mắt*), which is opposed to the more private, introspective "way of the heart" (*đạo tâm)* that emphasizes silence and meditation. The eye is also associated with an "outward gaze" that incorporates other religious icons to reveal their shared aspects, while the more quietist "way of the heart" conforms to Sino-Vietnamese Taoist practices and is less syncretistic. Phạm Công Tắc was the leader of the largest visible, exoteric (*Phổ Độ*) branch, whose headquarters in Tây Ninh is the "mother church" for all Caodaists and a magnet for both pilgrims and tourists. He was one of three founding spirit mediums who received "instructions" for the construction of the

---

[2] Ashis Nandy, "The Politics of Secularism and the Recovery of Religious Tolerance," in *Secularism and Its Critics*, ed. Rajeev Bhargava (Delhi: Oxford University Press, 1998), p. 322.

Great Temple of Tây Ninh in the period 1926–34. Dictated by the Supreme Being using a phoenix-headed basket to trace his words, these "instructions" detailed the visual features of the temple, including elements of Hinduism and Islam in the grand format of a Gothic cathedral. Later, through his writings and sermons, Tắc would articulate this visual theology into a more this-worldly religious ideology.

As the Hộ Pháp ("Defender of the Faith") of the Tây Ninh Vatican or Holy See (Tòa Thánh), Phạm Công Tắc fashioned a modernist millenarianism designed to develop a new kind of agency, giving the Vietnamese people the confidence that they could change the course of history and were, in fact, destined to do so. He drew on the power of old prophecies that "One day, a country now in servitude will become the master teacher of all humanity."[3] Caodai teachings identified the left eye of God with dynamism, progression, and modernity (the masculine principle yang or *dương*); incorporated many of the organizational features of the Catholic Church; and encompassed Jesus into an Asian pantheon as the son of the Jade Emperor.

Born in the urban spaces of Saigon, Cholon, and Gia Dinh, Caodaism became the largest mass movement in French Indochina, building a following in the same areas as the Indochina Communist Party, and functioning at times as a political force in its own right.[4] But rather than arguing (as some French observers did) that this was a political "party masquerading as a religion," I place Caodaism instead within the ethnographic record of new religions that promote the emblems, narratives, and technologies of modern nation states.

Building on Phạm Công Tắc's autobiographic reflections and writings, I present a case that links stagecraft (his dramatic visual presentations) to statecraft (creating "Vietnam" as an autonomous religious space, "a state within a state"). This utopian project supported the struggle for independence by providing a new repertoire of concepts for imagining national independence, and a separate apparatus of power to try to achieve them.[5] Rather than stressing Phạm Công Tắc's political actions, which have been well documented in earlier studies,[6] I focus instead on an interpretation of Caodaism's architecture, which presents the key figures of the "revealed pantheon" of Caodaism visually, and then elaborates their roles in words. Tắc himself invested many visual symbols with ideologized interpretations, as can be seen by reading his sermons, séance transcripts, and commentaries.[7] His legacy came back under the

[3] Hương Hiếu (religious name of Nguyễn Thị Hiếu, wife of Cao Quỳnh Cư), *Đạo Sử Vols. I and II* [History of the religion], p. 242. Originally published by Tòa Thánh Tây Ninh, Vietnam. Reprinted in 1997 by Thánh Thất Dốc Đa in Westminster, California, from the mimeographed text by the author, a female cardinal who participated in the first séances with Cao Đài in 1968.

[4] Jayne Werner, "Vietnamese Communism and Vietnamese Sectarianism," in *Vietnamese Communism in Comparative Perspective*, ed. William Turley (Boulder, CO: Westview Press, 1980), pp. 107–37.

[5] This insight comes from conversations with Caodaists in California, France, and Vietnam from 2002 to 2010, and also from conversations with Jeremy Jammes in France in 2005, and the reading of his 2006 dissertation, a work that straddles Vietnamese and diasporic communities and contributed greatly to my understanding of Caodaism. Jérémy Jammes, Thèse de Doctorat, "Le Caodaisme: Rituels médiumiques: Oracles et exegeses, Approche ethnologique d'un mouvement relirigieux vietnamien et de ses réseaux," Paris: Université Paris X Nanterre.

[6] S. Blagov, *Caodaism: Vietnamese Traditionalism and Its Leap into Modernity* (New York, NY: Nova Science Publishers, 2001); and Werner, "Vietnamese Communism and Vietnamese Sectarianism."

[7] Đỗ Văn Lý, *Tìm Hiểu Đạo Cao Đài* [Understanding Caodaism] (Perris, CA: Cao Đài Giáo Việt Nam Hải Ngoại, Overseas Vietnamese Community of Caodaists, 1989); Đồng Tân, *Nhân Vật*

spotlight in 2006, when a huge controversy erupted over whether his remains should be brought back to communist dominated Vietnam. The tensions between the flexible, tolerant, and syncretistic theology of Caodaism and its links to ideologized factions were played out in this debate over the appropriate place to bury its most famous spirit medium.

Phạm Công Tắc was an important religious innovator, who created a new style of mediumistic séance and a new type of scripture. After many centuries of Sino-Vietnamese phoenix writing, his séances received messages not in Chinese characters traced in sand, but in the Romanized cursive of *quốc ngữ*, literacy that made it possible to receive dictation in both Vietnamese and French. The Romanized script was supremely well adopted to the bicultural and bilingual milieu of the early spiritist circles of young colonial subjects educated in French language schools. As a spirit medium, however, he never claimed "authorship" of these innovations, which were all attributed to divine guidance. But the model that he presented for conversations with divinities, rather than serving as a simple vehicle (the "voice" or "hand" of the spirit dictating a message), was to have profound implications for Caodai doctrine.[8] It developed in new directions over the almost thirty-five years during which he played a pivotal role in articulating Caodai teachings, and his subtle finessing of the issue of authorship was one of his most significant leadership strategies.

Caodaism's formation of an alternative apparatus of power can be seen to have a kinship with other indigenous movements against occupying states, like the Native American prophet Handsome Lake, who led a Seneca millenarian group and claimed to have conversed in a trance with the first US president, George Washington, speaking at his house as he played with his dog on the veranda.[9] By incorporating

---

Cao Đài Giáo [Caodai personages: Biographies of prominent Caodaists] (Carlton, Victoria: The Caodai Cultural Association, 2006); Hue Nhân (pen name for Vo Thành Châu), *Khai Dao: Tu Khoi Nguyen den Khai Minh* [The inauguration of the faith: From its first beginnings to the official declaration] (Ho Chi Minh City: Co Quan Pho Thong Giáo Ly Dai Dao, Nhà Xuât Ban Tôn Giáo, 2005); Phạm Công Tắc, *Con Đường Thiêng Liêng Hằng Sống* [The divine path to eternal life], Sermons from 1947–1949, trans. Dao Cong Tam and Christopher Hartney, The Sydney Centre for Caodaism Studies, online archive, www.personal.usyd.edu.au/~cdao/tam.htm, accessed May 29, 2012; Trần Văn Rang, *Đại Đạo Danh Nhân* (The Famous adepts of the great way) (Tây Ninh: Tòa Thánh Tây Ninh, 1971); Trần Mỹ-Vân, "Japan and Vietnam's Caodaists: A Wartime Relationship, (1939–45)," in *Journal of Southeast Asian Studies* 27,1 (1996): 179–83; Trần Mỹ-Vân, "Japan through Vietnamese Eyes 1905–1945," in *Journal of Southeast Asian Studies* 30,1 (1999): 126–54; Trần Mỹ-Vân, "Vietnam's Caodaism, Independence, and Peace: The Life and Times of Phạm Công Tắc (1890–1959)," in *Academica Sinica: Prosea Research Paper 38* (2000): 1–28; Trần Mỹ-Vân, *A Vietnamese Royal Exile in Japan: Prince Cuong De 1882–1950* (London and New York, NY: Routledge, 2006).

[8] The goal of a religious visionary may, in fact, be somewhat more like the goal of a novelist, seeking not so much to change reality but to replace it—to offer another life, endowed with its own attributes, that is created to discredit real life, to offer an alternative to the mundane. These visions serve to "re-enchant" the world, to place it within a wider celestial framework, and to infuse it with meanings beyond those ordinarily perceived. Political utopias often disappoint because their goals cannot be reached during the lifetime of their proponents. Religious utopias, which always project these goals onto another world, are not discredited by the same process.

[9] Alice Beck Kehoe, *The Ghost Dance: Ethnohistory and Revitalization, Death or Renewal?* (New York, NY: Holt, Rinehart, and Winston, 1989), pp. 32–33; Anthony F. C. Wallace, "Revitalization Movements: Some Theoretical Considerations for Their Comparative Study,"

and appropriating certain elements of the power of the colonial masters, religious leaders create a competitive model that derives its persuasive force from its capacity to both imitate and assimilate other forms of power. By appropriating and incorporating French heroes like Victor Hugo and Jeanne d'Arc, the Caodai Holy See mirrored to French colonial power the imagined modern nation that its construction was to bring into being. Its master planning, its intricate administrative hierarchy, are proof of this new religious movement's ability to create something new, to capture modernity in both its Asian and European aspects—its institutions, forms of knowledge, modes of power, and radiant future—by means of creating an alternative likeness. The copy itself becomes an original, a new model for a new order of being.

Phạm Công Tắc's career should not, however, be taken as the prototype for all of Caodaism. Ralph Smith famously described Tắc as "the most prominent, but not necessarily the most important" Caodai leader, and the controversies surrounding the return of his body to Vietnam reawakened these debates.[10] Many contemporary Caodaists express ambivalence about Phạm Công Tắc's later political prominence, although they all acknowledge his importance during the formation of the new religion. As Đồng Tân, one of his most stringent critics, notes, "He was the main person that God used during the early years of the Great Way."[11] But signs of schism began very early because of what some critics have called his "strong personality," his efforts to establish exclusive religious authority, and his efforts to use spirit messages to mobilize the masses against colonial rule.[12]

One Caodai historian has argued that Phạm Công Tắc "wanted to be Richelieu to Bảo Đài's Louis 13th, serving as a religious advisor to a secular king."[13] Others claim, even more critically, that he came to imagine himself more like Louis the Sixteenth: "Le Caodaisme, c'est moi"—eclipsing the ideal of spreading mystical enlightenment through the fold and monopolizing contact with the divine, restricting contact to specially trained mediums in a college of mediums designated with his own patronym.[14] At the same time that some of his followers identify him as a reincarnation of Jesus[15] or Buddha,[16] others argue that he corrupted the original intent of the Caodai Religious Constitution (which he himself received as a medium

---

American Anthropologist 58,2 (1956): 264–81; Anthony F. C. Wallace, *Death and Rebirth of the Seneca* (New York, NY: Knopf, 1970).

[10] Ralph B. Smith, "An Introduction to Caodaism, Part 2: Beliefs and Organization," *Bulletin of the School of Oriental and African Studies* 33,3 (1971): 574.

[11] Đồng Tân, *Nhân Vật Cao Đài Giáo*, p. 106.

[12] His critics within Caodaism do not deny Phạm Công Tắc's charismatic powers, but instead argue that his own spirit became too strong to be a vessel for God's messages. Reports of Tắc successfully healing patients with his hands and exorcising evil spirits are presented to show how he followed a mystical formula established by older religious traditions (*huyền thoại cựu giáo*), which was not consistent with the modern form of Caodaist teachings. See Đồng Tân, *Nhân Vật Cao Đài Giáo*, pp. 44–46, 49.

[13] Đỗ Văn Lý, personal interviews in Chatsworth, CA, 2005.

[14] Đồng Tân, *Nhân Vật Cao Đài Giáo*, p. 46.

[15] Denise Chong, *The Girl in the Picture: The Story of Kim Phuc, Whose Image Altered the Course of the Vietnam War* (New York, NY: Viking, 2000).

[16] Danny Pham, "The Caodai Holy See in Pictures," unpublished manuscript, 2006, shared with the author.

and published) and compromised the faith by tying it to political and military agendas.

My goal is not to resolve these debates, but to situate them in relation to anthropological and postcolonial theories about nationalism, anticolonial resistance, and the leaders who operate in both the spiritual and the temporal spheres. Phạm Công Tắc's career has sometimes been compared, both favorably and unfavorably, to that of M. K. Gandhi, in India. He was an exceptional figure, whose influence has never been replicated, but his leadership was deeply divisive. Today, eight hundred of the thirteen hundred Caodai temples in Vietnam belong to the Tây Ninh "mother church," and almost all of them reverently display images of the Hộ Pháp at the rear of their temples, facing the altar of the Left Eye of God. For five hundred other temples (serving almost half of all Caodaists in Vietnam), Tắc is an important but problematic foundational figure, whose legacy is both positive and negative. Like Gandhi, Tắc tried to use "Orientalism" (a Western discourse about the differences between East and West) against empire, but the ways in which he did so balanced uneasily between asserting the powerful, progressive dynamics of a masculine, Asian perspective (*dương*, associated with the left) and integrating elements of Europeanized Christianity into a new universal doctrine.

"READING" CAODAI ARCHITECTURE: A FIRST LOOK

According to Caodai scripture, each feature of the Holy See was mandated by instructions received in spirit séances, most of them coming from the "Invisible Pope," Lý Thái Bạch, who is himself the spirit of the eighth-century Chinese Taoist poet Li Bai, known for his love of nature and inebriated versifying. From the front, the vast structure resembles a Gothic cathedral (Figure 1), with a nave, separate entrances for men and women, and a series of nine ascending levels advancing towards an octagonal inner sanctuary, where the Left Eye of God is represented on a huge globe (Figure 2). Open latticework windows with a lotus-enclosed eye design line the sides (Figure 3), and twelve dragons coil on pastel columns of lotus flowers.

Figure 1: Tây Ninh temple, side view. Photograph by Janet Hoskins

Figure 2: Dignitaries dressed in red (for Confucianism but also Catholicism), yellow (for Buddhism), and turquoise (for Taoism) kneel in front of the globe with the Left Eye of God on it. Photograph by Janet Hoskins

Figure 3: The interior of Tây Ninh's Great Temple, showing the dragons and flowers that curl around pillars to represent the moment when divine titles will be bestowed upon the most virtuous and devoted disciples, the "Dragon Flower Assembly." Photograph by Janet Hoskins

Figure 4: These statues were erected in the Great Temple in the 1970s to honor the three founding mediums. Phạm Công Tắc stands in the center, wearing the golden armor of a general. To his sides are his sacred and secular assistants, Cao Quỳnh Cư and Cao Hoài Sang, holding a fan and Taoist whisk for purification.
Photograph by Janet Hoskins

The relatively "European" exterior opens up onto an intensely Asian interior in which hierarchical rank and levels of spiritual attainment are mapped vertically and horizontally as disciples approach the altar. The pope and his six cardinals sit on special thrones in front of the altar, while the three founding spirit mediums stand with their backs to the entrance, in front of the "*khí*" character (for breath or vital force), with Phạm Công Tắc in the center, dressed in the splendid armor of a Chinese general, carrying an exorcist's staff in his left hand and the beads of compassion in his right (Figure 4).

Caodai commentators describe this "combination of three principal architectures" as modeling the dimensions of a syncretistic theology: "The Catholicism is marked by its verticality (bell tower and drum tower), the Buddhism by its horizontality (the Nine Sphere Palace in the middle and the Octagonal Palace in the rear), and the Islamism by its sphericity."[17] The "verticality" of the "Catholic front" was presented to French authorities to command their attention, but the more sacred spaces are inside, and illustrate ascending levels of spirituality. The highest

---

[17] Hum Dac Bui and Ngasha Beck, *Caodai, Faith of Unity* (Fayetteville, AR: Emerald Wave, 2000), p. 13.

ranking dignitaries are seated at the opposite end of the Gothic exterior, nearest to the Octagonal Palace (Bát Quái Đài), which is named after the eight trigrams used in Taoist divination. This is where the invisible spirits reside, since their coming together was prophesied in the *Dao de Jing*. Two spheres rise over the roof of the Holy See: the Islamic-like onion dome over the center (where disciples kneel on cushions as they meditate to music, topped with a map of the world and the dragon horse used to carry the deceased in funeral processions), and the Octagonal Palace at the back (hovering over the globe with the divine eye, topped with the Hindu figures of Brahma, Shiva, and Vishnu). Tellingly, the Hindu deities are described as earlier forms of the Buddha, and the "sphericity" of Islam encircles earlier Asian traditions since Mohammed is seen as carrying forward the same basic message as these spiritual predecessors.

Figure 5: Canopy with Global Eye. Photograph by Janet Hoskins

Above the Great Eye hangs a pediment in front of a blue curtain, picturing the world's spiritual leaders on five levels (Figure 5). Buddha sits at the apex, flanked by Lao Tzu on his right and Confucius on his left, with Lý Thái Bạch below him and the female Boddhisattva Quan Âm to his right and the red-faced warrior Quan Cong on his left. Below them, on the third level, is Jesus, and then below him is Khương Thái Công, a figure representing the veneration of local spirits and heroes. Buddha represents the ideal of enlightenment, while Lao Tzu and Lý Thái Bạch stand for the "way of the immortals" (*đạo tiên*), Jesus for the "way of the saints" (*đạo thánh*, which includes Judaism and Islam), and the final level for the "way of humanity." When asked why Jesus is placed three levels below Buddha, most Caodaists say it is because he came after Buddha in history, but since the eighth-century Taoist poet Li Bái is also placed higher than Jesus, this "chronological" order becomes hard to defend. Instead, it is argued that each "way" is valid and valuable for those who follow it, and the Jade Emperor (Cao Đài) sent all these spiritual leaders.

The statue of Phạm Công Tắc by the entrance stands on a lotus blossom in front of a Naga throne, with seven Naga heads emerging from it. His throne bears a striking resemblance to a famous Cambodian colonial monument, the "Naga bridge," designed by the French architect Fabre and finished in 1892 to span a newly built canal leading to the Buddhist Vat Pnum temple, designated as Phnom Penh's *"pagode national."*[18] Modeled on a serpent's arching body, the Naga bridge features seven hooded Naga heads flanking each end, and is situated in the center of the French administrative district, where Phạm Công Tắc was employed in the customs office from June 1927 to May 1928.[19] In Theravada Buddhist tradition, the seven-headed snake Muchalinda was said to have sheltered the meditating Buddha from a powerful storm by coiling himself around the Buddha and stretching his hoods out to form an umbrella over the Buddha's head to shelter him from the rains. The bridge design fuses the reverence for snakes common in indigenous Southeast Asia, where they often represent the original owners of the land and guardians of fertility, with Buddhist ideas of protecting and honoring the Buddha.[20]

The snakeheads on Phạm Công Tắc's throne are arranged quite differently from those in Phnom Penh, and suggest the influence of Christian theology, in which the snake is an emblem of evil. Half of them are identified as representing "poisonous emotions which can raise their heads to destroy good deeds and bring people into a sea of hardship for many generations."[21] Phạm Công Tắc is pictured with the snakeheads representing the three "positive emotions" (joy, happiness, and love) rising upwards behind his head, showing that these emotions should be nurtured.[22] His hands push down the two snakeheads representing unclean thoughts and sexual urges, and his feet stand ready to push back those representing anger and ambition.

During his lifetime, Phạm Công Tắc would sit on this throne in the golden armor of his high ceremonial costume (Figure 6), flanked by the two other mediums who assisted him at the first séances. After his death, the statue erected in his place stands higher on its lotus column and seems to have risen above these worldly temptations, and he now holds a golden staff in his right hand to drive away evil, and the rosary beads of compassion in his left hand. His throne presents a visual statement in which a moral discourse (distinguishing between good and bad emotions) is projected onto an image of power borrowed from Khmer Hindu icons and incorporated into French-designed "Buddhist" decorations in Phnom Penh.

---

[18] Penny Edwards, *Cambodge: The Cultivation of a Nation, 1860–1945* (Honolulu, HI: University of Hawaii Press, 2007), p. 47.

[19] Tran, "Vietnam's Caodaism," p. 10.

[20] Pacific Asia Museum, *Visions of Enlightenment: The Art Of Buddhism*, Pacific Asia Museum, exhibit catalogue, 2006.

[21] Nguyễn Văn Hồng, *Giới Thiệu Tòa Thánh Tây Ninh của Đạo Cao Đài qua hình ảnh* (Westchester, CA: Cơ Quan Truyền Giáo Cao Đái Hải Ngoại, 2006).

[22] Ibid.; Pham, "The Caodai Holy See in Pictures."

Figure 6: Phạm Công Tắc, photographed in 1950, sitting on his Naga throne and keeping the evil serpents under control as the good ones rise up behind his head. Photograph archived by Trần Quang Cảnh, used with permission

Visitors enter the temple through two doors, men entering on the left side of the divinity and women entering on the right, in a section called the Hall of Tranquility (Tịnh Tâm Điền), where they should calm themselves before the ceremony. On the inside wall of this section is a large mural showing three saints signing a contract between God and Humanity: Sun Yat Sen (1866–1925), the Chinese nationalist who is the patron saint of Asian self-determination, is on the left holding an ink slab. Victor Hugo (1802–85), the French novelist, poet, and spiritist, known for his compassion for the oppressed, is in the middle, writing in French *"Dieu et Humanite, Amour et Justice."* The Vietnamese poet and prophet Nguyễn Bỉnh Khiêm (1491–1585, called the "Nostradamus of Vietnam") is on the right, painting the same message in Chinese characters (Figure 7). Each of these figures was seen as predicting the advent of Caodaism: Sun Yat-Sen because he led the first successful Asian nationalist struggle, Victor Hugo because he foretold the advent of a new fusion of Eastern and

Western philosophies in a transcript of séances received in 1835,[23] and Nguyễn Bỉnh Khiêm because he spoke of a "great new spiritual pathway" that would appear in the southland. These saints are said to watch human activity from the White Cloud Lodge in heaven, and they also represent the coming together of Chinese, French, and Vietnamese literary traditions among the colonized intellectuals of Saigon.

Figure 7: Mural featuring Sun Yat Sen, Victor Hugo, and Nguyễn Bỉnh Khiêm.
Photograph by Janet Hoskins

Hugo's spirit was first contacted in séances held by Phạm Công Tắc in Phnom Penh, and Hugo was eventually appointed the "spiritual head of the foreign mission," designated to advise the expansion of the faith in other Francophone colonies. Hugo dictated messages both in French (using alexandrine verse) and in Vietnamese (using the classic seven-eight verse pattern). His French verses criticize the colonial conquest ordered by his great enemy, Napoleon III, and call on France to remain true to the freedoms of her humanitarian heritage. "Here in Indochina, we are under the power of potentates," he begins, with the "colonial government

---

[23] Hugo's séance transcripts were not published until thirty years after his death, when they appeared in Gustave Simon, ed., *Chez Victor Hugo: Les Tables Tournantes de Jersey* (Paris: Louis Conard, 1923). These séances were the subject of many articles in French Indochinese newspapers, and inspired others to try their hand at spiritism.

bowing to the Catholic rod ... As a son of France, at least for one lifetime, I have come to know how deeply her ideals have been betrayed" by the persecution of followers of the new faith.[24] Hugo is not, strictly speaking, "deified," but incorporated into a "republican pantheon" of great men and women modeled in many ways on the Panthéon mausoleum in Paris. This was not a tactical cover but a cosmopolitan reference to assert the parity between colonizer and colonized, and make claims to universal values in the same spirit as those of the French Republic.

In 1934, Phạm Công Tắc claimed that Hugo's spirit supported his excommunication of dissident branches, so after that time none of the other Caodai branches has honored Hugo in their pantheon. In a sermon delivered in 1948, Phạm Công Tắc revealed that Hugo was the reincarnation of the famous Vietnamese poet Nguyễn Du, and so completed the process of "indigenizing" Hugo's legacy and incorporating him into Vietnamese literary history. Today, his image (duplicated in most of the eight hundred Tây Ninh temples in Vietnam and dozens in the diaspora) remains a visual reminder of humanist ideals and the support that Caodaists received from the Committee for the Rights of Man and other Paris-based critics of colonialism in the period from 1931–36.

The visually eclectic elements of Caodai theology had attracted a large following, which began to fragment into different ideologically oriented factions during the divisive years of anticolonial struggle. Many other denominations of Caodaism formed their own Holy Sees, interpreting the "divine instructions" received in 1926–34 in their own ways. They built variations on the Gothic cathedral frame with minor changes (e.g., using statues instead of ancestral tablets on the altar, painting the outside a rose color or white instead of yellow). The dome-like roof of the "Sacré Coeur" in Paris was the architectural inspiration for a splinter group that worshipped the eye inside the symbol of the heart. The strategic flexibility of a visual theology allowed the "blueprint of Caodai belief" to be constructed in different colors and sizes, while retaining its identifiable characteristics of the eye and a syncretistic pantheon.

USING ORIENTALISM AGAINST EMPIRE: VISUAL THEOLOGY BECOMES INFUSED WITH ANTICOLONIAL IDEOLOGY

When the American scholar Virginia Thompson visited French Indochina in 1935, she found Caodaism to be "the one constructive indigenous movement among the Annamites" and was particularly full of praise for what the Hộ Pháp had done in Tây Ninh, providing schools, printing presses, and weaver's looms with a "Gandhiesque flavor about creating a community which is self-sufficient."[25] Both Phạm Công Tắc and Gandhi promoted cultural nationalism as a major strategy of anticolonial resistance. The notion of a return to pure, indigenous traditions, with emphasis on certain forms of moral and ethical strength, was important in preparing people to resist an apparently overwhelming colonial power. Influenced by Social Darwinism, Gandhi argued that Indians had brought on the degeneracy of India

[24] Trần Quang Vinh, *Les Messages Spirites de la Troisième Amnistie de Dieu en Orient* (Tây Ninh: Sainte Siège du Caodaisme, 1962), pp. 58–59.

[25] Virginia Thompson, *French Indo-china* (New York, NY: The Macmillan Company for the American Council Institute of Pacific Relations, 1937), pp. 474–75.

through their own moral faults and complicity by following foreign consumer fashions. Phạm Công Tắc drew on an earlier tradition of prophecies that the Vietnamese had brought colonialism on themselves as a punishment for their sins, but had now paid their karmic debts over a hundred years of French domination. Because they bore this burden with courage and grace, they would be rewarded for their suffering under the colonial yoke by becoming the "spiritual masters of mankind."

The grandiose architecture of Tây Ninh was modeled in part on the *folies de grandeur* of French cathedrals and opera houses. The home of the École Française d'Extrême Orient (constructed in Hanoi at the same time as the Tây Ninh Caodai temple) was praised for pioneering a hybrid "Indochinese" style, and featured an Orientalist facade with a somber European interior, rather neatly inverting the "divine blueprints" of the Caodai Holy See. Construction of the Holy See continued over a twenty-year period (1934–54), interrupted in 1940 when French forces arrested Phạm Công Tắc for prophesying a "Great War" in Europe that would bring an end to the French colonial empire. Exiled to colonial prisons in Madagascar for five years, Phạm Công Tắc returned to Vietnam in 1946 as part of a negotiation with a Japanese-trained Caodai militia that had helped to overthrow the French in Saigon in March 1945. In return for serving as a peacekeeping force in collaboration with the French, Caodaists were given weapons to defend themselves against the Viet Minh (their former comrades-in-arms during the August revolution, who had then turned against non-communist nationalists).

While Phạm Công Tắc (like Gandhi) was usually seen as preaching a "counter-modernity," and spoke of restoring traditional values, it is also true that "his counter-modernity proved to be the most modern of all those of anticolonial activists."[26] In the final decade of his life, the Hộ Pháp began to promote his message through the media, using the society of spectacle as his secret weapon. He gave a series of press conferences, met with foreign reporters, and traveled to Geneva and to Japan, Taiwan, and Hanoi as a "spirit medium diplomat" who desperately opposed partition.

Bernard Fall visited Phạm Công Tắc in August 1953 to ask for his perspective on the decolonization process. The Caodist leader impressed Fall deeply, as noted in a recently published letter Fall wrote to his wife:

> The man had a piercing intelligence and his approach to things is very realistic. I learned more about Indochina than I'd learned before in three and half months. To think that he was sitting there with me telling me about the need for French help after he'd spent five years in French banishment in Madagascar. The man was fascinating and I can see why two million people think he's the next thing to God himself—and that includes a lot of educated Europeans.[27]

Fall famously described him as "the shrewdest Vietnamese politician," but remained skeptical about whether Phạm Công Tắc could use his religious base to reconcile the

---

[26] Robert Young, *Postcolonialism: An Historical Introduction* (London: Wiley Blackwell, 2001), p. 334.

[27] Dorothy Fall, *Bernard Fall: Memories of a Scholar–Soldier* (Washington, DC: Potomac Books, 2006), pp. 77–78.

increasingly polarized forces of what became the governments of Hanoi and Saigon.[28]

In 1953–54, Phạm Công Tắc gave a series of press conferences praising both Bảo Đại and Hồ Chí Minh and calling for national unity. When the French were defeated at Điện Biên Phủ in 1954, he called for a reconciliation of the southern republic with the northern communists. Phạm Công Tắc believed that his religion of unity would provide the ideal setting for negotiations to bring Vietnam's different political groups together, and he hoped for French and American backing for this to proceed. He attended the Geneva Conventions and tried to work behind the scenes to convince others, but this proposal was doomed to defeat when the French and Việt Minh agreed to the "temporary measure" of a partition at the seventeenth parallel.

Phạm Công Tắc and many other Caodaists had been willing to work with Bảo Đại, but as Ngô Đình Diệm moved to consolidate his own power with US backing, the militia associated with nonaligned nationalists were forcibly dissolved. In October 1955, Ngô Đình Diệm ordered Caodai General Phương to invade the Holy See and strip Phạm Công Tắc of all his temporal powers. Three hundred of his papal guardsmen were disarmed, and Phạm Công Tắc became a virtual prisoner of his own troops. On February 19, 1956, a number of other religious leaders and his daughters were arrested, but he himself managed to slip away. He made contact with his followers from Phnom Penh several weeks later, and lived out the last three years of his life in exile in Cambodia.

Phạm Công Tắc insisted that Caodaism needed to remain "independent" (*độc lập*), refusing to align with either side and seeking a peaceful path through the decolonization process. Caodaists had long nourished a utopian vision of living as an autonomous community, owing deference neither to the French colonial government nor to the Việt Minh. During the period 1946–54, Caodaists came close to realizing that dream. The French agreed to create a "state within a state," where Caodaists handled their own administration, collected their own taxes, enjoyed religious freedom, and received French weapons and funding for their troops. This mini-theocracy within the province of Tây Ninh lasted for almost a decade, dramatically enacting the nationalist dream of autonomy, and carving out its own separate space of power in the margins of the embattled French colonial administration.

Phạm Công Tắc's critics argued that he sacrificed the unifying appeal of the faith in order to become an activist driven more by ideology. His final writings lament the tragedy of partition, suggesting that Caodaists, and all Vietnamese, should seek expiation for "their divisiveness."[29] His deathbed request to the Cambodian King Sihanouk was that his body would not be returned to Vietnam until the country was "unified, or pursuing the policy of peace and neutrality to which I gave my life." But even as he saw many of his hopes crushed, the Hộ Pháp still knew how to use people's sense of guilt creatively: He promised his followers a moral victory by drawing on the non-martial self of the apparent victors to create in them doubts

---

[28] Bernard Fall, "The Political–Religious Sects of Viet-Nam," *Pacific Affairs* 28,3 (1955): 249.

[29] In the spirit message from Lý Đại Tiên received by the Hộ Pháp on April 9, 1948, Tắc is asked "not to feel hurt that the army was established in his absence," but instead to accept it as part of a Divine mechanism. He is, however, cautioned that his main trials lie ahead, since "this divisiveness does not help to save the world" (*mà lại đố kỵ chẳng dám cứu đời*), and "if the Vietnamese people do not respond to the call to religion, they cannot be saved." Trần Quang Vinh, *Hồi Ký Trần Quang Vinh và Lịch Sử Quân Đội Cao Đài* [Mémoir and history of the Caodai Militia] (Maryland: Thánh Thất Vùng Hoa Thịnh Đốn, 1992), pp. 188–89.

about their victory. On an ethical plane, his final words echoed Romain Rolland's formula, "Victory is always more catastrophic for the vanquishers than for the vanquished."[30] The suffering of the defeated can enhance their moral character and make them strong, while the triumphant celebrations of their opponents open the way for corruption and decadence.

2006 CONTROVERSY ABOUT RETURNING TẮC'S REMAINS

In November 2006, in response to US government criticism of Vietnam's suppression of religious freedom, the Vietnamese government decided to jump start the normalization of Caodaism by "repatriating" the body of Phạm Công Tắc after "fifty years of exile" (since he left for Cambodia in 1956). This occurred during the same week that US President George W. Bush flew to Hanoi for the ASEAN conference. It seems to have been negotiated as a concession to respond to the American government's removal of Vietnam from the list of "countries of particular concern" for violations of religious freedom, and it came just months before Vietnam was admitted into the World Trade Organization (WTO). For years, Caodaists had said that Phạm Công Tắc would be returned to Vietnam once Caodaists were free to hold séances and organize their worship services as they had before 1975. But this was not yet the case. A huge controversy erupted in overseas Caodai communities, with some Caodaists embracing this gesture as a "reconciliation" of their long troubled relation to a Marxist state, and others condemning it as an empty and inappropriate move at a time when full religious freedom and self-determination had not yet been granted. Discussion of this issue directly addresses the problem of whether charisma has to "anchored" in a specific location (here, the Holy See in Tây Ninh) in order to be efficacious, or whether it operates from a higher, de-territorialized spiritual realm.

For thirty years after 1975, many Caodai temples were closed, as thousands of South Vietnamese officers, medical personnel, and civil servants were forced to do hard labor in government "reeducation camps." The Tây Ninh Holy See was occupied by North Vietnamese tanks for some time, and then gradually reopened and used for short-term "reeducation classes" for religious leaders and followers. The original administrative structure was disbanded and replaced by a government-approved Governance Committee. At the dawn of the "Renovation" reforms that restored Vietnam to a market economy, funds to rebuild the temple and renovate its grounds began to come in from overseas Caodaists, and by the late 1990s the Holy See reemerged as a splendid, newly painted tourist attraction, surrounded by restaurants built to serve the thousands bused in from Saigon hotels. Graham Greene's vivid description of Caodaism in the widely read novel *The Quiet American* (filmed on site in 1958 and again in 2003) also helped to stir international interest.

Returning Phạm Công Tắc's remains to Vietnam disturbed the purity of exile enjoyed by those who resisted any collaboration with the communist government, since their own exile had been symbolically linked to the exile of the body of their most famous leader. Others, however, argued that there would be a spiritual efficacy to bringing his body to his final resting place within the Holy See, since then his "spirit would be better able to administer the religion from above," and his followers would feel closer to him and more willing to make pilgrimages to pray at his tomb.

---

[30] Ashis Nandy, *Exiled at Home* (Oxford: Oxford University Press, 2005), p. 123.

Some overseas Caodaists argued: "It is a central doctrine of spiritism that the location of the body is no impediment to communication with the soul of the deceased," so moving his remains would not help. But their critics countered that since spirit séances had been strictly forbidden by the Socialist Republic of Vietnam since 1976, the "return" of Phạm Công Tắc's remains to Tây Ninh was a step towards rebuilding relations with the liberalizing government, and publicly asserting that he was, in fact, a Vietnamese patriot who had struggled and suffered for the independence of the nation. (Caodaists in other denominations claimed to have received messages from Phạm Công Tắc's spirit both endorsing and criticizing the move, but since none of these occurred within the "Cung Đạo," or sacred medium's sanctuary within the Holy See, they could not be considered official.) There were rumors that the tomb in Phnom Penh would be found to be empty, either robbed by thieves seeking gold or intentionally vacated by the Hộ Pháp because his soul was reluctant to return to a communist Vietnam. But, in fact, his body was found to be surprisingly intact, with skin and hair still visible under the tightly wound coverings, and it was photographed and rewrapped for transport.

A huge ceremony attended by some 100,000 people greeted the return of Phạm Công Tắc's remains, which were carried in a dragon boat hearse across the border, and across the Mekong, and arrived on November 30, 2006. For the first time in over thirty years, the main gates of the Holy See were opened to allow the dragon boat to enter, and his body spent one night outside the tomb while thousands of Caodaists gathered for prayers. The next day it was placed in his tomb, flanked by the tombs of his two assistant mediums (whose statues stand on either side of his in the sanctuary). After the conclusion of the ceremony, religious leaders announced that they would meet to revise the government-imposed administrative structure and (it was hoped) move closer to the "divinely ordained Religious Constitution" that had been revealed to Phạm Công Tắc and his two assistants during the "age of revelations," from 1926 to 1929.

The colorful spectacle of this vast funeral cortege was an effort to reinvigorate a visual theology that needed to be reestablished as a "faith" as opposed to an ideology. In a religion-as-faith, most followers see their daily practice as something that can protect them, and from which they can receive solace and guidance. In a religion-as-ideology, followers come to see it more as something that they have to protect and promote. Belief is important in both cases, and contemplating visual icons such as the divine eye can strengthen belief. In a religion-as-faith, there is an idea that if you believe in it, it will work for you, while the logic of a religion-as-ideology is that if you believe, you should work for it. The strategic ambiguity of visual symbolism allows followers to choose both their own interpretations and their own orientations in their style of worship.

SETTING THE STAGE FOR A NEW NATION STATE

The lively debates that I witnessed about the repatriation of the Hộ Pháp's remains in November 2006 reflect several dimensions of the interactions between visual elements and written doctrine that have been important in Caodaism's history. Understanding Phạm Công Tắc as a performer who drew upon various "repertoires" and fused them into an efficacious enactment of a discourse of power allows our analysis to come closer to that of contemporary scholars of East Asian religion, who have argued that Confucianism, Taoism, and Buddhism are—as

Caodai scriptures teach—closer to "repertoires" than to "religions," since their doctrines are not mutually exclusive. They are more properly understood as cultural resources from which individuals have marshaled different ideas and practices at different times.[31] So the ambiguity of a visual theology is well suited to the fusion of the "three religions," and able to encompass and incorporate elements of Christianity, Hinduism, and Islam as well.

Phạm Công Tắc's role in constructing the Holy See could be interpreted as a way of visualizing charisma, trying to contain and enshrine it within a new architecture providing a concrete shape for the dream of national unity. His own power as a spirit medium was volatile, unstable, and revolutionary, but he wanted it to endure as something institutionalized, stable, and foundational. As Geertz notes:

> This is the paradox of charisma: that though it is rooted in the sense of being near to the heart of things, of being caught up in the realm of the serious, a sentiment that is felt most characteristically and continuously by those who in fact dominate social affairs, who ride in the progresses and grant the audiences, its most flamboyant expressions tend to appear among people at some distance from the center, indeed often enough at a rather enormous distance, who want very much to be closer. Heresy is as much of a child of orthodoxy in politics as it is in religion.[32]

Caodai architecture, considered "heretical" by the Catholic mission whose power it sought to usurp, was intended to incarnate a more enduring, centered, and well-established structure of authority. And the paradox of Caodai history is that, in spite of the trials of an anticolonial struggle, Cold War divisions, and three decades of a secular, authoritarian government, the Holy See has managed to do that.

Today, the ideal of independence that so inspired early Caodaists has had to make peace with a state where religion has generally been in disfavor. But recent reforms have allowed many temples to reopen and—with renovations and fresh coats of paint—opened the doors of a colorful, syncretic pantheon to a new generation of followers. This distinctively Vietnamese visual theology remains a compelling blend of the many historical influences on Vietnam—its early Hindu kingdoms, the Chinese education system, and Buddhist ideals of virtue—and is still flexible and ambiguous enough to be embraced by new interpretations.

---

[31] Robert Campany, "On the Very Idea of Religions in the Modern West and in Early Medieval China," *History of Religions* 42,4 (2003): 287–319; Robert Campany, "Secrecy and Display in the Quest for Transcendence in China, ca. 220 BCE–350 CE," *The History of Religions* 45,4 (2006): 291–336.

[32] Clifford Geertz, "Centers, Kings, and Charisma: Reflections on the Symbolics of Power," in *Local Knowledge: Further Essays in Interpretive Anthropology*, ed. Clifford Geertz (New York, NY: Basic Books, 1983), pp. 143–44.

CHAPTER 4

MATERIAL RELIGION AND ETHNIC IDENTITY: BUDDHIST VISUAL CULTURE AND THE BURMANIZATION OF THE EASTERN SHAN STATE

Klemens Karlsson

To be facing a Buddha image is like being in the presence of the Buddha himself. This may not be obvious to the Western viewer, but to the local Buddhist people, who are aware that the image has been consecrated, it is apparent that an image of the Buddha is more than just a lifeless sculpture. A key property of religious visual culture is that it evokes a sense of the sacred.[1] Making images or venerating and offering before them is a form of motion that allows believers to connect with the sacred, but it is also a way to establish a sacred space and a religious environment. Beautiful objects can attract people and make them feel that they are close to something sacred. According to David Morgan, members of an imagined community "need symbolic forms such as songs, dance, images, and food to allow them to participate in something that is larger both spatially and temporally than their immediate environment."[2]

Buddha images and religious buildings are also, as we will see, important visual objects that can act as emblems of ethnic identity and nationalism. They can put in motion political manifestations, such as the border conflict between Thailand and Cambodia at the ancient Khmer Preah Vihear temple site, where Buddhist monks on both sides held rituals in support of their respective governments, while accusing the other side of using black magic. This conflict over an ancient Hindu temple has been used for nationalistic purposes by politicians, monks, and the military on both sides.

Ethnicity and religion are among the most important markers of group identity. Ethnic and religious groups serve many functions, and people affiliate with these groups for many reasons. Ethnicity and religion are both essential aspects of the way people perceive their place in the world. In addition to a positive identity, feelings of

---

[1] Claire Mitchell, "The Religious Content of Ethnic Identities," *Sociology* 40,6 (2006): 1149.

[2] David Morgan, *The Sacred Gaze: Religious Visual Culture in Theory and Practice* (Berkeley, CA: University of California Press, 2005), p. 59.

certainty, and a sense of belongingness and inclusion, they provide a cultural worldview and meaningfulness.[3] According to Claire Mitchell, there appears to be a complex two-way relationship between the religious and ethnic bases of identity, where each can inform and provoke changes in the other.[4] The intertwining of religious and ethnic identity is particularly visible among ethnic groups of Southeast Asia, and the group identities of Thai, Burmese, and others are intimately connected with Buddhism. Ethnicity and religion have a tendency to merge into each other in such a way that it is nearly impossible to separate them.

Conflicts based on ethnic-religious identity are frequent throughout the world, with religious architecture and visual objects often serving as "powerful means of imagining a common identity."[5] Arguably, it is nearly always clearly defined religious traditions that confront each other. Here, however, we will see how ethnic-religious identity can be expressed in a conflict between two ethnic groups nominally sharing the same religious tradition. Most Buddhists in Upper Southeast Asia, e.g., the Burmese, the Thai, the Shan, and the Lao, belong to the same Theravāda tradition of Buddhism. Their canonical texts and doctrines, originating in the Mahāvihāra tradition of Lanka, are nearly identical, and the differences lie mostly in the rituals, in how the *vinaya* rules are observed and in the materialistic aspects of religion.

The present paper has as its primary concern the exemplification of the way religious visual culture may serve as a marker of ethnicity and nationalism. Examples are taken from Buddhist visual culture in the Eastern Shan State of Myanmar. The visual objects considered in this discussion are two very special Buddha statues that can, in different ways, convey Burmese ethnic and religious identity and be seen as elements in the Burmanization of the Shan State. In order to understand the role of these objects, this paper will also discuss, from a perspective of Southeast Asian history, the genuineness of Buddha statues and the reason why some Buddhist images and religious buildings are more sacred than others.

THE TAI KHUN AND THE ETHNIC CONFLICT IN THE EASTERN SHAN STATE

The Eastern Shan State lies east of the Salween River within the Shan State of Myanmar, bordering on Thailand, China, and Laos. The Tai Khun, i.e., the Shan people native to the Eastern Shan State,[6] have had a long and close relationship with neighboring Tai peoples in northern Thailand, Sipsongpanna, and northern Laos.

Defining ethnic groups in Southeast Asia, just as in many other places, is not an easy task. Southeast Asia is a region of constantly shifting ethnic boundaries, and ethnicity cannot be treated as a primordial given. On the contrary, ethnic groups everywhere constantly redefine themselves and are similarly redefined by others. Michael Moerman notes that ethnicity is impermanent in that individuals,

---

[3] Meykel Verkuyten and Ali Aslan Yildiz, "National (Dis)identification and Ethnic and Religious Identity: A Study among Turkish-Dutch Muslims," *Personality and Social Psychology Bulletin* 33 (2007): 1448–62.

[4] Mitchell, "The Religious Content of Ethnic Identities."

[5] Morgan, *The Sacred Gaze*, p. 221.

[6] Tai people in Myanmar are called Shan by the Burmese. The Thai in Thailand call them Tai Yai. They call themselves Tai and recognize numerous subcategories within this ethnic designation. The Tai people traditionally living east of the Salween River call themselves Tai Khun.

communities, and areas change their identification.[7] According to him, Tai tribal names are political in origin. People define and redefine themselves in relationship to others.[8]

People select their own history in the context of others, and it is necessary to view every social entity as part of a larger system. The self-definition of a people includes attributions made by its neighbors. An ethnic group is a socially constructed community that often defines itself by its origin or language. Thus, a chosen history is one of the main elements in creating a self-definition and prescribing its boundaries for others. I am therefore following Santasombat when he emphasizes that the ethnic identity of a particular Tai group is constructed in a continual process, not only by external forces and labeling by outsiders with whom the Tai interact, but also by their own socio-cultural process of creating a self-definition.[9] I will define Tai Khun primarily as those who define themselves, and are defined by others, as descendants of the city-state of Chiang Tung.

Chiang Tung,[10] the capital of the Eastern Shan State, was established in the middle of the thirteenth century by King Mangrai, a Tai ruler from the royal family of Chiang Mai. It was attached to the loosely connected state of Lan Na, which consisted of a few large and many smaller autonomous or semi-autonomous principalities or city-states (*muang*) with fluctuating boundaries, subordinated to a Buddhist ruler. These city-states paid tribute to local overlords in kind, and their rulers were required to come to Chiang Mai annually in order to "drink the water of allegiance" in the presence of the king.[11] From that time, Chiang Tung was part of the northern Tai cultural area, and there were close connections between Chiang Tung and the main cities in Lan Na. Having been part of Lan Na is, to the Tai Khun people of Chiang Tung, a "chosen glory" (to use a term from Catarina Kinnvall).[12] In 1558, the whole of Lan Na fell to the Burmese, but the connections between the different Tai peoples living in the Upper Mekong area were not severed until 1774, when Lan Na swore allegiance to Siam and Chiang Tung remained as a tributary to the Burmese kingdom, together with the rest of the Shan State.[13] Since that time, Chiang Tung has been subject to intense cultural Burmanization, but still less so than the rest of the Shan State. The descendants of the Mangrai dynasty of Chiang Mai continued to rule Chiang Tung until the aristocratic system was ended by the Burmese military government in the mid-twentieth century.[14]

---

[7] Michael Moerman, "Ethnic Identification in a Complex Civilization: Who Are the Lue?" *American Anthropologist* 67 (1965): 1215–30.

[8] Heather A. Peters, "Ethnicity along China's Southwestern Frontier," *Journal of East Asian Archaeology* 3,1–2 (2002): 78.

[9] Yos Santasombat, *Lak Chang: A Reconstruction of Tai Identity in Daikong* (Canberra: Pandanus Books, 2001), p. 15.

[10] Chiang Tung is the Tai rendition of the city name. It can also be given as Keng Tung, among other spellings; the official Burmese transcription is Kyaingtong.

[11] Volker Grabowsky, *The Northern Tai Policy of Lan Na (Babai-Dadian) between the Late Thirteenth to Mid-Sixteenth Centuries: Internal Dynamics and Relations with Her Neighbours*, ARI Working Paper 17 (Singapore: Asia Research Institute, National University of Singapore, 2004), p. 34.

[12] Catarina Kinnvall, "Globalization and Religious Nationalism: Self, Identity, and the Search for Ontological Security," *Political Psychology* 25,5 (2004): 741–67.

[13] Sai Kham Mong, "The Shan in Myanmar," in *Myanmar: State, Society, and Ethnicity*, ed. Narayanan Ganesan and Kyaw Yin Hlaing (Singapore: ISEAS, 2007), p. 258.

[14] Sarassawadee Ongsakul, *History of Lan Na* (Chiang Mai: Silkworm Books, 2005), p. 100.

By the middle of the thirteenth century, Buddhism was introduced to Chiang Tung by King Mangrai. Later, in the fourteenth and fifteenth centuries, two different reformist orders, Suan Dok and Pa Daeng, were introduced from Chiang Mai to Chiang Tung. The chronicle of Wat Padaeng describes in detail the trip that a Tai monk took to Lanka in the fifteenth century for the purpose of establishing a new Buddhist order.[15] After his reconsecration in Lanka, he traveled to Ayutthaya, Sukhothai, and Chiang Mai. This new order was eventually introduced in Chiang Tung, where it established itself at the Wat Padaeng monastery, which is still standing.

Today, a traditional Tai Khun Buddhist tradition, with its canonical writings in Tai Khun letters and with forty traditional Tai Khun monasteries located in the Chiang Tung urban area, exists side by side with the Shan and the Burmese Buddhist traditions. These three traditions are distinguished by ethnicity, and their practitioners do not cooperate in rituals. They have their own respective religious festivals and rituals, and the religious buildings have easily identifiable features. Besides visual culture, Tai Khun Buddhism has at least two very important characteristics compared to Burmese and Shan Buddhism. Full moons are not celebrated on the same days as in the Burmese and Shan traditions because Tai Khun Buddhism uses an old calendar system. Further, the recitations in Pali differ in rhythm and intonation compared to recitations made by Burmese and Shan monks, because Tai Khun canonical scriptures are written in Tai Khun letters.[16]

James Finch declares that "the eastern Shan State has developed a unique style of sacred art."[17] This is especially true when compared to Burmese visual culture, but the Tai Khun style is also rather different from that of the rest of the Shan State. Finch seems, however, to be unaware of the historical and cultural divergence between the Tai Khun and the rest of the Shan people. In traditional Tai Khun monasteries, the Buddha images are of a special Tai Khun style, very similar to that of the Tai Lue in Sipsongpanna. Further, the interior of a Tai Khun assembly hall (*vihan*) is characterized by walls and wooden pillars with gold stenciling on a red background and banners (*tong*) hanging from the ceiling, just like in a Tai Lue monastery. Different forms of visual representations of the legend of Prince Vessantara are nearly omnipresent in Chiang Tung traditional monasteries, just as in the rest of the Tai Buddhist cultural sphere. Especially, a pair of wooden animals (an elephant and a horse), placed in front of the main Buddha and representing the gift of Prince Vessantara, plays a prominent part in Tai Khun visual culture.[18]

---

[15] Sai Saimong Mangrai, *The Padaeng Chronicle and the Jengtung State Chronicle Translated* (Ann Arbor, MI: University of Michigan, 1981).

[16] For an account of the features of Tai Khun Buddhism, see Klemens Karlsson, "Tai Khun Buddhism and Ethnic-Religious Identity," *Contemporary Buddhism* 10,1 (2009): 75–83; and Paul T. Cohen, "Buddhism Unshackled: The Yuan 'Holy Man' Tradition and the Nation-State in the Tai World," *Journal of Southeast Asian Studies* 32,2 (2001): 227–47.

[17] James Finch, "Hidden Burma: The Sacred Art of the Eastern Shan State," *Arts of Asia*, 36,5 (2006): 143.

[18] For an account of the art and material religion of Tai Khun, see Klemens Karlsson, "Shan Ethnic-Religious Identity: Object, Art, and Material Religion in the Eastern Shan State," in *Shan and Beyond: Essays on Shan Archaeology, Anthropology, History, Politics, Religion, and Human Rights*, ed. Montira Rato and Khanidtha Kanthavichai (Bangkok: Institute of Asian Studies, Chulalongkorn University, 2011), pp. 117–24. For an account of the importance of the legend of Prince Vessantara in Tai Buddhism in Northeast Thailand and Laos, see the article by Sandra Cate and Leedom Lefferts in this volume.

During the colonial period, the Shan people in British Burma enjoyed an extensive degree of autonomy. Burma proper was a directly administered British colony, while the many small Shan states became protectorates, and each Shan hereditary ruler (*saopha*) was responsible for administration and law enforcement, with an armed police force, civil servants, magistrates, and judges serving in his state. The British plan was originally to stop at the Salween River, as they wanted to avoid sharing a border with France, but the plan was later changed and in 1890 the Shan state of Chiang Tung became part of the British Empire.[19] In 1922, the British created the Federated Shan States, but this came to an end when the Japanese occupied most of Southeast Asia in 1942. Soon after Word War II, Burma received independence from Britain and an agreement to unify the country was signed between Burmese nationalists and some of the leaders of the frontier peoples. The Panglong Agreement of 1947 is the key document governing post-war relations between the frontier peoples and the Burmese central government. The Shan people were granted the right to secede from the Union of Burma after a ten-year trial period.[20]

In 1949, Kuomintang (KMT) forces invaded Chiang Tung from Yunnan and sought refuge in the Shan hills. There were as many as 12,000 KMT soldiers inside Burma, and the Burmese army was unable to oust them. This conflict meant that the Shan became wedged in-between two armed forces, both of which were foreign to the local people. For many Shan peasants, it was the first time they had come in direct contact with any Burmese. The result was a strong Shan nationalist movement, and by 1959 some Shan had taken up guerrilla warfare against the Burmese army. In 1962, General Ne Win and the military took over the Burmese government, and the Shan have been engaged in an intermittent armed conflict ever since. At present, there is a cease-fire agreement between the Government of Myanmar and most of the armed rebellion forces.[21]

The Burmese military regime claims to rule in accordance with the three main national causes: "the non-disintegration of the union, the non-disintegration of national solidarity, and the perpetuation of national sovereignty."[22] Military leaders present Buddhism as a bedrock and the basis for national unity and solidarity. The military regime in Myanmar uses Buddhist religion as a powerful political tool to legitimize its power and authority.[23] In an effort to popularize its vision of Myanmar

---

[19] Ratanaporn Sethakul, "Political Relations between Chiang Mai and Kengtung in the Nineteenth Century," in *Changes in Northern Thailand and the Shan States 1886–1940*, ed. Prakai Nontawasee (Singapore: Institute of Southeast Asian Studies, 1988); Ongsakul, *History of Lan Na*, p. 175.

[20] Martin Smith, *Burma: Insurgency and the Politics of Ethnicity* (London: Zed Books, 1999), p. 79.

[21] During a certain numbers of years the Government has been negotiating with the ethnic cease-fire armies to make them a government-run Border Guard Force and thus engage them in the political process. After the general election on November 7, 2010, and the by-elections held on April 1, 2012, there has been a drastic change in Burmese politics with renewed negotiating between the Government and ethnic armies, but it is still too early (May 2012) to know whether the changes will result in a lasting and permanent peace.

[22] Curtis W. Lambrecht, "Oxymoronic Development: The Military as Benefactor in the Border Regions of Burma," in *Civilizing the Margins: Southeast Asian Government Policies for the Development of Minorities*, ed. Christopher R. Duncan (Ithaca, NY: Cornell University Press, 2004), pp. 150–81.

[23] Janette Philp and David Mercer, "Politicised Pagodas and Veiled Resistance: Contested Urban Space in Burma," *Urban Studies* 39,9 (2002): 1587–1610.

and its national history, the government finances archaeological preservation and reconstruction of sacred sites throughout the modern nation-state.[24] There is a continuing process of Burmanization, especially of minority areas, as a way of manifesting the government's dominance over and subordination of ethnic culture and religion among minorities. The palace of Chiang Tung was a symbol of independence for the Shan, and the Tai Khun in particular, and intimidated the Burmese rulers, who consequently destroyed it in the middle of the 1990s. This destruction is an obvious example of the Burmanization of minorities.

THE MAHĀMUNI BUDDHA OF CHIANG TUNG

The Mahāmuni (*Maha Myat Muni*) Buddha image of Chiang Tung is situated in a temple hall in the center of the city and is a quite spectacular image. It is a huge sitting Buddha, golden in appearance and seated on a throne, clad in Burmese royal attire and regalia. It was made in the 1920s as a copy of one of the most famous Buddha images in Burma, the Mandalay Mahāmuni Buddha, which is subject to extensive ritual veneration.[25] A ritual is performed every morning at the temple in Mandalay, with monks washing and applying gold-leaf to the image.[26] A similar but simpler variant of this ritual takes place every full and new moon at the Chiang Tung Buddha image (see Figure 1). This image is maintained by the Board of Pagoda Trustees, which consists of prominent Tai Khun laypeople, though the people who venerate the image are from all ethnic groups. Monks from different monasteries may be invited to the washing ritual, but always from one ethnic monastic commmunity (*sangha*) at a time.

The original Mahāmuni Buddha in Mandalay was constructed in Arakan (Rakhine State), the western part of today's Myanmar. The mythical tradition places the construction of the Mahāmuni image as far back as the lifetime of the Buddha. Historians judge that the image may be from the fifth century and was probably first installed in the royal shrine of one of the early kings of Arakan. The image has been highly venerated throughout Burmese Buddhist history. It is told that many kings attacked Arakan with the intention of obtaining the Mahāmuni image. King Anawratha of Pagan is said to have failed in his attempt to move the image to his capital.[27] Burmese political history of the eighteenth century, especially regarding the kingdom of Bodawpaya, has been closely connected to the Mahāmuni Buddha image. King Bodawpaya was the most powerful of all Konbaung kings, and his reign was a period of military expansion. In 1784, after his invasion of Arakan, he took the Mahāmuni image to his new capital at Amarapura, in present-day Mandalay. The image still resides in Mandalay and is regarded by the Burmese as a national treasure, legitimizing the political power of the present military government.

---

[24] Juliane Schober, "Buddhist Just Rule and Burmese National Culture: State Patronage of the Chinese Tooth Relic in Myanmar," *History of Religions* 36,3 (1997): 236.

[25] There are copies of the Mahāmuni Buddha in several places in the Shan State, e.g., Tachileik and Hsipaw.

[26] Juliane Schober, "In the Presence of the Buddha: Ritual Veneration of the Burmese Mahamuni Image," in *Sacred Biography in the Buddhist Traditions of South and Southeast Asia*, ed. Juliane Schober (Honolulu, HI: University of Hawaii Press, 1997), pp. 259–88; U Thaw Kaung, *Selected Writings of U Thaw Kaung* (Yangon: Myanmar Historical Commission, 2004).

[27] Schober, "In the Presence of the Buddha."

Figure 1: Ritual veneration of the Chiang Tung Mahāmuni Buddha, January 2006.
Photo by Klemens Karlsson

According to the legend of the Mahāmuni, the Buddha once flew, with five hundred of his followers, to visit King Candasuriya at Dhanyawadi. It is told that Indra made the image, just outside the palace of King Candasuriya, and that after its construction, the Buddha breathed life into it.[28] This story is a version of an old Buddhist legend about the origin of the first image of the Buddha. It expresses the view that the Buddha visited Myanmar and that the Mahāmuni image is a true and exact likeness of him. For this reason, it is believed that the image can act as an adviser to the ruler who is in possession of it, and it thus serves to legitimize that ruler.

The construction of the Chiang Tung replica was not an act of some prominent Burmese person. Instead, the making of the image was commissioned by the hereditary ruler of Chiang Tung, Sao Kawn Kiao Intaleng, together with the abbot of Wat Zaing Ngarm. Officials were sent by the *saopha* to Mandalay to oversee the casting of the image, which was done by U Tit and his workers in 1921. Thereafter, the image was brought in pieces to Chiang Tung by boat and bullock cart and

---

[28] Pamela Gutman, *Burma's Lost Kingdoms: Splendours of Arakan* (Bangkok: Orchid Press, 2001), pp. 29–39.

installed in a temporary building. In 1926, the image was finally installed in its present building (Wat Phra Sao Luang) in the center of town.

As the original image is a prominent part of Burmese national identity, to copy the Mahāmuni Buddha can be seen as an example of cultural Burmanization. At the time of the replica's construction and installation in Chiang Tung, increasing connections were being established between the Eastern Shan State and the Burmese culture, and the Buddha can be perceived as a representation of those ties. The Mahāmuni image stands as a reminder of a time when the Shan states enjoyed a measure of independence and were keen to have good relations with the Burmese.

The history and myth of the Mahāmuni Buddha is an example of the way art and visual culture can express ethnicity and political hegemony. The image establishes a link with sacred Buddhist history, with the Buddha himself, and with the Burmese history of military conquest. It is therefore remarkable that the long-lasting civil war in the Shan State, in which the Shan State Army South (SSA-S) is fighting the military government, has not prevented Tai Khun and Shan from continuing to venerate the Mahāmuni image and to consider it to be an exceptionally sacred image. By the time the Mahāmuni image was constructed, the country was under British rule and each Shan State enjoyed a measure of administrative independence as British protectorates. Chiang Tung had also suffered three Siamese invasions between 1849 and 1854, repulsing them with Burmese and Shan aid. Chiang Mai was at that time a power in decay and dependent on Siam.[29] As a result, Burmese influence in the area increased, and the ruler of Chiang Tung ordered the copying of a Burmese Buddha and not one of the highly venerated Buddha images from northern Thailand (for example, the *Phra Buddha Sihing*, in Chiang Mai).

Today, there is one specific piece of cloth that indicates that Burmese military leaders have symbolic control of the Mahāmuni image. A baldachin of orange cloth is placed at the top of the head of the Buddha. A piece of blue cloth with the names of the present military commander in Chiang Tung and his wife are stuck on the baldachin. Every time a new commander takes office in Chiang Tung, a donation ritual is made, and the names on the baldachin are replaced. Before the military coup in 1962, it was possible for ordinary people to donate robes to this Mahāmuni image as an act of merit. Today, it is strictly prohibited for ordinary people to donate clothes to the image.

The names on the baldachin imply that the military commander and his wife are the main donors contributing to the image and that everyone who enters the temple and donates flowers, food, or gold leaves does it under military protection. This symbolic control of the image manifests that all merit from venerations and donations made by ordinary people goes to the main donor, the present military commander.

However, during the daytime, a steady stream of local Tai Khun visitors can be observed contemplating and paying homage to the image, despite the symbols of Burmese control. The reason for this favorable reception is the belief that the connection between this image and the historical Buddha is particularly powerful, as it is believed that it was the Buddha himself who breathed life into the image. The image is therefore regarded by the Tai Khun as especially sacred, and to be sitting in front of the Mahāmuni Buddha is like being in the presence of the Buddha himself. As long as the Board of Pagoda Trustees remains in the hands of the Tai Khun, ethnic

---

[29] Sethakul, "Political Relations," p. 305.

Tai Khun Buddhists will almost certainly continue to venerate the image. There is reason to suppose that, in the future, the Burmese will want to obtain important positions on the Board of Pagoda Trustees as well, to gain greater control.

THE KHEMARATTHA STANDING BUDDHA

In recent years, the Burmese government has, in an effort to popularize itself, constructed religious buildings and Buddha images all over Burma. In the year 2000, the construction of a huge standing and pointing Buddha image was completed on Swamhsat Hill in the outskirts of Chiang Tung. The prominent image (see Figures 2 and 3), more than twenty meters tall from head to foot and illuminated in the evenings, can be seen from throughout the city.[30]

Figure 2: Khemarattha Standing Buddha. Photograph by Klemens Karlsson

At Tachilek, a border town close to Thailand, there is a copy, built in 1993, of Yangon's famous Shwedagon Pagoda (see Figure 4). Shwedagon is one of the most venerated Buddhist shrines in Burma and is connected with the establishment of Buddhism in early Burma. Shwedagon is connected with the life-story of the Buddha and the relic of the eight sacred hairs of the Buddha, but it also has a long history connected with Burma's kings and rulers.[31]

Both the enormous Buddha image and the pagoda were constructed on the initiative of the *Tatmadaw*, the Burmese military, and stand today as reminders of

---

[30] The image is called "Khemarattha Standing Buddha Image" in the official government organ *The New Light of Myanmar*, April 9, 2002. Huge standing and pointing Buddha statues have also been constructed by the government at other places around Myanmar, e.g., in Mongla at the Chinese border and Hsipaw in the Northern Shan State.

[31] Elizabeth Moore, "Shwedagon: Its History and Architecture," in *Shwedagon: Golden Pagoda of Myanmar*, ed. Narisa Chakrabongse (London: Thames and Hudson, 1999), pp. 144–48.

Burmese supremacy and sovereignty and as symbols of Burmese Buddhist legitimacy in a Shan and Tai Khun area. Both the Standing Buddha and the Tachilek Pagoda are constructed in the tradition of Burmese visual culture, with no connection to Tai Khun or Shan visual culture. An obvious example of a typically Burmese stylistic element is the eight planetary shrines associated with the days of the week constructed around both the Standing Buddha statue and the Tachilek pagoda, just like at the original Shwedagon Pagoda in Yangon. Another well-known motif often used in Burmese art is the Hamsa bird, a statue of which can be found on a tall pillar at the site of the Standing Buddha. The Hamsa is a sacred goose found in Hindu and Buddhist mythology and has been especially connected with the Mon people in southern Burma. At the pagoda there is also a shrine for the legendary monk Upagupta, a common figure in Burmese visual culture, but rare in Tai Buddhism and culture.

Figure 3: Khemarattha Standing Buddha. Photograph by Klemens Karlsson

The history of the Standing Buddha began in 1995, when, as the story is told, a couple of small Buddha sculptures were found in the ground at the site of the Chiang Tung Weather Department. The images were established to be very old, and it was decided to relocate the weather department and build a sacred site at the top of the hill. The construction of the statue between 1998 and 2000 was, according to the information plaque at its base, led by General Thein Sein and his wife, Daw Khin Khin Win.[32]

Figure 4: Shwedagon, Tachileik. Photograph by Klemens Karlsson

The statue, with its outstretched, pointing hand, resembles a famous statue on Mandalay Hill.[33] The Pointing Buddha at Mandalay was built by King Mindon in the mid-nineteenth century, and it is associated with Burmese nationalism. The statue was part of King Mindon's sacred building program that resulted in the erection of a royal palace, city walls, pagodas, and monasteries during the establishment of his new capital, which he built in order to express his role as a Buddhist protector and *cakravartin* (universal ruler). It is told that the Buddha visited Mandalay Hill and that an ogress worshipped him there. The Buddha then pointed at the foot of the hill and prophesied that a great Buddhist city would be established there 2,400 years later, and that the ogress would be reborn as the king who would establish that city. When King Mindon established Mandalay in the mid-nineteenth century, he associated himself with the ogress and the king who was envisaged by the Buddha.[34] Thus, the Pointing Buddha was the centerpiece of King Mindon's construction program as it connected with the Buddha himself and with his prophecy, portraying the king as

---

[32] From 1996 General Thein Sein led the Triangle Regional Military Command in Keng Tung. From 2007 until 2011, he served as the prime minister and after the 2010 general election he became Myanmar's first civilian president.

[33] The statue at Chiang Tung is not an official copy of the one at Mandalay Hill.

[34] Cynthia Warso, "The Pointing Buddha Image of Mandalay Hill: Gautama Buddha 'Shows the Way' in Late Nineteenth- and Early Twentieth-Century Burma (Master of Arts thesis, Northern Illinois University, 2004).

the one who would rescue the country from the British and establish a golden Buddhist Empire.

According to the legend of the origin of Chiang Tung, the Buddha and forty-nine of his followers visited Swamhsat Hill, which at that time was surrounded by a big lake, and left behind eight hairs from his head. He also made a prophecy, saying that a hermit would come along and drain the water from the lake and found a city in its place, and that a king would later establish a *sangha* there.[35] As already mentioned, Buddhism was introduced to the area by monks from Chiang Mai, and the city was established by a Tai king in the thirteenth century. However, in an attempt to establish a historical Burmese connection to the city, the information sign at the base of the Standing Buddha indicates that the supposedly first Buddhist building on the hill, the Anawratha Pagoda, was made by an ancient Burmese king in the year 734 (according to the Burmese calendar, or 1372 CE). The pagoda must have been named for the pagan King Anawratha, one of the main rulers and conquerors who figures in Burmese history. Nevertheless, according to several chronicles, this was the time when King Khaen Lek, the son of Chiang Mai ruler Ku Na, ruled Chiang Tung. It was also the time of the first Singhalese reformist order being established in Chiang Tung, after first having reached Sukhothai and Chiang Mai.[36] Thus, the authorities who constructed the statue wanted to declare that Buddhism, even in this remote area, was introduced by the Burmese, not by the Shan, Tai Khun, or Lan Na, despite historical evidence to the contrary.

There is seemingly a double meaning to the Standing Buddha. First, it symbolizes the origin of Chiang Tung and Buddha's visit to the hill and his prophecy that an important Buddhist city would be established there. The second meaning is a negative one: the statue can be regarded as a symbol of the way local people must live under the supremacy of the Burmese government. Some locals I have spoken to believe that the giant standing Buddha is a fake, not made in a proper way. There are rumors that the statue is dangerous and ill-omened, and people see symbolic significance in its having been struck by lightning not long after its construction. Therefore, some local people avoid walking near the statue because doing so, they believe, may bring misfortune.[37]

Local people avoid interacting with Chiang Tung's standing Buddha because it is placed outdoors and was not made according to local tradition. The image was fashioned in an unusual position with a pointing hand, which is not a traditional Buddhist position. Further, the image is placed outdoors, not inside a monastery or a temple. A consecrated Buddha image is traditionally placed at a monastery, inside a rectangular pillared hall (*vihan*) or ordination hall (*ubosot*). By comparison, Chiang Tung's Standing Buddha is placed on a hill, expressly so that it can be seen from all over the town. Therefore, people cannot avoid looking at the image. Another negatively perceived aspect is that the image was constructed in the tradition of

---

[35] For the details of this legend, see Sai Long Seng Lung, *Precise History of Tong Karasi: Four Hermits Creators of the Kengtung Region* (Kengtung: Khun Cultural and Literature Society of Kengtung, 1997); and Mangrai, *The Padaeng Chronicle*.

[36] Mangrai, *The Padaeng Chronicle*; and Sommai Premchit and Donald K. Swearer, "A Translation of Tamnan Mulasasana Wat Pa Daeng: The Chronicle of the Founding of Buddhism of the Wat Pa Daeng tradition," *Journal of the Siam Society* 65,2 (1977): 82–85.

[37] Asking questions of local people about controversial and political matters poses some risk for the locals. It is problematic in a country like Myanmar to confirm how widespread this opinion is. It is, therefore, impossible actually to know if this is a common perception.

Burmese visual culture, with a symbolic connection to King Mindon and Burmese nationalism. Local people know that the image was made recently by Burmese authorities, and it is easy for people to see that the image is of a foreign shape. Therefore, local people do not interact with the outdoor standing Buddha if they can avoid it, especially since there is a rumor that it was not consecrated through established practice.

There are many similarities between the Standing Buddha at Chiang Tung and the Pointing Buddha at Mandalay, and I argue that the Standing Buddha at Chiang Tung represent Burmese national Buddhism and ethnic-religious identity. The Standing Buddha in Chiang Tung and the Shwedagon Pagoda at Tachilek are emblems of Burmese identity, and also representative of the Burmese military government because those structures are connected with Burmese history and were built by the military regime, whose active support of Buddhism is part of an attempt to achieve political legitimacy (not unlike ancient Burmese rulers' motivations). Constructing sacred buildings and statues is a traditional way for rulers in Buddhist societies to establish legitimacy and to acquire merit in this life or the next. In conclusion, the destruction of symbols of Shan and Tai Khun independence (such as the Chiang Tung palace) and the construction of sacred buildings and statues connected to Burmese ethnic-religious identity are examples of the Burmanization of minorities.

BUDDHA IMAGES AS EMBLEMS OF ETHNIC-RELIGIOUS IDENTITY

To better understand the way Buddhist visual culture serves as a marker of ethnic-religious identity, it is important to look closely at the history of Buddhism, at the uniqueness of Buddhist visual culture, and at the genuineness of a Buddha statue.

Religious visual culture is an important factor in the spread of religions throughout the world, and whenever Buddhism has spread from one region to another, visual culture has been an important part of its transnational development and the success of its mission. From the beginning, Buddhist religious tradition was the product of a shared sacred Indian culture with sacred auspicious signs, local deities, and mythological creatures, and it interacted with different belief systems and cultural expressions.[38] Buddhist tradition has always been in a state of flux, and as Buddhism spread among different cultures throughout the Asian continent, it adopted many indigenous cultural manifestations. This adaptation to local customs eventually merged Buddhist tradition with ethnic identity, making them nearly inseparable, and resulting in the creation of local and national Buddhist traditions. This can be seen in the Buddhist expansion in China, Southeast Asia, and elsewhere.

While Buddhism today is a worldwide movement, it also consists of different national *sanghas* that remain under the authority of national governments, leading to an apparent opposition between a transnational Buddhism with universal lessons and national Buddhism with ethnic and nationalistic tendencies.[39] This opposition

---

[38] Klemens Karlsson, *Face to Face with the Absent Buddha: The Formation of Buddhist Aniconic Art* (Uppsala: Uppsala University, 1999), pp. 174–78, 187–92; and Klemens Karlsson, "The Formation of Early Buddhist Visual Culture," *Material Religion: The Journal of Objects, Art, and Belief* 2,1 (2006): 68–95.

[39] Thomas Borchert, "Buddhism, Politics, and Nationalism in the Twentieth and Twenty-first Centuries," *Religion Compass* 1,5 (2007): 529–46; and Thomas Borchert, "Worry for the Dai

can be clearly recognized in Buddhist art and visual culture, which, while it functions as a uniting force and is important to the spread of Buddhism, is also a kind of emblem of ethnic and religious identity and part of a process of enclosing and excluding peoples. Thus, the unique style of sacred art in the Eastern Shan State is a form of imagining and expressing a Tai Khun identity, especially in relation to the Burmese. Conversely, Burmese Buddhist art set up in the Shan State serves as a marker and emblem of Burmese identity.

It is told that the Buddha, after his awakening, traveled far with his disciples in the region of the Ganges, preaching the *dhamma* and visiting different communities. As we have seen, it is also told that the Buddha visited places in Southeast Asia by traveling through the sky using his supernatural powers. The sacred biography of the Buddha continues after his death in the shape of images. As described by Schober, the rituals and myths of the Mahāmuni Buddha place local context and actors within a universal Buddhist cosmology and establish a continuing biography of the Buddha in the Buddhist polities of Arakan and Upper Burma.[40] As the Mahāmuni statue was brought from Arakan to Mandalay and installed there as a palladium, so was, implicitly, the Buddha himself, in the form of the Mahāmuni, arguably as a symbolic captive of King Bodawpaya. Much later, the image, and, figuratively, the Buddha, were copied and installed in Chiang Tung.

Throughout the Buddhist history of Southeast Asia, Buddha images have traveled far and wide according to political circumstances, for rulers and conquerors needed Buddha images as tokens of legitimacy.[41] There are numerous examples of how important Buddha images have been captured in conflicts and installed in new capitals to legitimize the conqueror. The Prabang Buddha has been moved several times between Bangkok and Luang Prabang, and the famous Emerald Buddha has also been the subject of political conflicts before becoming a protector figure of the Thai people.[42] Such highly venerated Buddha images have often been used as emblems of political power and ethnic identity, and these images have become part of an ethnic-religious symbolic network. The Prabang Buddha has become intimately connected with Lao identity, the Emerald Buddha with Thai identity, and the Mahāmuni Buddha with Burmese identity. As with the Mahāmuni, there are several other stories told all over the Buddhist world about Buddha images made during the lifetime of the Buddha. These stories give good reason for the popular practice of venerating the Buddha through his contemporary visual manifestations.

One reason why some images have been regarded as more sacred than others is the occurrence of miraculous events, and there is almost always an extraordinary history connected to these highly venerated images. It is also important to consider the manufacturing and consecration of Buddha images, specifically when a Buddha image is to be considered as a true Buddha, whether when manufactured or only after its consecration. Donald K. Swearer has studied the rituals performed during

---

Nation: Sipsongpanna, Chinese Modernity, and the Problems of Buddhist Modernism," *Journal of Asian Studies* 67,1 (2008): 107–42.

[40] Schober, "In the Presence of the Buddha."

[41] Stanley J. Tambiah, "Famous Buddha Images and the Legitimation of Kings: The Case of the Sinhala Buddha (*Phra Sihing*) in Thailand," *Res: Anthropology and Aesthetics* 4 (1982): 5–19.

[42] Frank E. Reynolds, "The Holy Emerald Jewel: Some Aspects of Buddhist Symbolism and Political Legitimation in Thailand and Laos," in *Religion and Legitimation of Power in Thailand, Laos, and Burma*, ed. Bardwell L. Smith (Chambersburg, PA: Anima Books, 1978), pp. 175–93.

the construction and consecration of Buddha images, and, based on his research in northern Thailand, he points out that the rituals are made to infuse *dhamma* into the images in such a way that an image can represent the living presence of the Buddha in the same way as a relic.[43] The transformation of power to a newly constructed image involves the use of sacred threads that connect the copy to an already consecrated image, and in the extension back to the expected original first image of the Buddha.[44] It is believed that a Buddha image that has not been part of a consecration ritual is only a lifeless object, lacking the sacredness of a consecrated image. However, the ritual connected to the manufacturing of an image, described by Alexandra de Mersan, points to the fact that ritualized construction itself can give the image its sacred power.[45]

Figure 5: Buddha image with sacred threads, Chiang Rai, northern Thailand.
Photograph by Klemens Karlsson

---

[43] Donald K. Swearer, *Becoming the Buddha: The Ritual of Image Consecration in Thailand* (Princeton, NJ: Princeton University Press, 2004).

[44] Ordinary white cotton threads are commonly used to transfer sacred power from one object to another or from one person to another. See Figure 5 and Swearer, *Becoming the Buddha*, fig. 18–20.

[45] Alexandra de Mersan, "'The Land of the Great Image' and the Test of Time: The Making of Buddha Images in Arakan (Burma/Myanmar)," in this volume.

There are similarities, but also differences, between the Mahāmuni Buddha and the more recently made Standing Buddha at Chiang Tung. Both are extraordinarily large and conspicuous, and both are connected to the lifetime of the Buddha, but also to Burmese national pride and history of conquest. The most prominent difference lies in the history behind their construction. The Mahāmuni copy was made during a relatively prosperous period in Shan history, when the Shan enjoyed relative independence from British interference, and creating the copy may have been an attempt by the local ruler to legitimize himself as a representative of the Tai Khun and Shan people of Chiang Tung. The image may be regarded as a symbol of Burmese ethnic-religious identity, but the statue is not as controversial to local people as is the more recently constructed Standing Buddha. The Standing Buddha's appeal is compromised because it was made by the Burmese military government, arguably to express Burmese Buddhist identity and, in a symbolical way, to keep an eye on the people of Chiang Tung. The political dimensions of both statues are demonstrated by the fact that high-ranking generals and government administrators of the Burmese regime frequently pay homage to Mahāmuni and the Khemarattha Buddha because of the connection these statues have with Burmese identity, whereas old traditional Tai Khun monasteries, such as Wat Padaeng and Wat In, are less favored by Burmese officials.

These two statues illustrate how Buddha images function, how they differ, why some are treated with more respect than others, and what role Buddhist visual culture plays as a marker of ethnic-religious identity. The Mahāmuni image serves as an illustration of the concept that some Buddha images are more sacred than others because they have a special connection to the Buddha himself and are part of the sacred history of Buddhism. Thus, the principal reason for a Buddha image to be conceived as more sacred than others and as an effective emblem of ethnic identity is its authenticity. The image is supposed to be connected to the Buddha and to present an authentic likeness of him. Correspondingly, both of the images under consideration have specific connections with the Buddha through legend.

CONCLUSION

Visual culture is an important part of a living religious tradition, with veneration of sacred images being a form of spiritual motion in individuals that allows them to connect with the sacred. Visual culture can instigate the movement of people, both in relation to sacred sites and to one another, and it is also important to the popularity, and hence the spread, of religions. This may be especially true of Buddhism, for its expansion across Asia was marked by adaptation to local cultures in order to enhance its appeal among local people. Thus, Buddhist visual culture differs from place to place according to ethnic environment, leading to different material traditions even among ethnic groups that follow the same textual tradition. Adopting indigenous cultural manifestations merged local Buddhist visual culture with ethnic identity and, as a consequence, with politics and nationalism.

Some Buddha images are considered more sacred than others, often because of legendary connections to the life of the Buddha. Such images have been used to legitimize political power, and so have repeatedly been captured in wars and venerated by victorious rulers. Through such geopolitical motion, images acquire symbolical meaning, connecting them with a certain political authority or ethnic group. Religious images and visual culture are useful in validating the history of a people. For these reasons, Buddha images can serve to express local and national Buddhism and to convey ethnic identity.

This is the case in the Eastern Shan State, where Buddhist art and visual culture serve as markers of ethnic-religious identity in the conflict between the Burmese government and the Shan minority, despite the fact that Buddhism of the Theravāda tradition is dominant both among the Burmese and the Shan. This division is exemplified by the two Burmese Buddhas in Chiang Tung, situated in the middle of the Tai Khun cultural area. They establish links with sacred Buddhist history and with the Buddha himself, as they each have a mythical history connected to the historical Buddha. They also establish links with Burmese history and with Burmese ethnic-religious identity, because they are connected to significant royal rulers and important events in Burmese history. Both statues must thus be considered part of the Burmanization process, but as the Mahāmuni Buddha was made on the order of a local ruler during the colonial period, it enjoys greater acceptance among the locals than does the Standing Buddha, which was constructed during the last fifteen years by the (pragmatic) military government.

The connection with Burmese history and the symbolic control of the Mahāmuni image by Burmese military, manifested by the name of the present military commander on the baldachin, do not prevent local Tai Khun visitors from paying homage to the image. The authenticity of the image derives from the belief that it was the Buddha himself who breathed life into it. The image is therefore regarded as especially sacred, and to be sitting in front of it is like being in the presence of the Buddha himself. As the Mahāmuni image was made by the local Tai Khun ruler during a time when the Shan States enjoyed a measure of independence as British protectorates, and from that time been an important part of the religious life of Chiang Tung, ethnic Tai Khun Buddhists will almost certainly continue to venerate the image, especially since the image has a connection to the historical Buddha himself. Important, too, is that the Mahāmuni Board of Pagoda Trustees still remains in the hands of the Tai Khun, not the Burmese.

The Khemaratta Standing Buddha represents Burmese national Buddhism and Burmese ethnic-religious identity in a more distinct way. Local people avoid interacting with the Standing Buddha because it was not created according to local traditions. They know that the image was made recently by the Burmese authorities, the same authorities that destroyed the palace of Chiang Tung, and it is also easy for them to see that the image is of a foreign shape.

The Standing Buddha, and to a lesser extent the Mahāmuni, represents Burmese national Buddhism and Burmese ethnic-religious identity, and the Standing Buddha, especially, is an attempt by the government to legitimize its rule in this minority area. The images thus act as emblems of Burmese hegemony and Burmese nationalism, in a continuing process of Burmanization, especially of minority areas, as a way of manifesting the government's dominance over and subordination of ethnic culture and religion.

CHAPTER 5

HOLY WATER AND MATERIAL RELIGION IN A PILGRIMAGE SHRINE IN MALAYSIA[1]

Yeoh Seng Guan

In the grasping and enlivening of human existence, materiality, and its conceptual alter ego, immateriality, are both pragmatic and philosophical concerns. Not least in the specific domain of religious beliefs and practices, the differential configuration and dialectical interplay between these axes—the material and the immaterial—have historically coexisted and assumed variable juxtapositions and coexisted. In some cases, the sensorial elements of iconicity and tactility, experienced by people relating with the sacred, are preeminent in religious orthodoxy, while in others that relationship is fraught with uneasy tensions. For those skeptical of a reliance on material icons and artifacts in religious worship, perhaps their prime doctrinal concern can be framed in terms of the perceived fetishistic danger (as usually typified in popular religious practices) of the banal immanent reducing and diminishing the eternal transcendent. Both stances—the orthodox and the hetereodox—nevertheless lend themselves well to interrogations of material religion as scholars seek to apprehend the cultural specifics of religiosity and, more broadly, the role of sacred material objects in everyday "secular" life.[2] Thus, as programmatically outlined in the preface of the inaugural issue of *Material Religion: The Journal of Objects, Art, and Belief*:

> Religious identity and experience are deeply dependent on the material stuff
> and ordinary practices of belief ... religion is what people do with material

[1] I first conducted fieldwork at the St. Anne's shrine in Bukit Mertajam between November 1997 and August 1998, with the support of the Evans Postdoctoral Fellowship, Department of Social Anthropology, University of Cambridge, for which I gladly acknowledge my gratitude. Short follow-up visits were also made in July 2001 and July 2002. For this chapter, I carried out additional interviews on the subject of St. Anne's water. I wish to thank Julius Bautista for kindly inviting me to the workshop on "New Directions in the Study of Material Religion," held at the Asia Research Institute, National University of Singapore, in August 2008, and to the co-participants for fostering a lively and convivial atmosphere.

[2] For example, Webb Keane, "The Evidence of the Senses and the Materiality of Religion," *Journal of the Royal Anthropological Institute, Special Issue* (2008): S110–27.

things and places, and how these structure and color experience and one's sense of oneself and others.[3]

Scholars have analyzed not only the "meanings" believed sedimented and substantiated in ritual objects or their imageries, but also the appropriation and usage (or non-usage) of these objects in terms of their relational powers.

> By material religion we intend not simply what people think about their images but what the images or objects or spaces themselves do, how they engage believers, what powers they possess, and in what manner a community comes to rely on them for the vitality and stability of belief.[4]

The catalogue of materials (humanly crafted and otherwise), which may include images, objects, natural geological formations, or spaces that are recruited or appropriated for religious worship, is as long as it is diverse. Nevertheless, the generic usage and signification of these materials across different religious traditions recur and share resonances, and, in some cases, complicate more recent ethno-religious putative differences. In this chapter, I direct my ethnographic attention to one of the prized religious items—Saint Anne's water—sought after by pilgrims and devotees at a Roman Catholic pilgrimage shrine in northern Peninsular Malaysia. I suggest that its materiality not only conventionally destabilizes religious *orthopraxis,* but also illuminates what Edward Said has famously characterized colonialist culture to be—a culture of "overlapping territories and intertwined histories."[5] Expressed differently, while elucidating the "specific materiality" of Saint Anne's water, I also examine how various "plural materialities" are activated and set into motion, as pilgrims from different religious traditions temporarily inhabit the circumscribed sacred space of the shrine.[6] More to the point, I examine how religious items like Saint Anne's water are indexical of a trajectory of subjectivities that confounds contemporary societal configurations of cultural politics in multiethnic and multireligious Malaysia. By doing so, I draw attention to the analytical utility of Saint Anne's water in delineating a family resemblance of religious practices that have a longer historical and geographical presence in comparison to constructions of the contingent present.

GRANDMOTHER SAINT AND MOTHER GODDESS: THE MANY PERSONAS OF SAINT ANNE

In Peninsular Malaysia, of the few Roman Catholic churches dedicated to Saint Anne, the one in Bukit Mertajam town is singularly the most celebrated and well-known. Although the neo-Gothic church situated at the foot of a picturesque hillock

---

[3] D. Goa, D. Morgan, and C. Paine, "Editorial Statement," *Material Religion: The Journal of Objects, Art and Belief,* 1,1(2005): 4–9.

[4] Ibid., p. 8.

[5] Edward Said, *Culture and Imperialism* (London: Vintage, 1994).

[6] Daniel Miller, "Why Some Things Matter," in *Material Cultures: Why Some Things Matter,* ed. Daniel Miller (Chicago, IL: University of Chicago Press, 1998); and Daniel Miller, ed. *Materiality* (Durham, NC, and London: Duke University Press, 2005).

was erected in 1888, there had already been a chapel outpost set up in the mid-nineteenth century, in this same location, by Father Adolphe Couellan, a French priest from Les Missions Etrangères de Paris (Paris Foreign Missionary Society), to gather their flock of mainly Hakka-Chinese farmers and Tamil-Indian laborers residing in and near the fledging market town and in the many cash-crop plantations (sugar cane, pepper, rubber) opened up by British and French colonial planters.[7]

Saint Anne's Church. Photo by Yeoh Seng Guan, 1998

Parish records suggest that, while the annual feast of Saint Anne (held on July 26 in the Roman Catholic calendar), was celebrated after the inception of the church in Bukit Mertajam, it was essentially a localized affair. The appointment of the first local Chinese priest, Father Michael Seet, in 1918, planted the seeds of change, as he began to include the Bishop, priests, and Roman Catholics of neighboring parishes in the celebrations of the feast. Since that time, the church has progressively acquired a reputation as a popular pilgrimage destination, even reportedly drawing in regular pilgrims from Singapore, Thailand, and beyond. Contemporary records indicate that the numbers of pilgrims who make the journey have increased in more recent times relative to the past. In 1954, for instance, the *Malayan Catholic News* reported "more than a thousand pilgrims from Singapore and the Federation."[8] By comparison, between the early 1980s and the 1990s, local newspapers reported estimates of between 50,000 to 350,000 pilgrims. Better transportation networks, upward social

---

[7] For a brief parish history of the church, see http://www.stannebm.org/history.html.

[8] See "Statue of St. Anne is Carried Round Bukit Mertajam Town," *The Malayan Catholic News*, August 29, 1954; and "Record Post-war Crowd Packs St. Anne's Church," *The Malayan Catholic News*, August 25, 1957.

mobility, and the communicative powers of a growing stock of testimonies of Saint Anne's miraculous interventions over the decades are some of the likely reasons for the substantial increase in numbers of believers seeking to tap the spiritual magnetic powers of the shrine. Even allowing for the possibility that various social agencies, motivated by other considerations, have over estimated (or even underreported) these demographic numbers, it was evident that the constant stream of visitors and pilgrims was at least in the tens of thousands when I conducted fieldwork during the feast celebrations of 1997 and 1998.

The visible presence of a significant number of non-Roman Catholics at the shrine during the feast celebrations, cursorily indexed by their respective devotional postures and through a survey questionnaire conducted with 130 pilgrims, intrigued me as well as a number of local officials and shrine authorities I interviewed.[9] While contemporary Roman Catholic records do not often remark on the presence of non-Roman Catholic pilgrims from outside their fold at the feasts, interviews with elderly parishioners and veteran pilgrims suggest that non-Catholic celebrants have often taken part in the festivities, and that the shrine is of some significance in the non-Roman Catholic religious landscape. To be sure, the presence of adherents of other faiths in an array of large religious festivals—mostly involving street processions—in the present day provincial state of Penang (where Bukit Mertajam is situated) is not exceptional. For instance, during the Hindu festival of Thaipusam, in the nearby state capital city of Georgetown, it would be commonplace to see a significant number of Chinese shopkeepers who reside along the processional route giving respectful recognition and obeisance to the male deity (Lord Murugan) by breaking coconuts and offering *archanai* (ritual gifts) in return for his blessings and boons.[10] Similarly, on a less publicly conspicuous scale, I have witnessed the trans-religious incorporation of deities who promise prosperity, like the rotund Laughing Buddha and the White-Clad Goddess of Mercy (*Kuan Yin* in Chinese-Cantonese or *Guan Imm* in Chinese-Hokkien), as well as the adoption of various religious artifacts, like Chinese joss-sticks and geomantic *pa-kua* (literally, "eight changes"), artifacts hung on door lintels to ward off malevolent forces, into the family altars or roadside shrines of Hindu devotees. Compared with these instances of trans-religious intermingling, the participation of non-Catholics in the feast of Saint Anne is more striking and unexpected. Roman Catholicism is theologically and religiously exclusive, and the presence of non-Roman Catholic pilgrims hailing from the religious provenances of Daoism, Buddhism, Hinduism, and Sikhism are therefore seen as transgressive of its truth claims.

A stock of explanations was offered by pilgrims and shrine authorities alike to account for this religiously pluralistic state-of-affairs. Its detractors, usually Christian purists, however, also denounced the phenomena as "syncretistic," if not

---

[9] Yeoh Seng Guan, "Religious Pluralism, Kinship, and Gender in a Pilgrimage Shrine: The Roman Catholic Feast of St. Anne in Bukit Mertajam, Malaysia," *Material Religion: The Journal of Objects, Art, and Belief* 2,1 (2006): 4–37.

[10] See also M. E. Collins, *Pierced by Murugan's Lance: Ritual, Power, and Moral Redemption among Malaysian Hindus* (DeKalb, IL: Northern Illinois University Press, 1997). Jean DeBernardi has similarly studied the malleability of Chinese religious symbols in Chinese identity formation in Penang vis-à-vis national cultural projects. See J. DeBernardi, *Rites of Belonging: Memory, Modernity, and Identity in a Malaysian Chinese Community* (Stanford, CA: Stanford University Press, 2004).

"idolatrous," in nature.[11] Others characterized the feast as "becoming more like a mini-Thaipusam," with a carnivalesque atmosphere resembling those of Hindu religious festivities. The striking aspect of all these accounts, nevertheless, is their implicit recognition of the materiality of sacred power, whether embodied in terms of the "place" or the "person" believed to be in residence there. In terms of "place," the shrine could be variously read by Chinese pilgrims as auspiciously sited in terms of Daoist geomancy (*feng-shui*), and hence as exuding contagious *ling* ("efficacy"),[12] or, similarly, the topography of the pilgrimage center might be apprehended by Hindus as a sacred *tirtha*, a "crossing point," where divinities are eminently present. C. J. Fuller characterizes Hindu pilgrimage sites as constituting "a pivotal center, a microcosm of the universe, and a node of an areal religious unity in a set of interrelated symbolic senses."[13] In pilgrim accounts that emphasize the entity believed to be in residence at the shrine, rather than the shrine's location, the sentiments of the narrators tend to resonate with those of an elderly Indian parishioner of the church, John Lourdes, and a young Chinese Roman Catholic priest, Rev. Fr. John Khoo, based in Penang, whom I interviewed:

> John Lourdes: The feast has changed a lot. About 60 percent who come are non-Christians, and a great many Hindus have devotion to Saint Anne. They feel that she is a goddess. They normally say, "we have come here to see our Annamal. Everything we pray, we get." They want child, they get. They want husband or wife, everything they get.[14]

> Rev. Fr. John Khoo: People from other faiths come more because they want to have their favors granted and not only because they see Saint Anne as Mariyamman or Kuan Yin. These people have some serious problems ... Many times they keep coming because they have tried everywhere else, especially for childbirth.[15]

What is striking about both their comments is not only the charge that many of the celebrants mistakenly identify Saint Anne as a mother goddess, rather than an exalted human being, but also their descriptions of the transactional tenor that supposedly typifies the religious fervor of non-Roman Catholic pilgrims. Nonetheless, for many ordinary pilgrims with whom I spoke, Saint Anne is generically perceived to be the "patron saint of" or "mediator" for mothers, and is believed to have special intercessory powers and to show particular benevolence to women troubled by the vicissitudes and anxieties of motherhood, such as those involved in childbearing, sickness, and the upbringing and education of children. While popularized primarily through a growing, amoebic stock of personal testimonies, Saint Anne's powers are further reinforced through Roman Catholic

---

[11] Yeoh Seng Guan, "For/against Hybridity: Religious Entrepreneurships in a Roman Catholic Pilgrimage Shrine," *Asian Journal of Social Science* 37,1 (2009): 7–28.

[12] S. Sangren, *History and Magical Power in a Chinese Community* (Stanford, CA: Stanford University Press, 1987).

[13] C. J. Fuller, *The Camphor Flame: Popular Hinduism and Society in India* (Princeton, NJ: Princeton University Press, 1992), p. 209.

[14] Interview with John Lourdes (pseudonym), January 19, 1998.

[15] Interview with Rev. Fr. John Khoo (pseudonym), August 20, 1998.

hagiographic pamphlets (in different languages) distributed at the shrine, which extol her as a "family-oriented saint" who "oversees family happiness" and helps her devotees to find "good life partners and children," as well as "success in business and examinations."[16]

Saint Anne and Mary inside the shrine. Photo by Yeoh Seng Guan, 1998

For others who give more attention to the specific genealogy of Saint Anne, like Roman Catholic pilgrims, her responsiveness to petitions was simply attributed to her being a persuasive grandmother to a filial and eminently powerful grandson, Jesus Christ. Thus, while a number of those who attended the Bukit Mertajam shrine seeking Saint Anne's spiritual intervention were motivated by the saint's family resemblance to highly compassionate female deities or *bodhisattvas* found in various religious traditions (like Hinduism and Buddhism), many worshippers, in addition, understood this saint in terms of an idealized (and perhaps even fetishized) matriarchal bond with her "devotees" or "children," a familial quotidian experience and metaphor that connects readily across various religious and ethnic domains.

---

[16] Undated pamphlet, author unknown.

Despite the saint's compelling allure, my informants also recounted conundrums and obstacles that impeded those who wish to seek the help of Saint Anne at the shrine. Again, I turn to John Lourdes for leads.

> A lot of other Christians from other denominations as well as Buddhists also come, even Muslims. I know of some Muslims who are afraid to come personally. They use a second person or close friends to burn candles on their behalf. One time I remember a Malay lady coming in a big car to see the priest. I was told later that she was related to royalty and had studied in a convent before. She gave a donation to the church and left. Nowadays, it is difficult for Malays because there are a lot of spies watching. It is also difficult to distinguish between Indonesian Catholics and Malay-Muslims.[17]

I shall revisit this observation to discuss what it indexes about contemporary interreligious politics in Malaysian society after I have looked at one of the most sought after objects at the shrine—Saint Anne's water.

SAINT ANNE'S WATER

Before focusing specifically on Saint Anne's water as a particular kind of "sacred commodity," it would be pertinent to contextualize this particular item in terms of the circuits of sacred gifting created during the period when the shrine is most visited by pilgrims—the nine days' novena preceding the feast day.[18] At the main entrance of the shrine complex, pilgrims minimally purchase two items from an army of makeshift roadside vendors who line the entire stretch of the thoroughfare to the shrine. One is either a small bouquet or an Indian-style garland of flowers, and the other is a box of white candles. In the case of the latter, some pilgrims may choose to purchase exceptionally long candles—some of these extend up to six feet in length/height—as an indication of their devotional fervor. Inside the compact sanctuary, where dyadic statues of Saint Anne and a pubescent Mary are found perched up high on a pedestal, pilgrims stand or kneel in prayer with lighted candles for a few minutes facing these figures. They then advance to the front to present their gifts of flowers and candles to the wardens on duty, who act as intermediaries between the supplicants and Saint Anne. Upon request, pilgrims would receive, in return, smaller portions of flowers offered to Saint Anne earlier, by other pilgrims, from a rack placed at the edge of the altar area. Before pilgrims finally leave the sanctuary, they deposit money in old metal alms boxes placed at the altar, in full view of Saint Anne and Mary.[19] While money is the current dominant medium of "offering" to the saint, other kinds of items have been known to be deposited as well. These have included gold and silver jewelry, as well as small, metal, votive plaques pressed into the iconic likeness of human body parts like eyes, heart, hands, kidneys,

---

[17] Interview with John Lourdes, January 19, 1998.

[18] Cf. P. Gleary, "Sacred Commodities: The Circulation of Medieval Relics," in *The Social Life of Things: Commodities in Cultural Perspective*, ed. Arjun Appadurai (Cambridge: Cambridge University Press, 1986).

[19] In the past, Indian pilgrims from plantations were known to bring more organic forms of gifts, like cockerels, coconuts, bananas, rice, and cooking oil to the shrine.

and so forth, or shaped as whole human figurines.[20] According to pilgrims and shrine authorities, the intent of these votive offerings can be read as dual—either to provide an eloquent pictorial embodiment of the pilgrims' requests, or as a visual testimony to the fact that past prayers for healing or fertility had been answered. Quite a number of pilgrims I spoke to mistakenly held the view that the offering of votive objects was not of Roman Catholic provenance, and traced the origins of this practice solely to the intervention of Hindu visitors. In reality, votive objects are still very much part of both the pilgrimage cultures of Roman Catholic and Eastern Orthodox Catholic traditions in Europe.[21]

Some of the votive images deposited at the shrine. Photo by Yeoh Seng Guan, 1998

At the sanctuary, the gifting (and exchange) of flowers and candles is facilitated by volunteer wardens. However, two other items equally sought after by pilgrims are left unmediated. The first involves small packets of salt mixed with black peppercorns left anonymously behind by other pilgrims in the sanctuary area and even on any available spaces around the sanctuary. Except for comments that this practice is "traditional," "of Indian origin," and "from another religion," many pilgrims were often at a loss to explain to me the specifics of this cultural practice. Nevertheless, as pepper and salt are common household cooking ingredients, pilgrims reckoned that these items were to be consumed together with their food in order to benefit from its curative, purificatory, and apotropaic powers of the shrine. This practice appears to be dwindling in popularity, not least because it is frowned upon and discouraged by shrine authorities as "un-Catholic." Another item suffering the same fate is oil. A middle-aged, Chinese Roman Catholic priest, one of my

---

[20] For example, see "Statue of St. Anne is Carried around Bukit Mertajam Town," *The Malayan Catholic News*, August 29, 1954. When the dyadic statue of St. Anne and Mary was physically more accessible to pilgrims, it was reported that these votive figurines were placed at the feet of the saint. See "A Time for Hope and Devotion," *The Star*, August 9, 1988.

[21] For example, see M. L. Nolan and S. Nolan, *Christian Pilgrimages in Modern Western Europe* (Chapel Hill, NC: University of North Carolina Press, 1989).

informants, recollected that in the 1980s, when he first visited the shrine as a young seminarian, he was surprised to see oil being distributed in the same easily accessible manner as the packets of salt and pepper. He speculated that the small measures of oil must have been brought in by non-Roman Catholic pilgrims, given that consecrated oil in the Roman Catholic tradition is a rare religious commodity that can only be liturgically blessed by a bishop and is intended for important ritual purposes.[22]

Outside and adjacent to the sanctuary building, pilgrims avail themselves of another seemingly banal or quotidian substance—water—but without the theological predicaments attached to salt and oil. Like the aforementioned items, because this water is sited on sacred and auspicious ground, pilgrims impute transformative properties to it. Moreover, since it is explicitly publicized by the shrine authorities as Saint Anne's water (and identified as such in Chinese and Tamil script inscribed on notices), pilgrims help themselves to the water at a short, free-standing wall bearing a row of taps. Built a few years before my fieldwork, together with a water pump, the wall took the place of a sheltered well and made it unnecessary for attendants to draw up and dispense water to the large crowds of pilgrims.[23] At these taps, the pilgrims I witnessed performed a variety of ritual actions, and, once again, indexed their different faiths by these actions, as some wetted their faces, while others sprinkled drops of water over their heads or drank handfuls of water. Moreover, pilgrims familiar with the shrine would also bring empty plastic bottles and other receptacles (even plastic bags) to collect Saint Anne's water. Others could resort to buying smaller empty plastic containers sculpted in the dyadic likeness of Saint Anne and Mary, sold by the church youth group on duty near to the taps. According to local parishioners, Saint Anne's water stems from natural underground sources, not chemically treated piped water. The only human technological intervention is in the shape of a pump and the provision of a filter to facilitate easy accessibility. On a normal non-feast day, the flow of water is plentiful and unhindered, but during the nine days' novena preceding the feast day in July, the supply occasionally suffers because of the large crowds availing themselves of it. In consideration for pilgrims who traveled from afar and risked returning home empty-handed, shrine authorities also sell bottles of Saint Anne's water collected several days or weeks earlier, the price of which covers the cost of manufacturing the plastic containers; there is no charge for the water.

---

[22] In the Roman Catholic tradition, the act of blessing oil (a mixture of olive oil and balsam) is executed by the Bishop on Maundy Thursday (during the last week of Lent). The consecrated oil (*chrism* in Greek) is then used for the important ritual functions of baptism, confirmation of believers, and the institution of holy orders, as well as for consecrating churches and other ritual objects. This practice stems from the biblical notion of "anointment" in Judaism and is also practiced by the Eastern Orthodox Church and some Anglican and Lutheran Protestant churches. Refer to http://www.newadvent.org/cathen/03696b.htm (accessed April 3, 2012) for more details.

[23] Earlier containers—rectangular medicinal bottles—were simpler. The change mimicked the practice found in other major Roman Catholic pilgrimage shrines, like the celebrated Our Lady of Lourdes in France. Similarly, when a strikingly new and large church structure was completed in Bukit Mertajam in 2002 adjacent to the old shrine, the marble wall was replaced by a more elaborate wall resembling those found in European pilgrimage shrines, such as Lourdes.

Collecting Saint Anne's water into specially designed plastic bottles.
Photo by Yeoh Seng Guan, 1998

Following Marcel Mauss's pioneering work, this set of activities, together with those described earlier, can be characterized as essentially a "gifting transaction," in which the items collected tangibly materialize the ineffable attributes and powers of the giver.[24] In qualitatively differentiating this potent substance from "holy water" (I discuss the distinction below) by personalizing it as Saint Anne's water, the shrine authorities lend further credence to this transformative activity. What is given in asymmetrical exchange for these tokens of transubstantiated water, salt, flowers, and boons is the gratitude and loyalty of the pilgrim, in addition to varying amounts of money donated to the church coffers. Moreover, pilgrims' expressions of gratitude could also take on culturally specific embodied trajectories. For instance, ethnic South Indian Tamils have been known to perform a range of devotional labor, done in honor of Saint Anne (or her multiple personas). Tamil pilgrims/devotees commonly prepare cooked vegetarian food to be offered freely to others present in the shrine compound, they beg for alms (*madipitchay* in Tamil), which are later donated to the church, or unwrap candle wrappers for other pilgrims. Each of these actions entails different degrees of logistical and organizational complexity, while reinforcing the personalized nature of the pilgrim's vow to the saint. In a number of my conversations, pilgrims took evident pride in telling me that these activities have become an inter-generational "family tradition," originating with their forefather's or foremother's founding vow, and that they were perpetuating its trajectory and, by implication, continuing their family's relationship with the saint. In contrast to the Tamils' largely public expressions and performances of reciprocity, ethnic Chinese pilgrims are more inclined to offer money as their preferred medium of gifting and exchange. At its most intimate level, pilgrims could honor Saint Anne through simply narrating stories (firsthand or otherwise) to other pilgrims and strangers alike (such as this author), describing her interventions as glowing testimonies of her

---

[24] Marcel Mauss, *The Gift: The Form and Reason for Exchange in Archaic Societies* (London: Routledge, 1990 [1925]).

power and compassion. Indeed, for a number of pilgrims with whom I spoke, the saint's pervasive, immaterial, and yet tangible presence at the shrine is indexed by their hesitance, if not reluctance, to answer or engage with critically framed questions about her perceived identity and relational powers. Presumably, entertaining these doubts might attract the saint's displeasure and prompt her to withdraw her protective powers from supplicants confronted by the vicissitudes and vagaries of everyday living.[25]

The new wall of taps dispensing St. Anne's water. Photo by Yeoh Seng Guan, 2004

In light of the foregoing, how does the materiality of Saint Anne's water and similar substances like it (dis)articulate with the contemporary ethno-religious discourses of the modern Malaysian nation-state? As a point of departure, I begin with the theological and pastoral concerns of a few local Roman Catholic priests whom I had conversations with about Saint Anne's water. They conveniently stand in for the institution that they represent and for which they mediate. While not overtly dismissive, some were ambivalent about the water's purported widely efficacious properties. They stressed, instead, the need for lay Roman Catholics to hold firm to the sacraments and the core teachings of the church, rather than place their faith solely in miraculous interventions and boons as embodied in talismanic objects. These priests gave prominence to the moral and ecclesiastical duties as laid out in Roman Catholic orthodoxy in the light of the reforming spirit of the landmark Vatican II conciliar meetings held in the 1960s. Discursively, this stance is underscored by a semantic and theological distinction made between "holy water," which has been ritually transformed by the liturgical utterances of priests and is subsequently used for "blessing" people (and objects), and Saint Anne's water, which requires no similar human intervention (unless individual pilgrims specifically request it).[26] Through the transformative power of a priest's special

---

[25] It must be noted, however, that not all visitors to the shrine during this occasion go as pilgrims. "Undesirable elements," such as male youth gangs and thieves, take advantage of the festive atmosphere and large crowds to ogle young nubile girls (colloquially, to *cuci mata*, or "wash eyes"), or pick the pockets of pilgrims.

[26] Unlike the Roman Catholic consecration of oil, discussed earlier, which only takes place annually on Maundy Thursday, water can be blessed by an ordained priest throughout the year, when there is need for it, though this rite is usually carried out during the Easter season.

words, ordinary water is resignified and repositioned into a higher plane of the moral economy of religious meanings. Nevertheless, these same priests also conceded the possibility that the efficacy of Saint Anne's water, as in the well-known healing spring waters of the ecclesiastically sanctioned shrine in Lourdes, France.[27] The substantive difference between the two shrines, however, is that, unlike the Sanctuary of Our Lady of Lourdes, the Bukit Mertajam shrine has never been authenticated by a documented, miraculous appearance by the saint, even though local narratives describing the appearance of a "mysterious white-clad woman" in the shrine do circulate widely.

Notwithstanding the intricacies involved in ecclesiastically legitimating and institutionalizing sacred places, these concerns are not paramount for the ordinary pilgrim. For pilgrims, the grasping of Saint Anne's water as a natural substance and as a religiously objectified form proceeded along both common and unfamiliar trajectories. Indeed, apart from its purported efficacious qualities, the water had the added advantage of being readily portable, in addition to being malleable and durable. Moreover, unlike statues or amulets, which entail human intermediaries or artisans in the creative process of design and production, the primal and aniconic form of water enables worshippers to sidestep various doctrinal differences between religions while also threading through and connecting these differences.[28] This process is manifested in the myriad ways in which various pilgrims comprehend Saint Anne's water. Depending on the individual pilgrim's religious provenance and circumstances, Saint Anne's water could be drunk, applied to afflicted body parts, added to one's bath, and used to "cleanse" domestic spaces and a range of artifacts through sprinkling. Within homes, Saint Anne's water becomes a prized possession and would be stored at a special place, usually on the family altar alongside icons of divinity and other religious paraphernalia.[29] The plastic containers sculpted in the dyadic image of Saint Anne and Mary containing the water enact a material visualization and objectification of the saint's benevolent presence. Because Saint Anne's water is not readily accessible, it would be used sparingly in small amounts for special occasions and urgent circumstances (like life-threatening health situations or severe spiritual maladies). In this way, the special properties of Saint Anne's water not only mimic those of "holy water," as officially sanctioned by the Roman Catholic ecclesiastical authorities, but also extend beyond this provenance.[30]

As elsewhere, the belief that water is an apt container or conduit for acquiring and conveying transformative powers through utterances of special words and through contagious physical contact with sacred places or iconographic representations of the sacred (like statues of divinities) is ecumenically shared across the major religions found in peninsular Malaysia. On a wider geographical and ecological canvas, given the region's wet climatic conditions ("water from heaven"), which are regulated by seasonal monsoon winds, water has deeply imprinted the

---

[27] For a historical treatment of the shrine of Our Lady of Lourdes, see Ruth Harris, *Lourdes: Body and Spirit in the Secular Age* (London: Penguin, 2000).

[28] See also Laurel Kendall, Vũ Thị Thanh Tâm, and Nguyễn Thị Thu Hương, "Icon, Iconoclasm, Art Commodity: Are Objects still Agents in Vietnam?" in this volume.

[29] See also Daniel Miller, ed. *Home Possessions: Material Culture behind Closed Doors* (Oxford: Berg, 2001).

[30] Compare this to the Roman Catholic theology of the ritual transubstantiation of wine and bread (or wafer) into the blood and body of Christ during mass through the liturgical utterances and performance of the priest.

histories of most Southeast Asian kingdoms and territories, affecting trade and diasporic mobility, as well as shaping worldviews in indigenous classification systems, beliefs, myths, notions of healing, and so forth.[31] These different social and cultural vectors highlight the material conditions for an understanding of water in all its mythological and everyday, pragmatic religious dimensions. Thus, in the context of the domestic domain, a Hindu informant explained to me that a small pot of water, earlier chanted over by temple priests, is usually placed at her home altar for the purpose of repelling "ill desires" and "bad vibrations" emanating from "outside" the home and threatening to affect its occupants. An elderly Malay-Muslim informant described a similar ritual involving the ministrations of a Malay *bomoh* (shaman), who might include Quranic verses in his stock of incantations. While water transformed by the *bomoh* would essentially function as "medicine" to heal an array of physical and spiritual ailments, the desired efficacy of the transformed water is not always guaranteed, and is contingent on the special knowledge base and ascetic powers of the specific *bomoh*. Consistent with the instrumental slant of magical practices, the moral nature of the intentionality of the individual seeking the interventions of the *bomoh*, whether for "good" or "bad" purposes, is not foregrounded, although the consequences of the supplicant's intentions can accrue and rebound on him or her if higher spiritual powers will it.

Spiritually transformed water does not all have the same value. Water found in famed pilgrimage places is held to be already extraordinary and does not require human intervention. Thus, for Hindus, water from the Ganges river in India is especially desired because of its close association with the feminine divine and its preeminent powers to cleanse and to purify pilgrims.[32] Malaysian Hindu pilgrims who make a trip to the Ganges river invariably try to bring back small metal pots of its prized contents. Similarly, Malaysian Muslims who make the *haj* (pilgrimage) to Mecca frequently collect and bring home fairly large plastic bottles of "zam zam water" found inside the Grand Mosque. While different religions may characterize water according to their various respective mythic charters, its usage by pilgrims essentially shares similar resonances. Chief among them, as related to me by my Muslim informants, is water's purported curative and purifying properties, signaled by the distinctive taste of water from a particular source. Zam zam water has the additional feature of being able to address other kinds of anxieties or hopes that may be preoccupying the pilgrim and influencing his or her life at a particular point in time. When drinking zam zam water, the pilgrim brings to mind these concerns and hopes in order to set in motion a resolution in the as-yet-unknown future. Similar to mnemonic ritual devices found in other faiths, zam zam water, then operates for the Muslim pilgrim as a medium for thinking through and materializing one's biographical and spiritual state-of-being in the context of a grand scheme of things.[33]

Water need not always be imbued with sacred properties before it becomes efficacious for religious purposes. Before entering into the inner spaces of Hindu and

---

[31] For example, see Peter Boomgaard, ed., *A World of Water: Rain, Rivers, and Seas in Southeast Asian Histories* (Singapore: National University of Singapore Press, 2007).

[32] S. Darian, *The Ganges in Myth and History* (Delhi: Motilal Banarsidass Publishers, 2001 [1978]).

[33] See Liana Chua, "The Problem with 'Empty Crosses': Thinking through Materiality in Bidayuh Religious Practices" (this volume); and Janet Hoskins, *Biographical Objects: How Things Tell the Story of People's Lives* (New York, NY: Routledge, 1998).

Islamic places of worship, for instance, devotees use tap water to cleanse parts of their outer bodies; for Muslims, this act of ablution is a ritual prerequisite for approaching the sacred. Water also figures prominently in Theravada Buddhist temple rituals. Traditionally, Buddhist monks sprinkle water onto devotees as they chant from the sutras, and devotees gain merit by "bathing"—scooping several ladles of water onto—miniature statues of Buddha. In short, the fundamental and polyvalent substance of water is amenable for a range of purposes. While the significance of water may be nuanced according to the religious *habitus* that informs each act of devotion, the utility of water as a cleansing agent and a vehicle for supernatural agency is a generic motif easily grasped, appreciated, and acted upon.

It is in this light that the collection and gifting of Saint Anne's water assumes special significance. A number of non-local pilgrims with whom I spoke said that, in addition to collecting Saint Anne's water for their own use, they also made an effort to bring back the prized item for relatives, friends, neighbors, and work colleagues who could not make the trip for various reasons, such as ill health, lack of money and time, and so forth. Additionally, these souvenirs of Saint Anne's water could be offered as gifts, thereby manifesting personal concern and goodwill to a host of people, including non-Roman Catholics. Similarly, prayers and petitions (in the form of letters) could be recited or delivered to Saint Anne at her shrine on behalf of one's family or friends, thus enacting a kind of vicarious pilgrimage for "absentee pilgrims."

In particular, my Roman Catholic informants' accounts of Malay-Muslims stealthily participating in the feast or seeking the intervention of Saint Anne (or her perceived personas) were related to me with barely disguised pleasure. By the same token, given the current health of inter-ethnic relations in Malaysia, the religious and political significance of aiding Muslims as "absentee pilgrims" is not lost on them. In the distant past, these acts of mediation and goodwill were arguably not viewed as extraordinary or as transgressing religious norms. However, for the last three decades or so, various kinds of overlapping political and economic projects have radically reconfigured the Malaysian ethno-religious landscape. First, the developmentalist transformation of the country has not only materially and spiritually transformed territories, but also catalyzed the creation of new social classes among a wider segment of the multiethnic population—especially in the urban centers—and reshaped the use and exchange values of both "secular" and "religious" commodities. Another trajectory, arising from the "race riots" of May 13, 1969, has been determined by the transformative powers of the New Economic Policy (1971–90) and its subsequent mutations as a wide-ranging affirmative action program, crafted ostensibly to unravel the racialized and segregationist legacies of British colonial rule through a selective bio-political investment in ethnic Malays.[34] With the spawning of modernist subjectivities in an age of predatory capitalist "globalization," competing projects of nationalism and cosmopolitanism have marked and guided the country's development as well. On the one hand, the ethno-religious diversity of the country is magically represented as a cultural resource to stake out an imagined community based on an inclusive nationalist identity (i.e., *Bangsa Malaysia,* or the "Malaysian race") and cultural diversity (as exemplified by the "Malaysia, Truly Asia" slogan), distinct from the social imaginaries of

---

[34] Aihwa Ong, *Flexible Citizenship: The Cultural Logics of Transnationality* (Durham, NC, and London: Duke University Press, 1999).

neighboring Asian nation-states. On the other hand, the same period has also seen the buttressing of a Wahhabi-style reformist version of Islamic governance, as a result of which state-led efforts to "purify" syncretistic Muslim popular practices and "modernize" Islamic morality have engendered spillover effects into the domains of other non-Muslim ethno-religious groups.[35] Ostensibly enacted to avoid "confusing Malay-Muslims," these Islamic reforms range from prohibitions of the use of certain words, such as *Allah* and *doa* (prayer) in non-Islamic literature, to the banning and confiscation of Bibles translated in the Malay language, to difficulties in obtaining land for building places of worship and burial grounds for non-Muslims, and, more recently, to high-profile court cases that pit the jurisdictional powers of secular civil law against Islamic Syariah law.[36] Many local commentators have lamented the rise of Malay-Muslim ethno-religious supremacy and the consequent undermining of the civil liberties enshrined in the Federal Constitution, as well as the corresponding deterioration of inter-ethno-religious relations; such critics frequently contrast the current, divisive state of affairs to a nostalgic golden age.[37] Apart from law, the "Islamization" of Malaysian society has also been articulated through a closer attention to symbolic and material boundaries, which extend to everyday commensality. The systematic and comprehensive distinction between *halal* (permissible) and *haram* (not permissible) activities and consumption, which guides not only one's choice of cuisine but also extends to a broad range of modern consumer products, have been in increasing evidence.[38] The commodification of the *halal–haram* spectrum has even extended to the banal object of bottled water, whereby only items emblazoned with the prized "halal" logo are deemed to be fit for Muslim consumption. Certainly, seen in today's context, a gesture of goodwill of the kind briefly chronicled in the *Malayan Catholic Leader* of 1954—which described the Sultan of Johore donating a "beautiful and immaculate white statue of Our Lady of the Immaculate Conception" to a convent[39]—would be unimaginable for many Malaysians today, given that each sultan is recognized as the statutory and moral guardian of Islam in his respective state.

---

[35] Michael Peletz, *Islamic Modern: Religious Courts and Cultural Politics in Malaysia* (Princeton, NJ: Princeton University Press, 2002).

[36] J. Lee, *Islamization and Activism in Malaysia* (Singapore: Institute of Southeast Asian Studies, 2010).

[37] Inter alia S. Ackerman and R. Lee, *Heaven in Transition: Non-Muslim Religious Innovation and Ethnic Identity in Malaysia* (Honolulu, HI: University of Hawaii Press, 1988); P. Martinez, "Islam, Constitutional Democracy and the Islamic State in Malaysia," in *Civil Society in Southeast Asia*, ed. H. G. Lee (Singapore: Institute of Southeast Asian Studies, 2004); Andrew Willford, *Cage of Freedom: Tamil Identity and the Ethnic Fetish in Malaysia* (Ann Arbor, MI: University of Michigan Press, 2006); Yeoh Seng Guan, "In Defence of the Secular?: Islamisation, Christians, and (New) Politics in Urbane Malaysia," *Asian Studies Review* 35,1 (2011): 83–103; and Yeoh Seng Guan, "Managing Sensitivities: Religious Pluralism, Civil Society, and Inter-faith Relations in Malaysia," *The Round Table: The Commonwealth Journal of International Affairs* 94,382 (2005): 629–40.

[38] For example, Johan Fischer, *Proper Islamic Consumption: Shopping among the Malays in Modern Malaysia* (Copenhagen: Nordic Institute of Asian Studies Press, 2008).

[39] See "H. H. Sultan of Johore Donates Marian Statue," *The Malayan Catholic News*, August 29, 1954. In the late eighteenth century, the Sultan of Kedah had also gifted land and a house to a French Roman Catholic missionary. See "Land and House Given by Sultan Abdullah," *The Malayan Catholic News*, October 1, 1972.

CONCLUSION

Unlike the "natural symbols" of sun, fire, and earth, water "calls out" or "affords" differently because of its comparative malleability, portability, and accessibility.[40] For maritime and mainland Southeast Asian societies, water typically and effectively exemplifies the theme of "overlapping territories and intertwined histories" in a region largely marked by wet weather and extensive intercultural exchanges through centuries of long-distance trade.[41] A "sacred commodity" (or a fetish) like "holy water" bears material witness to these kinds of linkages. At the Bukit Mertajam shrine, the practice of collecting and sharing Saint Anne's water (and similar kinds of objects) across a spectrum of religious and ethnic groups thus enacts subaltern agencies and trajectories that, while giving credence, in part, to state-driven aspirations and the management of modernist "multiculturalism," also (dis)articulates with recent shifts in Malaysian cultural politics at the same time. The "plural materialities" of Saint Anne's water, as it moves from one person to the next, display attributes of the uncanny in not only confounding supposedly cultural wholes, but also in bearing witness to the fact that transsubstantiated religious materials can connect meaningfully among human subjects, just as they can be mobilized to divide. Reminiscent of what Patricia Spyer has termed to be the otherness of a "border fetish," the connective powers of the emblems (or fetish) of material religion do not always run in concordance with nation-state imaginaries and rationalities.[42] To track the cultural logic and material traces of the social lives and careers of such objects as they move and mutate over time and space is to see heterogeneous histories in motion.

---

[40] Mary Douglas, *Natural Symbols* (New York, NY: Vintage Books, 1973).

[41] Said, *Culture and Imperialism*.

[42] Patricia Spyer, "Introduction," in *Border Fetishisms: Material Objects in Unstable Spaces*, ed. Patricia Spyer (New York, NY: Routledge, 1998).

CHAPTER 6

"THE LAND OF THE GREAT IMAGE" AND THE TEST OF TIME: THE MAKING OF BUDDHA IMAGES IN ARAKAN (BURMA / MYANMAR)[1]

Alexandra de Mersan

This article is about the making of Buddha images today, in the Arakan (Rakhine) State of the Union of Myanmar. The Buddhist Kingdom of Arakan was independent until 1785, when it was conquered by the Burmese. Although their kingdom has not existed for more than two centuries, the Arakanese[2] still refer to it today and to its palladium, the protective Mahamuni Buddha bronze image, and thereby maintain a strong sense of historical and religious community among themselves. During fieldwork conducted in the late 1990s at Mrauk U, the former capital of the last Arakanese kingdom, I came to note the vitality of Buddhist statuary. Looking at these works, and reading many narratives on the images of Buddha in Arakan, I wondered why such images are so important. What do people do when they make Buddha images, and what does the study of this practice teach us about Arakan society? Why is it, for example, that high-ranking figures in the Burmese military are known to buy Buddha statues during their trips to Arakan State? In previous works,[3] I demonstrated how studying "material religion" is relevant to the understanding of relationships among ethnic groups in the nation-

---

[1] This article is dedicated to U Kyaw Tha Nyunt and U Maung Lon, masters craftsmen in Mrauk U. It is offered in memory of Sara U Kyaw Kyaw Hla, thanks to whom I discovered this domain. I wish to thank Bénédicte Brac de la Perrière for her readings and comments at several stages in the writing of the article.

[2] The Arakanese people are a Buddhist subpopulation belonging to the "Burmese-speaking family"—as they speak a dialect of Burmese—living mostly in the plains and valleys of the Arakan State, a coastal region of Western Burma/Myanmar. On the history of the kingdom of Arakan, see Jacques P. Leider, *Le royaume d'Arakan, Birmanie: Son histoire politique entre le début du XVè et la fin du XVIIè siècle* (Paris: École Française d'Extrême-Orient, 2004).

[3] Alexandra de Mersan, "L'expression du particularisme arakanais dans la Birmanie contemporaine," *Moussons* 8 (2005): 117–41; Alexandra de Mersan, "A New Palace for Mra Swan Dewi : Changes in Spirits Cults in Arakan (Rakhine) State," *Asian Ethnology* 68,2 (2009): 307–32.

building process in contemporary Burma.[4] In this chapter, I shall go beyond that point and focus on the fabrication itself, which highlights local values and embedded meanings independent of the national context, a focus which then raises the issue of the notion of "power."

This article is based on observation of several craftsmen in their workshops, and focuses on the making of a massive bronze Buddha image, the Lotaramuni image, in a monastery on the periphery of Mrauk U, during April 1999. The data gathered cover the entire, step-by-step process of making the Buddha image, from the original drawing of the future statue to its final consecration through the process of casting. Ancient and recent descriptions of the manufacturing process of such statues in Burma proper are available,[5] however, few studies focus on Buddhist rituals, in practice, in Burma. This is mostly because of the history of Buddhist studies, which for a long time considered practices and rituals as degenerate or corrupt, compared with "authentic," "original" texts,[6] but also because of, as Brac de la Perrière pointed out for Burma, an anti-ritualistic discourse in circulation among the Buddhists themselves.[7] Most of the studies on ceremonies associated with Buddha images in Theravada societies are concerned with the consecration ritual, and fewer concern

---

[4] Other authors have noted the building of a religious landscape in contemporary Burma, a development concomitant with the construction of infrastructures that are part of the nation-building process carried out by the military junta, which has promoted Buddhism through projects such as the erection of pagodas at strategic points and places—the "building a *mangala* [auspicious] country." See Gustaaf Houtman, *Mental Culture in Burmese Crisis Politics: Aung San Suu Kyi and the National League for Democracy* (Tokyo: Institute for the Study of Languages and Cultures of Asia and Africa, 1999); Juliane Schober, "Buddhist Just Rule and Burmese National Culture: State Patronage of the Chinese Tooth Relic in Myanmar," *History of Religions* 36,3 (1997): 218–43. See also Klemens Karlsson, "Material Religion and Ethnic Identity: Buddhist Visual Culture and the Burmanization of the Eastern Shan State" (this volume), or the study of the circulation of relics in Bénédicte Brac de la Perrière, "Urbanisation et légendes d'introduction du Bouddhisme au Myanmar (Birmanie)," *Journal des anthropologues* 61–62 (1995): 41–63; and Juliane Schober, "In the Presence of the Buddha: Ritual Veneration of the Burmese Mahamuni Image," in *Sacred Biography in the Buddhist Traditions of South and Southeast Asia,* ed. Juliane Schober (Honolulu, HI: University of Hawaii Press, 1997), pp. 259–88. I describe how Arakan, as a peripheral society of Burma, responds to this nation-building project.

[5] The technique for casting either a Buddha image or a bell is rather similar. Among those who have studied casting technique in Burma, with the exception of Shway Yoe, who does describe some rituals, most authors focus on the technique of casting itself. See Shway Yoe, *The Burman, His Life and Notions* (New York, NY: W. W. Norton, 1963 [1882]), pp. 198–210. See also Harry L. Tilly, *Monograph on the Brass and Copper Wares of Burma* (Rangoon: Government Printing, 1894); Max Ferrars and Bertha Ferrars, *Burma* (London: Sampson Low, Marston & Compagnie, 1901), pp. 103–5). For Thailand, see also Alexander Griswold, "Bronze-Casting in Siam," *BEFEO* 46,2 (1954): 635–39; Donna K. Strahan, "Bronze Casting in Thailand," in *The Sacred Sculpture of Thailand: The Alexander B. Griswold Collection, The Walters Art Gallery,* ed. Hiram W. Woodward, Jr. (Baltimore, MD: The Walters Art Gallery, 1997); and Donald K. Swearer, *Becoming the Buddha: The Ritual of Image Consecration in Thailand* (Princeton, NJ: Princeton University Press, 2004), pp. 49–50.

[6] Donald S. Lopez, *Curators of the Buddha: The study of Buddhism under Colonialism* (Chicago, IL: University of Chicago Press, 1995).

[7] Bénédicte Brac de la Perrière, "Les rituels de consécration des statues de Bouddha et de *naq* en Birmanie: Adaptation de formes rituelles indiennes,"*Purusartha* 25 (2006): 201–36.

themselves with the veneration of the Buddha images or remains.[8] I shall return to the ritual of consecration later on.

In the creation of the Lotaramuni image, several ceremonies and rituals took place, prior to its consecration, in the course of its production process. As there was little information on the subject, my research into the study of material religion, and more precisely, the relationship between myth and ritual as conveyed through the notion of "representation" in Buddhist popular practice, coupled with my study of the relevant rituals and local Buddhist society, possibly breaks new ground in Burma studies.

In comparing my data to local narratives—whether oral or written—I argue that, insofar as Buddha images are believed to contain powers, those powers are derived not only through the consecration ritual, but also, as my analysis reveals, throughout the fabrication of the image itself. Therefore, the collective act of producing Buddha images maintains the Buddha's dispensation (*sasana*), while "making radiate" the specific locality (i.e., Arakanese Buddhist society) throughout and beyond the Buddhistic universe.

BUDDHA IMAGES IN ARAKAN[9]

Theravada Buddhism is firmly rooted in local societies, particularly in a Southeast Asian context. Its implantation takes different forms contingent upon social and historical circumstances, such as the production of sacred objects and places. Hence, the legends related to the advent of Buddhism and the foundation of pagodas may differ in comparative strengths depending on the place in question.[10]

---

[8] About the consecration ritual, see the very stimulating work of Swearer, *Becoming the Buddha,* in which he demonstrates how the image of the Buddha is instructed in the life of the Buddha and empowered with his supernormal attainments. See also Juliane Schober, "Paths to Enlightenment: Theravada Buddhism in Upper Burma" (PhD dissertation, University of Illinois at Urbana, 1989), pp. 152–53 and see footnote 14. Regarding the veneration of Buddha images in Burma, see Schober, "In the Presence of the Buddha," and Juliane Schober, "Venerating the Buddha's Remains in Burma: From Solitary Practice to the Cultural Hegemony of Communities," *The Journal of Burma Studies* 6 (2001): 111–39; as well as John Strong "Veneration of Images," in *Encyclopedia of Religion*, ed. Mircea Eliade (New York, NY: Macmillan Publishing, 1987), pp. 97–104.

[9] Alexandra de Mersan, "Espace rituel et construction de la localité: Contribution à l'étude ethnographique d'une population de la Birmanie contemporaine: les Arakanais" (PhD Dissertation, l'École des Hautes Études en Sciences Sociales, Paris, 2005), fourth part.

[10] Frank E. Reynolds, "Buddhism as Universal Religion and as Civic Religion: Some Observations on a Recent Tour of Buddhist Centers in Central Thailand," in *Religion and Legitimation of Power in Thailand, Laos, and Burma*, ed. Bardwell L. Smith (Chambersburg, PA: Anima Books, 1978); Kevin Trainor, *Relics, Ritual, and Representation in Buddhism: Rematerializing the Sri Lankan Theravada Tradition* (Cambridge: Cambridge University Press, 1997); and Schober, "Venerating the Buddha's Remains." Swearer in recent works stresses also this fact: "The Buddha also lives in the form of particular Buddha images that have their own sacred stories (*tamnan*)." See Swearer, *Becoming the Buddha*, pp. 5, 231. See also Donald K. Swearer, "Presencing the Buddha in Northern Thailand: Perspectives from Ritual and Narrative," in *Buddhist Legacies in Mainland Southeast Asia*, ed. François Lagirarde and Paritta Chalermpow Koanantakool (Paris: Publications de l'École Française d'Extrême-Orient, 2006), pp. 277–84. Meanwhile, Strong has emphasized the role of relics (which he names "relics of the still living Buddha") in spreading Buddhism. See John Strong, "Les reliques des cheveux du Bouddha au Shwe Dagon de Rangoon,"*Aséanie* 2 (1998): 79–107; and John Strong, *Relics of the Buddha* (Princeton, NJ, and Oxford: Princeton University Press, 2004).

Or, in Schober's words, these narratives and traditions are about "Mapping the sacred in Theravada Buddhist Southeast Asia."[11]

In Arakan, the legend of the Mahamuni Buddha image—the ancient palladium of the Arakanese kingship—has been the founding myth of Arakanese society for at least the last two centuries.[12] This is largely because such a legend (in its various versions) describes the advent of Buddhism at this specific locality, which, like many other Theravada societies, defines itself as Buddhist ("to be Arakanese is to be Buddhist," as "to be Burmese or Shan is to be Buddhist," and so on). This is also because, at the same time, this legend establishes a social, moral, and political agreement among the Arakanese based on Buddhist kingship.

There are many versions of the Mahamuni legend.[13] Briefly summarized, it relates that King Candasuriya, founder of Dhaññawati, the first capital of Arakan, was honored by the visit of Buddha Gautama who taught his Law (*dhamma*). The king, his family, and all inhabitants were overjoyed, and then converted enthusiastically to this new teaching. Before leaving the country, the Lord Buddha accepted the king's request, to make an effigy of him in remembrance of his teaching. Metal[14] was collected, and with the help of celestial beings, the image was cast over a period of seven days. This image was believed to be an original likeness of Gautama Buddha, enlivened by the Buddha himself and reflecting his features as if it were his "younger brother." Due to the likeness of the historical Buddha, as a "living-double" or a twin, the statue was thought as endowed with great powers. These powers are conceived as "power protection."[15] The image and its shrine were thus greatly revered for centuries. It functioned as the palladium of Arakanese kings until the Burmese seized the statue and brought it back to their capital after their conquest of

---

[11] Juliane Schober, "Mapping the Sacred in Theravada Buddhist Southeast Asia," in *Sacred Places and Modern Landscapes: Sacred Geography and Social-Religious Transformations in South and Southeast Asia*, ed. Ronald A. Lukens-Bull (Tempe, AZ: Arizona State University, 2003), pp. 15–17. Schober describes this process in terms of "locating the Buddha's presence in this world in rituals and myths that narrate often competing cultural hegemonies (what I call 'local society')." See p. 1.

[12] See Alexandra de Mersan, "Espace rituel," pp. 356–82; and Jacques P. Leider, "Relics, Statues, and Predictions: Interpreting an Apocryphal Sermon of Lord Buddha in Arakan," *Asian Ethnology* 68,2 (2009): 333–64. Arakan was known as "the Land of the Great Image," according to the British judge Collis, a public officer who wrote about Mahamuni in Maurice Collis, *The Land of the Great Image, Being Experiences of Friar Manrique in Arakan* (London: Faber and Faber, 1943).

[13] The tradition reported by E. Forchhammer, *Papers on Subjects Relating to the Archaeology of Burma: Arakan* (Rangoon, Government Printing, 1891), pp. 2–7, is probably most widely known. However, in my research on Arakan, I have also taken other kind of sources and narratives into consideration: oral and written (such as poetry, songs, and so on), and paintings and sculptures, some of which are also expressions of popular Buddhism and of local practices and representations. So although these narratives and artworks are the expressions of various social actors within this society, they demonstrate a shared cohesiveness.

[14] More specifically, "materials," as some versions indicate, can include diamonds, precious stones, and clay as components of the statue.

[15] On "power" as "power protection," see Nicola Beth Tannenbaum, *Who Can Compete against the World? Power-Protection and Buddhism in Shan Worldview* (Ann Arbor, MI: Association for Asian Studies, 2001 [1995]).

the kingdom of Arakan. Nowadays, located in Mandalay, it is one of the most venerated Buddha images in Burma.[16]

In Arakan today, in the act of producing new Buddha images, affiliated with the Mahamuni image—as well as through devotions, rituals, and donations—society perpetuates its own social and religious order through what I have called its "mythical space."[17] Images are linked to the Mahamuni in different ways, such as their shape or their story.[18] I shall return to this below. I want to stress here the need to take into consideration the context in which a Buddha image is produced or emerges, as in this case, direct links are traced to the original Buddha himself.

PARTICULARITY AND HIERARCHY OF BUDDHA IMAGES

There exists a hierarchy that distinguishes among the various kinds of Buddha images in terms of their value, quite specific to the societies that produced and ritually deploy them. Some are considered more effective and efficacious than others. When questioned about the relative powers attributed to different images, the Arakanese usually answer that, if Buddha images possess powers (*tan khui*), they have acquired them only through the ritual of consecration.[19] In other words, ritual transforms the material representation and turns it into a Buddha, an object of veneration (*anegaza ma tan bhura ma phrac*).[20] However, further observation suggests that, in practice, this transformational process is more complex. As we shall see, in some cases we can observe that the fabrication process itself has been partially ritualized, which indicates that something else is at stake before the consecration ceremony. As noted earlier, there are several descriptions and analyses of ritual consecration in Theravada societies.[21] In brief, in ritual, powers of the Buddha are

---

[16] On the veneration of the image now in Mandalay and on an analysis of its myth, see Schober, "In the Presence of the Buddha."

[17] See de Mersan, "Espace rituel," pp. 349–429.

[18] The Lotaramuni image is linked to Mahamuni because it is a copy of the Candamuni image, which is said to have been built with the metals left over from Mahamuni.

[19] Schober, "In the Presence of the Buddha," p. 276, has also pointed out the difference between principles, as expressed in discourses, and perception on the powers of the various Buddha images. She considers that difference of power is to be seen through stories told about them.

[20] In the Arakanese dialect, as in the Burmese language, the same word, "*bhura,*" can be applied to the Buddha himself, to a consecrated pagoda (stupa, *cedi*), to a monk, and to a consecrated Buddha image. In Mrauk U, people refer to a verse (*suttan*, pali), called "*satthu bimba suttan*"("the preaching on an image in metal"), to explain that "whatever the material used, only after *anegaza* can people worship the image as if they were worshipping the Buddha himself." However, the sole version I found of this verse indicates, only, that good merits are obtained for future life by those who make a Buddha image in metal; this verse does not emphasize the technique of manufacture or the material, as its title suggests.

[21] The ritual observed in Arakan, which is rather simple, is similar to the one in Lower Burma described by Brac de la Perrière. It is worth noting that in both cases there is no "opening-eye" ceremony, which is not the case in Central Burma and elsewhere as described for Southeast Asia. See Brac de la Perrière, " Les rituels de consécration," pp. 206–12. In Arakan, however, contrary to what is described in Lower Burma by Brac de la Perrière, the image is said to be enlivened (*a sak swan re*) through the words pronounced by the monks over it (*anegaza*), which are thought to be the first words spoken by the Buddha Gautama after his Enlightenment. This first preaching is the setting in motion of the Wheel of the Law (*dhamma*). Words—and then life—are infused into the image through an unction (*bhisik* in Arakanese, or *bhiseka* in Pali) by

brought to or infused into the image through the words pronounced over it. However, once consecrated, not all images are invested with the same value and efficacy. In Arakan, it is said that only the "Five Muni" can be genuinely called part of the "great left-over" (*maha kyan*), in reference to the fact that these images are supposed to have been made with metal left over from the Mahamuni.[22] In the case of the original Mahamuni image, its greater powers are due in the first place to its direct association with the historical Buddha. Also, its powers mainly derive from the Buddha's own glory during his actual lifetime.[23] They come also from the composition of the statue itself, for the Mahamuni Buddha was fabricated by craftsmen who had mastered the process enabling them to combine more or less precious materials brought to them by inhabitants from all over the kingdom, indicating their active part in the myth.[24] Materials represent the localities from which they were derived, or at least indicate or emphasize locality as a value, because the metalworking minerals originally come from the ground.

To my knowledge, no large series of images, cast in metal, equivalent to the mass-produced images, can be found in Arakan. Buddha images are still issued from artisanal means of production. To understand the differences in the powers attributed to various images, several elements, which are not mutually exclusive and are even often combined, need to be taken into consideration, namely: narratives (*samuin*)[25] and miraculous events associated with a particular image; its brightness when cast in metal; its size, which in a way is associated with the preceding idea of miracles and which, here, also highlights the need to evaluate the context of an image's emergence; the image's physical resemblance to the Buddha Gautama himself (as noted with the Mahamuni image)[26]; the social status of the main donor

---

throwing water and sometimes grains of paddy at the statue. The importance of this ritual in Burma appears to be relatively recent, as Shway Yoe notes that its celebration is a matter of individual choice and opinion, although the Sulangandi Buddhist sect considers it superfluous. See Shway Yoe, *The Burman*, p. 198. On the ritual in different Theravada societies, see Adhémar Leclère, "Le Lakkhana préas Putthéa rûp, ou Canon de la Statue du Buddha au Cambodge," *Comptes-rendus des séances de l'Académie des Inscriptions et Belles-Lettres* 42è année, 3 (1898): 368–76; Richard Gombrich, "The Consecration of a Buddhist Image," *Journal of Asian Studies* 26,1 (1966); Stanley J. Tambiah, *The Buddhist Saints of the Forest and the Cult of Amulets* (Cambridge: Cambridge University Press, 1984), chapter 17; François Bizot, "La consécration des statues et le culte des morts," in *Recherches nouvelles sur le Cambodge*, ed. François Bizot (Paris: École Française d'Extrême-Orient, 1994), pp. 101–35. See Swearer, *Becoming the Buddha*, last chapter; and Brac de la Perrière, "Les rituels de consécration," pp. 212–16, for a comparison among these various sources.

[22] They are also called "Noble Alive Image" (*rup rhan to*).

[23] Regarding the Mahamuni image, different traditions say, also, that the Buddha originally breathed upon the image or endowed it with emanations of the warmth of his own body. This necessarily leads us to explore whether this Buddha image, in particular, is to be considered a relic, what Strong calls "relics of the Still-Living Buddha." See Strong, *Relics of the Buddha*, chap. 3. Schober associates this event with the physical likeness of the statue with the Buddha, in reference to what is called the "Twin Miracle." See Schober, "In the Presence of the Buddha," pp. 269–73; and Strong, *Relics of the Buddha*, pp. 177–78.

[24] See de Mersan, "Espace rituel," pp. 365–67.

[25] See Strong, *Relics of the Buddha*; and Swearer, *Becoming the Buddha*.

[26] This point has been made by Stanley J. Tambiah, "Famous Buddha Images and the Legitimation of Kings: The Case of the Sinhala Buddha (*Phra Sihing*) in Thailand," *Res: Anthropology and Aesthetics* 4 (1982): 5–19. See also Schober, "Mapping the Sacred," pp. 15–17.

who sponsored the making of the image (whether a king or an influential layman)[27]; and the nature of the materials employed (use of precious metals or gems, or their greater or lesser durability). I will focus here on this latter point—the material nature of the image, its composition.[28]

The significance of the attributes of the materials from which a particular Buddha image is made—the celebrated Emerald Buddha, the Phrakeo Morakot, in Bangkok, is an excellent example of a Buddha figure renowned for the substance from which it was made—has already been addressed.[29] In Arakan, because the Mahamuni image figures as the ultimate reference, the more famous and powerful Buddha images are made from metal and, more specifically, bronze, usually cast by means of the well-known "lost-wax" (*cire-perdue*) technique. The entire process, from the beginning, can be broadly described in the following way: a rough image is made out of clay; the desired image is then modeled in wax on the clay base to the proposed thickness of the metal. A second clay shell is then placed over this; a number of holes are made in the base of this outer casing. When the clay has dried, the mold is heated, and the wax runs out, leaving the space ready for casting. The molten metal is then poured in through the holes in the mold, and eventually the next phases of gathering several component parts of the statue, brazing, and polishing take place, and then transportation of the statue, sometimes the enshrinement of relics inside the image, and, finally, consecration. However, if "becoming the Buddha" is the consequence of the latter ritual, there is also a lengthy process of ritualization involved during manufacture, if casting takes place in the monastery, as we shall see. This ritualization helps us gain a greater understanding of what a statue is made out of, what its nature is, and on what its powers are based.

MAKING A MAJOR BUDDHA IMAGE WITHIN THE MONASTERY GROUNDS[30]

Whenever the founding or casting of a Buddha image was carried out in a craftsman's workshop, I never witnessed or recorded any special rituals, except the closing of doors during the melting and pouring of the bronze, and also, once, a

---

[27] Tambiah, "Famous Buddha Images and the Legitimation of Kings"; Schober, "Buddhist Just Rule"; and Strong, *Relics of the Buddha*, chap. 6, p. 237. These sources note the role of such powerful statues in the legitimation of Buddhist rulers (whether palladiums as Mahamuni or Phrakeo Morakot, the "Emerald Buddha" in Bangkok). Their "possession" is thought as indicating the high level of morality and spiritual purity of the owner.

[28] There are other ways to differentiate among images of the Buddha. Very interestingly, Brac de la Perrière ("Les rituels de consécration," p. 207) underlines the fact that some of these figures are mobile and can be used for processions, whereas other are fixed; the fixed image can be considered as a substitute for the *dhamma* that the Buddha taught and inscribes the *dhamma* in a place; the mobile image creates or reaffirms links between social and religious units such as villages, or countries. See also Schober, "Buddhist Just Rule" and François Robinne, "Jeux d'échelle et enjeux: dynamiques identitaires des cérémonies processionnelles en Birmanie bouddhique," *Aséanie* 22, (2008): pp. 121–50.

[29] See, for example, Robert Lingat, "Le culte du Bouddha d'émeraude," *The Journal of the Siam Society* XXVII,I (1934): 9–38; and Frank E. Reynolds, "The Holy Emerald Jewel: Some Aspects of Buddhist Symbolism and Political Legitimation in Thailand and Laos," in *Religion and Legitimation of Power in Thailand, Laos, and Burma*, ed. Bardwell L. Smith (Chambersburg, PA: Anima Books, 1978), pp. 175–93.

[30] This work with rituals has been described in detail in my doctoral dissertation; see de Mersan, "Espace rituel," chap. 13.

ceremony performed just before a large image was taken to its final destination. However, when a major Buddha image has to be produced *in-situ* (i.e., where it will be fixed), because of its great size and weight, or because of inherent technical limitations, the work will be undertaken within a specially erected enclosure[31] inside the monastery compound. The progress of the work at this place implies collective contribution and participation, and the ritualization of the fabrication process. Conversely, if there is to be a collective contribution, the process has to be carried out at the monastery itself, which is the core of a community's social and religious life. These moments spent at the monastery, where inhabitants gather to watch the casting process, participate in ceremonies, and make donations, are particularly emotional. The master craftsman, his family, and a team of craftsmen will stay there throughout the founding process. In the case of the Lotaramuni image, that meant they remained on site during eight full days. The enclosure is said to protect both visitors and other workers from the real (or "visible") danger associated with such work, but also, so it appears, to protect them from other, sometimes invisible, threats.[32] Thus, as "impurity" creates danger, every day before starting work, a ritual "shampoo" is applied to the craftsmen and to their tools as well. Also, as in alchemy, danger is believed to be created whenever one works with air and fire generates power.

As a preliminary step, the complete Buddha image is divided into eight components, each one of which will then be cast individually during the period spent in the temporary compound. After the pieces have been brought inside, a ritual cleansing ceremony is held during which nine monks recite prayers (*parit*) in order to prevent the approach of or ward off any evil beings. This act that purifies the site has various aspects in common with other purification rites observed in several cases (the Arakanese New Year's rite and others).[33] Ordinarily, in Arakan State, as elsewhere in Burma, the exact time and date of all such ceremonies is determined in accordance with astrological considerations.

Indeed, as is true throughout Burma, the Arakanese conception of the world is linked to the configuration of the planets within the cosmos and concerned with their influence on human destiny in daily life. According to this view, the eight planets are

---

[31] This lattice-fence enclosure, which has a special diamond-shaped design, called *rajamat*, is commonly featured in many occasions associated with Buddhism or kingship, where the point is to make a fence against evil; such a fence is used, for instance, when repairing or restoring a pagoda. An example and analysis are given in the present volume. See Sandra Cate and Leedom Lefferts, "Becoming Active/Active Becoming: Prince Vessantara Scrolls and the Creation of a Moral Community."

[32] Most often, the type of the threat or danger is not detailed or explicit. Similar threats seem to be involved in gold-beating work, such as that done in Mandalay, which is performed within an enclosure. Denise Bernot, personal communication.

[33] In these cases, the place to be purified is always closed off or delimited. See also Frederic K. Lehman (Chit Hlaing), "Monasteries, Palaces, and Ambiguities: Burmese Sacred and Secular Space," *Contributions to Indian Sociology* 21,1 (1987): 169–86, especially p. 184 about the idea that power to be efficient must be bounded. This reading of *parit* or *kammawaca* is one of the most common ritual activities of monks in Burma and other Theravada countries; for Burma, see Melford Spiro, *Buddhism and Society: A Great Tradition and Its Burmese Vicissitudes* (Berkeley, CA: University of California Press, 1970); Schober, *Paths to Enlightenment*; and Brac de la Perrière, "Les rituels de consécration," p. 210–12.

associated with the eight points of the compass and the days of the week.[34] Qualities, numbers, and other special characteristics are attributed to each of these planets. These elements form a totality, and together represent a "magic square" (*an*), which serves as a base for astrological calculations, and which is in everyday use. This schematic representation of the cosmos, made up of the eight cardinal points, forms a Buddhist entity, with the Buddha at its center represented by the number nine, which is particularly auspicious (*mangala*). This explains why, on such occasions, the numbers (of monks for the ceremony, of casting days, of pieces to melt, and so on) are all chosen in relation to their auspiciousness.

Offering dedicted to Sasana and planets. Photograph by Alexandra de Mersan

The next day, a further ceremony is celebrated for the erection of the pole, which will be used to help bear the weight of the crucible containing the molten metal. A rite such as this is mandatory for pacifying powerful spirits of the land each time a pole is placed in the ground, such as when building a house or erecting a shrine to the village spirit. This reminds us that spirits of the land are its owners, the lords of it.[35]

On the following day, just prior to the first casting, a third auspicious and protective ceremony is held, with offerings (*sasana pwe*) dedicated to the religion and

---

[34] For astrological calculations, Wednesdays count for two days so that they are under the influence of two planets.

[35] See Frederic K. Lehman, "The Relevance of the Founders' Cult for Understanding the Political Systems of the Peoples of Northern Southeast Asia and its Chinese Borderlands," in *Founders' Cults in Southeast Asia: Ancestors, Polity, and Identity*, ed. Nicola Tannenbaum and Cornelia Kammerer (New Haven, CT: Yale University Southeast Asia Program Monograph Series, 2003), pp. 15–39; de Mersan, "A New Palace"; and Alexandra de Mersan, "La construction rituelle du territoire à travers la tradition orale: Etude d'une incantation aux esprits d'Arakan (Birmanie)," *Aséanie* 26 (2010): 31–55.

to planets.[36] This ceremony is to ensure the success of casting the image and to ensure the long life of the Buddha dispensation (*sasana*). Then, the pouring of the metal can begin and is performed over several days.

The pouring of the metal into one part of the statue.
Photograph by Alexandra de Mersan

Finally, on the day when the bronze will be fused for the last piece of the complete Buddha statue, members of the monastery committee organize a small celebration, during which they sing and dance. This joyful ceremony marks the conclusion of the casting phase.[37]

In summary, the melting and casting processes are delimited—and as such, protected—both in time and space inside the monastery. To achieve success in these perilous operations, rites are performed that establish a proper relationship between the spirits of the land and the forces of the cosmos, through astrological calculations,

---

[36] There are eight (plus one) different plants in the offering, each one associated by its initial consonant with a planet and a day of the week. For details on astrology, see Maung Htin Aung, *Folk Elements in Burmese Buddhism* (London: Oxford University Press, 1962); Lucien Bernot, *Les paysans arakanais du Pakistan Oriental: l'Histoire, le monde végétal, et l'organisation sociale des réfugiés Marma (Mog)* (Paris: Editions Mouton & Co., École Pratique des Hautes Etudes, 1967), pp. 154–97; and, for a recent application elsewhere in Burma, in Shan State, see François Robinne, *Fils et maîtres du Lac: Relations interethniques dans l'État Shan de Birmanie* (Paris: CNRS Editions/Editions de la Maison des Sciences de l'Homme, 2000), pp. 117–26.

[37] For details, see de Mersan, "Espace rituel," pp. 397–419.

offerings, and rituals. These are key elements of the Arakanese ritual system. Having observed all the above-mentioned ceremonies, the celebrants are clearly convinced that something important has been accomplished through this process, an accomplishment that has been made possible and confirmed through the ritualization of the fabrication. The expression used in the process of melting and then pouring the metal is *cak swan*, for which several translations are possible. *Swan* means "to pour, to cast"; *cak* is a circle, a wheel, but is also the word used to designate actions with machinery, as in manufacturing. In this respect, the analogy between the terms for the pouring (*cak swan*) and the consecration (*a sak swan*), which means "to enliven," would indicate that animation of the image has already started with this ritualization. The simultaneity of the fabrication and consecration ritual, as detailed in an Arakanese text[38] and elsewhere in Southeast Asia,[39] would also support this idea.

Parts of the statue, with metal poured, are exhibited outside the compound to the devotees. Photograph by Alexandra de Mersan

A description of the fabrication of an image made specially in former times for the "king-making ritual" also indicates the need of limiting the space and time involved with purification and auspiciousness rites.[40] These rituals were performed by different ritual specialists, mostly astrologers, from India (*punna*), who used to officiate at the royal court.[41] Although these specialists do not exist anymore in

---

[38] San Tha Aung, *The Buddhist Art of Ancient Arakan: An Eastern Border State beyond Ancient India, East of Vanga and Samatata* (Rangoon: Daw Saw Saw, 1979), pp. 66–71. In the description given by this Arakanese scholar, San Tha Aung, the consecration (*anegaza*) occurs when the pouring of the metal begins.

[39] See note 42.

[40] San Tha Aung, *The Buddhist Art*.

[41] See Jacques P. Leider, "Specialists for Ritual, Magic, and Devotion: The Court Brahmins (*Punna*) of the Konbaung Kings (1752–1885)," *Journal of Burma Studies* 10 (2005–06): 159–202.

Arakan, as such, rites observed for the making of Lotaramuni, as well as the actual pouring of water on the Buddha image (*bhiseka*) for its consecration in Arakan, are reminiscent of ancient court practices. In the case of Lotaramuni, rites are not performed in direct reference to the former ritual for making this special statue, but they do adopt aspects of this royal ritual that are related to the planets and to astrology. That they still evoke the former Arakanese kingship might be explained by the fact that the Mahamuni image not only was a palladium, but it legitimized the king in his function. And finally, these rites remind us that, in this Buddhist kingdom, as in other Theravada societies, the king was conceived as the religion's first protector and propagator. As noted above, the ritualization of the construction of a Buddha cast at a monastery is described elsewhere—not only documents concerned with Arakan.[42] Following Swearer in his study on Buddha images, we recognize that it is important to localize observations, or to settle elements of context, to understand the meaning of such an event for the local community.[43] Thus, although kingship has ended in Arakan for the last two centuries, it is brought to the fore by these specific rituals, which underline and reenact its fundamental role in the myth of the origin of Arakanese society.

Ordinarily, although the making of a major image of this kind requires a principal donor, throughout the days of the foundry work within a temple compound, the members of the monastery committee invite all the local inhabitants to make further donations. These donations, regarded as being especially meritorious, can be in the form of money, or might include old objects in bronze, or zinc bars, along with jewels or precious metals (especially silver and gold) that will be remelted and recast. Jewels and precious metals are reserved for the most auspicious part of the image, corresponding to the top of the Buddha's head (*mani' to*). As the image is being enlivened through consecration, becoming a Buddha, the highest part of the body is thus logically considered as the noblest one.

Therefore, even if there is a "basic recipe" for alloying bronze, its final composition, and its metallurgical—and subtle—nature, depend on the type and composition of these donations. The ritualization of the process indicates that the nature of the "power" of the final image is not only acquired via the powers of the Buddha infused through the consecration ritual, but might exist before consecration as a result of the rites performed and materials used during the making of the statue.

Key aspects of the melting of the metal can be seen as an alchemical process, as both metal-working and alchemy share similarities with works using metal, fire, and air, which, as pointed out previously, generate power.[44] As Arakanese, and many Burmese, are familiar with alchemy, it would be interesting to compare, in greater detail, the aims and techniques of the alchemical process with those involved in the

---

[42] See Griswold, "Bronze-Casting in Siam," and Swearer, *Becoming the Buddha*. Both sources describe the construction of a Buddha image at a monastery, with similar ceremonies conducted during each process: the establishment of a closed or enclosed space inside a bamboo fence of special design, and establishment of the propicious time in connection with planets, as well as to astrological and auspicious considerations.

[43] Swearer, *Becoming the Buddha*.

[44] The practice of alchemy and the manufacture of a Buddha Image are linked, also, because each is precisely a process about making/giving life. See Schober, "Venerating the Buddha," p. 118, and Swearer, *Becoming the Buddha*, p. 214. Both suggest a similar idea. On this subject, see also the recent work of Guillaume Rozenberg, "The Alchemist and His Ball," *Journal of Burma Studies* 14 (2010): 187–228.

making of a Buddha bronze image. As writings on alchemy in Burma emphasize, one step vital to the success of the process requires mastering the combination and manipulation of materials that, once subjected to the action of air and fire, form a ball of matter that is usually known in Western literature as a "philosophers' stone," and which confers supernatural powers on the practitioner, depending on his spiritual perfection.

Metal and jewels offered as donations to be melted and incorporated in the statue.
Photograph by Alexandra de Mersan

With contributions coming from all around the city where a Buddha bronze statue is being made, and the very wide range of people gathering for such an event, we can truly say that a good part of the locality is contained in the image. The moral and spiritual level of the locality then will be spread through material Buddhism. This is made quite clear in narratives and discourses, whether oral or written, concerning the Mahamuni Buddha image, which detail its composition and emphasize the different materials provided by local inhabitants, lords, or kings for its creation.[45] The story of Mahamuni thus correlates with the casting process.

When a massive bronze image is cast *in situ* in a monastery, the local population is given the opportunity to participate collectively and become involved in the reenactment of its founding myth. Thus, while the manufacturing of a Buddha image makes a spiritual contribution to the perpetuation of Buddhism, it is, at the same time, the material expression of a specific society's deep connection to its particular traditions. As a matter of fact, during the fabrication of a statue that I observed,

[45] See examples in de Mersan "Espace rituel," pp. 374–75.

monks who were invited for the consecration came from other monasteries in the town and from elsewhere in the State of Arakan.

Lotaramuni image, a few days after its consecration ritual.
Photograph by Alexandra de Mersan

A striking point that a number of authors have raised in recent studies of popular Buddhism, or of practices and attitudes found in Theravada Buddhism (for example, the consecration ritual, the location of relics, and the veneration of the Buddha), is that local practices contribute to the diffusion or the extension of the Buddha and/or his teaching (*dhamma*). In so doing, these practices constitute localized communities,[46] as I have demonstrated here in reference to the making of a

---

[46] See Schober on Buddha images. Schober also speaks about the narratives related to various images, which constitute a "hegemonic discourse among competing social entities." See Schober, "Venerating the Buddha's Remains," p. 123; and Schober, " Mapping the Sacred," as

collective Buddha. These rituals and donations also contribute to these specific communities' self-expression, or to their own perpetuation, through elements specific to each of them. In other words, in the absence of kingship, locality has assumed the role formerly played by the king as first among laymen, which maintains the Buddhist dispensation.

As noted above, the casting process is called *cak swan*. Significantly, a monk indicated to me a meaning establishing a link between *cak* and the *cakkavattin*, which, as some may recall, was in Arakan as in other Buddhist societies of Southeast Asia, and a model of a conquering Buddhist ruler who had to start the wheel of the *dhamma* turning to spread the Buddha's teaching.[47]

CONCLUSION

We have seen how the process of making a Buddha image contributes to the general conceptualization of a hierarchy among the material forms of Buddhism, and, more precisely, among Buddha images. In this process, what precedes the actual consecration ritual reveals that the composition of the image itself contributes to its potency.

Let us return, finally, to an elementary question: "What do people do when they make Buddha images?" The response is, of course, made up of multiple strands and not exhaustive: laymen who contribute to the making of a Buddha statue seek to increase their religious merit for a better rebirth in a future life, while they simultaneously increase their social prestige. The activity offers them the possibility of putting themselves under Buddha's protection, and it establishes or strengthens social relationships in a community of laymen during the ritualization of the manufacturing process. My research has further emphasized the need to consider local practices and beliefs more deeply, particularly in analyzing local notions of "power." The making of a Buddha bronze image in a monastery is a collective contribution, which allows a precious and powerful statue to be constructed from all individual contributions melted in the crucible. In doing so, the statue materializes and strengthens what constitutes Arakanese society, in reference to the Mahamuni image, namely, a specific moral and spiritual community. The notion of power seems to be essential in many contemporary discourses at the "symbolic level," reflecting also the confrontation or competition between inhabitants and the political regime.

Thus, through the production of its characteristic Buddha statuary, the Arakanese society is perpetuated by means of Buddhist iconography expressive of its Mahamuni image palladium and the reenactment of its myth. In the context of nation-building inside Burma today, this is also the only way the Arakanese can freely express their "specificity" without fearing repression from the military regime claiming the primacy of "national unity" as opposed to "localized particularity." However, as demonstrated here, although in a way the local making of a Buddha

---

well as the study on relics by Strong, *Relics of the Buddha*, p. 18, and a study of the consecration ritual by Swearer, *Becoming the Buddha*.

[47] See Stanley J. Tambiah, *World Conqueror and World Renouncer: A Study of Buddhism and Polity in Thailand against a Historical Background* (Cambridge: Cambridge University Press, 1976); and Tambiah, *The Buddhist Saints of the Forest and the Cult of Amulets*. On this aspect, in Arakan see also Jacques P. Leider, "Forging Buddhist Credentials as a Tool of Legitimacy and Ethnic Identity: A Study of Arakan's Subjection in Nineteenth-Century Burma," *Journal of the Economic and Social History of the Orient*, 51, 3 (2008): 409–59.

statue can serve an Arakanese nationalist cause, Arakanese religious action is not necessary undertaken in opposition to Burmese hegemony. In any case, this example helps us to understand that the policy to promote Buddhism by the Burmese regime in its search for legitimacy is contested, to a certain extent, by other special Buddhist traditions, such as those we have observed in Arakan State.

CHAPTER 7

THE PROBLEM WITH "EMPTY CROSSES": THINKING THROUGH MATERIALITY IN BIDAYUH RELIGIOUS PRACTICES

Liana Chua

When people in my fieldsite—a Bidayuh village in Sarawak, Malaysian Borneo—talk about and "do" (*nai*) Christianity, their first recourse, it invariably seems, is to objects and substances. For many, Christian practice entails crossing themselves with holy water, consuming communion wafers, lighting candles, amassing a kaleidoscopic array of sacred pictures, rosaries, and medallions, and getting all sorts of objects, ranging from Bibles to false teeth, blessed. These and other similarly object-centered procedures are routine features of both Anglicanism and Catholicism, the two majority denominations in the area, and are depicted as the "correct" way to pray and to be good Christians. Bereft of these material features, Christianity would seem curiously barren to these Bidayuhs.

The notable—and, to many Anglicans and Catholics, perplexing—exceptions to this rule are the twenty-five or so village households that claim membership in the Sidang Injil Borneo (SIB), or Borneo Evangelical Church.[1] Introduced to the area in the 1990s,[2] the SIB stresses scriptural familiarity and individualized religiosity. Its

---

[1] The successor to a multi-denominational organization introduced to Sarawak by Australian missionaries in the early twentieth century, SIB is now a non-denominational church with branches rapidly spreading across East and West Malaysia. For more information on its history and mission, see Matthew Amster, "Community, Ethnicity, and Modes of Association among the Kelabit of Sarawak, East Malaysia" (PhD dissertation, Brandeis University, 1998); and Shirley Lees, *Drunk Before Dawn* (Sevenoaks: OMF Books, 1979).

[2] By this time, the majority of villagers were either Anglican or Catholic, most of whom had converted since the 1960s. The village's first SIB adherents broke away from the Anglican church; many now assert that they did so because they wanted truly to understand the Bible and the meaning of Christianity. Histories of Christianity in Sarawak can be found in Peter Kedit, Aeries S. Jingan, D. Tsen, T. Chung, Heidi Munan, and Y. John, *150 Years of the Anglican Church in Borneo 1848–1998* (Kuching: Bishop of Kuching, 1998); Keat Gin Ooi, "Mission Education in Sarawak during the Period of Brooke Rule 1840–1946," *Sarawak Museum Journal* 42,63 (1991): 282–373; John Rooney, *Khabar Gembira: A History of the Catholic Church in East Malaysia and Brunei (1880–1976)* (London and Kota Kinabalu: Burns and Oates Ltd. and Mill

gatherings consist of "praise and worship" songs, Bible readings, and spontaneous eruptions of prayer, unmediated by the paraphernalia and physical protocol that characterize Anglican and Catholic services. While the disparities between the three village churches generally have little bearing on daily life, I sometimes found them crystallizing in discussions about religious protocol.

An altar in a Catholic home. Photograph by Liana Chua, 2008

It was during one such conversation, which centered on funerary practices, that my thirty-year-old Catholic friend explained why she would never "become SIB." Struggling to articulate her point, she finally described their services with the English words "empty cross." "They have nothing," she said, "No Jesus, no Mary, no pictures, no praying—only singing and text Bible." In her experience of Christianity, objects and substances were not mere accessories to its proper observance, but the

Hill Missionaries, 1981); Graham Saunders, *Bishops and Brookes: The Anglican Mission and the Brooke Raj in Sarawak 1848–1941* (Singapore: Oxford University Press, 1992).

very things that made it possible. Such sentiments, I soon discovered, were not uncommon in the village—an observation corroborated, perhaps, by the fact that the local SIB congregation had remained fairly small since its establishment.[3] The question that underlies this chapter, then, is why the SIB's style of highly textual and relatively immaterial religiosity has not become more popular in the village—why, that is, such misgivings persist about "empty crosses." One place to seek elucidation would, of course, be the object-centered discourses and practices dominating the majority's experience of Christianity. At first glance, these seem to indict Bidayuhs of being stalwart materialists: a charge also levied against them by nineteenth- and early-twentieth century Christian missionaries, officials, and scholars. Such observers often saw in *adat gawai*—the complex of rice-based rituals and practices indigenous to Bidayuh communities—evidence of crude dependence upon materiality. Indeed, they might have felt vindicated by the comments of my Catholic friend, which reveal the apparent persistence of an "externalist" bias throughout the conversion process.

My intention is not to contradict this general point, but to reassess the conclusions towards which it edges. While acknowledging the object-centeredness of past and present Bidayuh religious practices, I am less willing to "explain [them] away," as did earlier observers, as signs of fetishism, or more forgivingly, of misplaced faith in materiality.[4] Rather, I shall argue that although objects and substances are vital focal points in Bidayuh religious practices, they are not necessarily the ends to which such practices are directed. Instead, materiality must be viewed as simply one aspect of most Bidayuhs' experience of "religion" as a constitutive process concerned with capacities and effects. To this end, I take up Amira Henare, Martin Holbraad, and Sari Wastell's recent call for anthropologists to acquire analytical insights by "thinking through things" as their informants do. By this I do not mean to undertake the "methodological fetishism" famously advocated by Arjun Appadurai by focusing on objects as artifacts of and keys to apprehending predetermined socio-cultural phenomena like politics or religion.[5] My aim, rather, is to ask what Bidayuhs might mean—rather than what academic observers assume— when they talk about and engage with the material stuff of *adat gawai* and Christianity. I shall suggest that thinking through these things offers a useful heuristic means of understanding Bidayuh religious practices—and, to return to our opening puzzle—understanding why empty crosses can be trouble.

CROSSES, EMPTY AND FULL: THE OBJECTS OF RELIGIOUS CONVERSION

For most of the last 150 years, Bidayuhs—who constitute Sarawak's second-largest indigenous group—have lived in villages in the mountains surrounding the state capital, Kuching, cultivating rice and trading in pepper, rubber, cocoa, bird's nests, and other produce. It is around this predominantly agricultural system that the

---

[3] Conversely, "conversions" between Anglicanism and Catholicism are much more common, and usually due either to personal choice or marriage.

[4] Amiria Henare, Martin Holbraad, and Sari Wastell, "Introduction," in *Thinking Through Things: Theorizing Artefacts Ethnographically*, ed. A. Henare, M. Holbraad, and S. Wastell (London: Routledge, 2007), p. 1.

[5] Arjun Appadurai, ed., *The Social Life of Things: Commodities in Cultural Perspective* (Cambridge: Cambridge University Press, 1986).

rituals, observances, and concepts known collectively as *adat gawai* revolve.[6] Briefly, *adat*—a concept with cognates across the Malay world—means both "customary law" and "way of life," while *gawai* conflates "festival," "ceremony," and "feast,"[7] the core events at which such *adat* is observed.[8] *Adat gawai* was followed by the vast majority of Bidayuhs until the 1970s, and is still practiced today by thinning pockets of elderly people.

While its manifestations vary among villages, *adat gawai*'s fundamental principles and mechanisms remain broadly consistent. Its key aims are pragmatic: to engender the well-being, safety, and prosperity of the community through labor-intensive rituals, prescriptions, and proscriptions that suffuse daily life. These rituals and guides range from animal augury to the imposition of communal "prohibition" or "taboo" periods (lasting from a day to several months) on movement, food consumption, and work. Cumulatively, such practices establish, maintain, and manipulate relations with a multitude of entities, including *Tăpa*, the creator and "supreme being,"[9] spirits of trees, stones, animals, waterways, and ancestors, malicious influences, and, most importantly, the rice spirit (*simangi padi*), whose well-being is conflated with that of persons, households, and the village.

Since the 1960s, Bidayuhs have converted in burgeoning numbers to Christianity;[10] today, the vast majority of them adhere to one denomination or another. In most areas, this shift was precipitated by Sarawak's entry into *dunia moden*—"the modern world"—in 1963, when it gained independence from Britain as a state of Malaysia. Although Anglican and Catholic missionaries had been working in the area since the mid-nineteenth century, they had hitherto enjoyed minimal success[11] due to the mutually reinforcing relationship between *adat gawai* and the agricultural system.[12] Post-independence changes, however, swept up Bidayuh communities in a nationwide wave of "developmentalism" that brought

---

[6] I use *adat gawai* as a phrase that encompasses the practices, assumptions, and constituents of the Bidayuh pre-Christian "lifeworld," as described by Fiona Harris, "Growing Gods: Processes of Religious Change in Sarawak, Malaysia" (PhD dissertation, University of Edinburgh, 2001), p. 9. The following descriptions draw on a combination of fieldwork experience, historical sources, and comparative studies of *adat gawai* in other Bidayuh areas. See William Geddes, *The Land Dayaks of Sarawak: A Report on a Social Economic Survey of the Land Dayaks of Sarawak Presented to the Colonial Social Science Research Council* (London: HM Stationery Office for the Colonial Office, 1954); Harris, "Growing Gods"; Pamela N. Lindell, "The Longhouse and the Legacy of History: Religion, Architecture, and Change among the Bisingai of Sarawak (Malaysia)" (PhD dissertation, University of Nevada, Reno, 2000); and Patrick Rigep Nuek, *A Dayak Bidayuh Community: Rituals, Ceremonies, and Festivals* (Kuching: Lee Ming Press, 2002).

[7] William Nais, *Daya Bidayuh–English Dictionary* (Kuching: Persatuan Kesusasteraan Sarawak, 1988), p. 155.

[8] Adat Bidayuh, *Adat Bidayuh 1994 (Piminyu Biatah)* (Kuching: Percetakan Nasional Malaysia, 1994), p. 25.

[9] Geddes, *The Land Dayaks*, p. 24.

[10] More details on Bidayuh processes of conversion can be found in Liana Chua, *The Christianity of Culture: Conversion, Ethnic Citizenship, and the Matter of Religion in Malaysian Borneo* (New York, NY: Palgrave Macmillan, forthcoming); Harris, "Growing Gods"; and Lindell, "The Longhouse and the Legacy of History."

[11] Ooi, "Mission Education," pp. 312–13; Saunders, *Bishops and Brookes*, pp. 196–97.

[12] Harris, "Growing Gods," p. 79; and Peter H. Howes, "Why Some of the Best People Aren't Christian," *Sarawak Museum Journal* 9,15 (1960): 488–95.

infrastructure, cash crops, education, and healthcare into rural areas, and drew villagers towards cities and towns in search of schooling and employment.

In the 1960s and 1970s, such movements depleted the villages' agricultural workforces, and exposed many young Bidayuhs to alternatives to *adat gawai*. Conversion to any form of Christianity was tantamount to a "conversion to modernity,"[13] enabling the converts to follow their new educated, urbanized trajectories unburdened by the restrictive, labor-intensive demands of *adat gawai*.[14] Subsequently, these Bidayuhs became Christianity's most effective proponents in their home villages, persuading clusters of friends and family to convert. Most people's decision to become Christian had little to do with doctrinal or "intellectualist" concerns.[15] As rice-cultivation receded over the next few decades, it became less critical, and also more challenging, to observe *adat gawai* and its numerous regulations on a communal basis. With typical pragmatism, and bolstered by the conviction that it was better to ditch old rituals than do them badly, many older *gawai* practitioners "followed" their children into Christianity, thereby affirming its status as an *adat* more suited to the demands of *dunia moden*.

Although I describe *adat gawai* and Christianity heuristically as religious practices, it is important to note that neither occupies a purely "religious" niche distinct from other aspects of society. While my informants are aware of the official Malaysian term for "religion" (*agama*)—a concept that applies primarily to monotheistic, scripture-based traditions such as Islam[16]—it would be more appropriate to describe their experience of both *adat gawai* and Christianity as *adat*, in the encompassing sense that would refer to a way of life. Like *adat gawai*, Christianity has become a social and temporal regulator of village life in an increasingly urbanized, wage-centered world. Churches are weekly nodes of sociality for both town-based Bidayuhs—many of whom attend village services on weekends—and their village-based counterparts, at which communal announcements are made and administration is carried out. Christianity also spills into houses, schools, and farms, particularly via communal prayer gatherings held on specific occasions, such as birthdays, deaths, before impending examinations, or following the acquisition of new vehicles. Amid all this activity, the fundamental preoccupation with generating, maintaining, or restoring the well-being of individuals and the community through *adat* remains unchanged. Like *adat gawai*, much Bidayuh Christianity might be described as resolutely "this-worldly" in its scope and manifestations.[17]

This apparent attachment to material trappings was something that certain missionaries to the nascent Bidayuh Christian populations recognized, and not without apprehension. In a pessimistic 1969 article, David Sidaway of the Bunuk Anglican Dispensary grumbled that the "faith" of new converts remained "coloured

---

[13] Peter Van der Veer, "Introduction," in *Conversion to Modernities: The Globalization of Christianity*, ed. Peter van der Veer (London and New York, NY: Routledge, 1996).

[14] For an argument about why Bidayuhs have not embraced Islam in the same way, see Liana Chua, "Fixity and Flux: Bidayuh (Dis)engagements with the Malaysian Ethnic System," *Ethnos* 72 (2007): 262–88.

[15] Robin Horton, "African Conversion," *Africa* 41,2(1971): 85–108.

[16] The relationship between *adat* and *agama* in the Bidayuh context is discussed more fully in Chua, *The Christianity of Culture*, Chapters 2 and 4.

[17] Max Weber, *The Sociology of Religion*, trans. Ephraim Fischoff (Boston, MA: Beacon Press, 1963).

by their former traditional beliefs" from a world in which magic and superstition are everything.[18] Much of his ire was directed at "pagan" trappings, such as sacrificial animals, stones, bamboo, soul bottles, amulets, and charms, but he seemed equally troubled by people's apparently injudicious attachment to material stuff. He noted, for example, that both Christians and non-Christians would simultaneously employ Western medicine and traditional charms, "pagan feasts and ... useless magic," to cure illnesses, and he complained that "[i]n fact talismanic objects can be worse than useless on occasions when tied very tightly around a child's neck, wrists, waist, or ankles."[19]

Sadis (offerings) at an *adat gawai* ritual. Photo by Liana Chua, 2005

His words echoed those of his predecessors, many of whom were familiar with the notion—formulated first-hand or through ecclesiastical and scholarly

---

[18] See David Sidaway, "Influence of Christianity on Biatah-speaking Land Dayaks," *Sarawak Museum Journal* 17,34–35 (1969): 139–52, especially p. 139. Not all missionaries, however, were as dismissive of "native" traditions and processes of conversion. See, for example, Howes, "Why Some of the Best People Aren't Christian."

[19] Sidaway, "Influence of Christianity," p. 149.

literature[20]—that Borneans' "religion … was inseparable from their material wants."[21] As another observer of Bidayuh society put it:

> Worship resolves itself into a species of bribery, so many meals of rice or fowls offered to the *"antus"* [spirits] that they may cease to bring down sickness, or may give good crops of paddy. The native has no idea whatever of any influence on his own spirit; material good, what he can get is all, not what he can be.[22]

Such comments depicted Bidayuhs and other "primitive" people as reliant on materiality to give shape to and engage with forces that they could not otherwise apprehend.[23] Interestingly, other missionaries put the same presumption to more benevolent use. Some Catholic priests, for example, recalled incorporating *gawai* paraphernalia into church services in the 1970s, using bead necklaces and leaf bundles to sprinkle the congregation with holy water in replication of *gawai* blessings. Such practices were depicted as a means of preserving the "good" elements of "local culture," as *adat gawai* and other pre-Christian practices were glossed, to help ease the converts' transition. Over time, this policy of "inculturation"—sanctioned by various Christian authorities in the West[24]—became the norm in Bidayuh areas, overtaking other missionaries' sporadic efforts to make converts destroy, sell, or discard these objects.[25]

Whether they viewed objects as dangerous pagan relics or useful intermediary tools, both sets of missionaries shared concerns about the place, hazards, and potential of materiality in Bidayuh religious practice. These concerns appeared to pivot on a fundamental distinction between the realms of the abstract and the material, and the concomitant Cartesian depiction of the latter as a mere bearer or manifestation of the former. I suggest that Bidayuhs' apparent tendency to invest their faith in materiality evoked among their observers the specter of fetishism, a concept that has historically offered a compelling explanatory framework for missionaries, travelers, officials, and scholars encountering similar phenomena

---

[20] For example Charles Hose and William McDougall, *The Pagan Tribes of Borneo* (Singapore, Oxford, and New York, NY: Oxford University Press, 1993 [1912]); Henry Ling Roth, *The Natives of Sarawak and British North Borneo* (Kuala Lumpur: University of Malaya Press, 1980 [1896]); Walter W. Skeat, *Malay Magic: Being an Introduction to the Folklore and Popular Religion of the Malay Peninsula* (London: Macmillan, 1900).

[21] E. V. R. Westerwoudt, *Felix Westerwoudt: Missioner in Borneo*, trans. T. W. Lefeber (Maryknoll, NY: Catholic Foreign Mission Society of America, 2002 [1924]) p. 39.

[22] Eda Green, *Borneo: The Land of River and Palm* (London: Borneo Mission Association, [1909]), http://anglicanhistory.org/asia/sarawak/green/04.html, accessed October 2, 2011.

[23] Ironically, the material stuff of *adat gawai* served a similar purpose for certain missionaries, literally objectifying "the old ways," in a manner that made it possible to damn or discard them.

[24] Michael V. Angrosino, "The Culture Concept and the Mission of the Roman Catholic Church," *American Anthropologist* 96,4 (1994): 824–32, especially p. 824; Fenella Cannell, "Introduction," in *The Anthropology of Christianity*, ed. Fenella Cannell (London and Durham, NC: Duke University Press, 2006), p. 26.

[25] Chua, *The Christianity of Culture*, Chapter 5; Valerie Mashman and Patricia Nayoi, "Emblems for Identity: Ethnic Costume, Catholicism, and Continuity: A Pinyawa'a Bidayuh Study at Kampong Gayu," in *Borneo 2000: Proceedings of the Sixth Biennial Borneo Research Conference*, ed. Michael Leigh (Kota Samarahan: Institute of East Asian Studies, 2000).

around the world. Essentially a "derogatory term for the illusions of Others,"[26] the term "fetishism" implies "untranscended materiality:"[27] the tendency of the observed to misattribute an inherent agency or intentionality to stocks and stones, thereby "confound[ing] the proper boundaries" between human or divine agency and "mere objects."[28] Anxiety over such proclivities, I suspect, was one reason that certain missionaries jettisoned *adat gawai* objects while more indulgent ones tried neutralizing them within a Christian framework.

For Bidayuhs to become proper Christians, then, they had to divest themselves not of objects per se, but of their "primitive" misapprehensions about the relationship between subject and object, spirit and flesh, agency and its bearer. Embedded in the missionaries' concerns about materiality, however, was a deeper question: had Bidayuhs "really" converted when they retained such strong attachments to "external" trappings?[29] Such questions reflected the enduring "interiorist bias"[30] of early modern European discourses on religion and conversion,[31] which located "true" religion in the insubstantial, privatized realm of belief, spirit, and intention. On this count, it would appear that my Bidayuh acquaintances have not been model converts. Contrary to (neo-)Weberian expectations, even the most literate and self-consciously "modern" Anglicans and Catholics are keenly interested in the material and performative aspects of Christianity.

Physical and verbal protocol, candles, incense, and pictures play central roles in both Anglican and Catholic services, with the congregation genuflecting, bowing, reciting oral formulae, and crossing themselves with great seriousness. Texts such as hymnals and the Bible are occasionally referred to during services by literate attendees, but are often more significant as authoritative objects to be displayed at home or venerated in church. Catholics and Anglicans alike collect a range of portable objects, including rosaries, medallions, and pictures, which they hang in cars or accumulate alongside crosses, candles, and holy water on the ubiquitous household altars. Such items are often deployed to deal with illness and injury: on several occasions, I witnessed people dabbing ailing body parts with holy water, while on another, I found an elderly Catholic man wearing a rosary ring to alleviate chest pains that pills had not cured. Shortly afterwards, he consulted a *gawai* healer and was given further substances to combat his problems.

One way to account for these practices is, admittedly, to invert the disparaging logic of earlier missionary accounts. Rather than label Bidayuhs as unreformed fetishists in thrall to their superstitions, an analyst might posit that such instances

---

[26] Patricia Spyer, "Introduction," in *Border Fetishisms: Material Objects in Unstable Spaces,* ed. Patricia Spyer (New York, NY: Routledge, 1998), p. 3; Roy Ellen, "Fetishism," *Man* (n.s.) 23: 213–35, especially pp. 213–16.

[27] Peter Pels, "The Spirit of Matter: On Fetish, Rarity, Fact, and Fancy," in *Border Fetishisms: Material Objects in Unstable Spaces,* p. 91; and William Pietz, "The Problem of the Fetish, I," *Res* 9 (1985): 5–17.

[28] Webb Keane, *Christian Moderns: Freedom and Fetish in the Mission Encounter* (Berkeley, CA, and London: University of California Press, 2007), p. 77.

[29] Sidaway, "Influence of Christianity," p. 151.

[30] Robert W. Hefner, "Introduction: World Building and the Rationality of Conversion," in *Conversion to Christianity: Historical and Anthropological Perspectives on a Great Transformation,* ed. R. W. Hefner (Berkeley, CA, and Oxford: University of California Press, 1993), p. 17.

[31] See, for example, Van der Veer, "Introduction," pp. 3–5; and Talal Asad, "Anthropological Conceptions of Religion: Reflections on Geertz," *Man* 18 (1983): 237–59, especially pp. 244–45.

reveal cultural continuities in their religious engagements with materiality (or material engagements with religiosity). The drawback of this approach, however, is that it merely reaffirms the material/immaterial dichotomies upon which missionary misgivings were based. My contention, by contrast, is that it is erroneous to extrapolate from Bidayuhs' object-centered discourses and practices that (im)materiality lies at the heart of their religious practices. To find out what does, we need to think through, rather than peremptorily pigeonhole, the objects, actions, and other things through which Bidayuhs experience both sets—Christian and *gawai*—of *adat*.

THINKING THROUGH THINGS

In their introduction to *Thinking Through Things*, Henare, Holbraad and Wastell refuse to define a "thing": a crucial acknowledgement of the fact that "things" are not everywhere the same, and, more importantly, not always the bounded, physical objects of purportedly commonsense Western thought.[32] Rather than beginning with "a set of pre-determined theoretical criteria"—such as a Cartesian dichotomy between material things and concepts—anthropologists should, they argue, allow the "things encountered in fieldwork ... to dictate the terms of their own analysis."[33] As an example, they refer to Holbraad's work on *aché*: a powder that Cuban diviners say *is* their divinatory power.[34] Analyzing the situation through a framework in which concepts (power) and things (powder) are ontologically and irredeemably distinct may foster the opinion that diviners have obeyed a "peculiar cultural logic" by imputing power to what is really ordinary powder.[35] Holbraad, however, argues that taking the diviners' claims seriously entails discarding both the a priori concept–thing dichotomy and the anthropologist's assumption of epistemological superiority ("we can see what they can't"), and accepting as an *analytical premise* that powder *is* power.[36] The thing through which he thinks is thus not an inert, material substance that we might recognize as "powder," but an entity that is simultaneously and irreducibly concept and material stuff: *aché*, powerful powder.[37]

This does not imply that Cuban diviners live in a radically different world where powder can only ever be power: for the most part, I imagine, powder simply is powder. The agenda of *Thinking Through Things* is not to fetishize alterity, but to deal productively with unfamiliar phenomena in a way that does not reduce them to refractions of the analyst's "more familiar conceptions"[38] or elements of a thoroughly "Other" society. This is the methodological impulse that I would like to adopt in approaching Bidayuh religious practices. As I shall explain, the things of *adat gawai* and Christianity through which I think are neither straightforwardly material objects, nor components of some exotically different cosmology. My aim here is to use them as heuristic means[39] of understanding the nature and mechanisms of both

---

[32] Henare et. al., *Thinking Through Things*, p. 6.

[33] Ibid., p. 5.

[34] Ibid., p. 5–6.

[35] Ibid., p. 5.

[36] Ibid., pp. 204–6.

[37] Ibid., p. 206.

[38] Ibid., p. 1.

[39] Ibid., p. 5.

sets of religious practices, and to apply those insights, in turn, to the question of "empty crosses."

KNOWING AND CREATING THROUGH THINGS

One way to begin thinking through the things of *adat gawai* and Christianity is to think through the story of the origin of *adat gawai*,[40] a condensed version of which I recount here. Encapsulated by this tale are certain principles and mechanisms that will be central to our exploration of both sets of religious practices.

According to the story, *adat gawai* was first given to human beings in the distant past by a woman who ascended to the heavens and then returned to share the lessons she had learned there. All this was arranged by *Tăpa*. In the heavens, the woman met an old lady who chanted (*băris*) for her, and clothed her with a skirt, hat, and bead necklace so that she, too, could *băris* in the future. Then the woman descended to earth, carrying paddy seeds, betel quid, yeast plants, knowledge, the skill of sowing, and other things. She returned to her house and farm, and taught her husband to plant rice by showing him how to perform the relevant actions with the right tools. She then taught humans how to do *gawai* rituals, which revolved around rice planting, telling them about coconuts, different types of bamboo, offertory bundles of paddy stalks, how to make grids and fishing rods, and so on. From then on, humans followed *adat gawai*: sacrificing chickens and pigs, dibbling and sowing like people in the past, because *Tăpa* had given *adat gawai* to them. If they did it correctly, good things would result: rainfall, large rice harvests, a safe and healthy village. Further conversations with the storyteller and other informants revealed that such actions were vital not only in maintaining relations with the relevant *gawai* spirits, whose complicity enabled people to achieve their aims, but in sustaining their very existence in the village.[41]

Imbued in this story, which I was told by a senior *gawai* practitioner, is a constitutive logic that locates the agentive capacity to generate religious realities and effects at the level of human action. Although *adat gawai* originates as a gift from god, its continued presence, reproduction, and effect in the world are reliant on the words, actions, and objects of its adherents. In the recent past, this logic was echoed in the techniques by which *adat gawai* was "given" to children. Older women, for example, would teach their daughters and granddaughters to *băris*, then press cooked rice and salted fish onto their lips to help their mouths retain the chants. Such chants could later be reformulated to incorporate new elements, such as archaic Malay dialects,[42] and, more recently, charismatic Christian *glossolalia*.[43] As I explain elsewhere, the chants' origin and semantic intelligibility were less important than what they helped to *do* in the context of the ritual—namely, summon spirits. Such

---

[40] Similar stories from other Bidayuh villages can be found in Lindell, "The Longhouse and the Legacy of History," p. 98–99; and Nuek, *A Dayak Bidayuh Community*, pp. 133–41.

[41] The exception to this rule appears to be *Tăpa*, who also gave the world *adat Kristen* and is worshipped through it. For many of my acquaintances, *Tăpa* just *is*; his existence precedes and is independent from processes of creation.

[42] Peter Aichner, "Adat Begawai among the Land-Dayaks," *Sarawak Museum Journal* 6,6 (1955): 588–89.

[43] Carol Rubenstein, "The Flying Silver Message Stick: Update 1985–86 on Long Songs Collected 1971–74," *Sarawak Museum Journal* 42,63 (1991): 61–158, especially p. 64.

practices and innovations reflected the broader understanding, I suggest, that *adat gawai*, having been given to humans, is now what they make of it.[44]

A similar conviction—possibly inherited from *adat gawai* or fomented by missionary teaching—underlies contemporary Christian practice. Although the existence of Jesus, Mary, and other named personages is not contingent on a single village's actions as *gawai* spirits are, it is still vital to maintain good relations with them. To ensure this, my informants often emphasize the need to pray correctly, for it is through prayer that things are made to happen. Consequently, the effectiveness of both *gawai* rituals and Christian prayer is attributed less to the whim of God or spirits than to how well *adat* has been "done." A Catholic woman illustrated this concept to me by pointing out how the weather during *gawai sawa*—the post-harvesting *gawai* festival—had become much hotter and drier over the years. In the past, when everyone followed *gawai*, their prayers would bring light rain and cool weather during this period. Because practitioners' numbers and skills had since declined, she said, *adat gawai* was no longer being done properly, with detrimental consequences.[45]

This awareness that "doing makes it so" has, I suggest, given many Bidayuhs a sense of their capacity to accomplish things through religious praxis, as well as their culpability when things do happen. Yet this does not mean that they privilege human agency over everything else. As I shall now explain, human action and intention are necessary, but not sufficient, factors in engendering religious effects.

THINGS THAT COME IN PACKAGES

For the most part, the objects and substances of *adat gawai* and Christianity are ordinary physical entities that most Bidayuhs would happily slot into a Cartesian framework if presented with one. In specific contexts, however, these materials can be combined with other elements, including objects, words, and actions, to generate certain effects. As the story above reveals, *adat gawai* is not simply an abstract set of propositions, but, simultaneously, technique, knowledge, and material object, all united by their original status as gifts from god. None is self-contained: for *adat* to be brought into being, each gift must be combined with others. The woman can thus only *băris* when wearing the correct clothing, while rice-planting is learned by performing the prescribed actions with the correct items.

It is at this point of constitution that such elements become what I shall call the "things" of *adat gawai* and Christianity: things that are defined not by their (im)materiality, but by their *effects*. To *băris* in rituals, for example, is necessarily to conjoin material item (clothing) and immaterial performance (chants), thereby creating a new entity that is simultaneously clothing and chant. In this way, chanted words become *băris* chants, and clothing and chant transform each participant into a *dayung băris* (literally, chanting woman). On their own, the clothing and paraphernalia can be handled without fear of consequence: they are not *adat gawai* things. Such was the case when tourists first visited my fieldsite in the 1960s and

---

[44] Chua, *Objects of Culture*, pp. 95–118.

[45] This is also because *gawai sawa* is now observed annually as a public holiday throughout Sarawak on June 1. In previous decades, each village would hold its own celebrations just after the end of harvesting, between March and early May, when the weather was marginally cooler and wetter.

1970s. Although *adat gawai* was widely practiced at the time, villagers willingly let visitors don and handle their ritual paraphernalia when posing for photographs. This was safe, I was told, because the objects in themselves were not dangerous. The tourists, being ignorant of the requisite chants and actions, were just "playing," and unlikely to make anything happen.

Dayung băris chanting at an *adat gawai* ritual. Photo by Liana Chua, 2005

The same applies to the ubiquitous blue-and-white Chinese trade porcelain bowls historically obtained through trade networks and possessed by Bidayuh households as heirlooms or receptacles. They acquire agentive powers, however, when they are used in *gawai* ceremonies as offering holders and to summon nearby spirits to the ritual site. The latter ceremony is performed by the senior *dayung băris*, who kneels before the "altar" (*sangar*) on which the offerings are hung, and taps a small metal blade against the bowl's rim while reciting an invitational chant, thereby generating a specific sound recognized by spirits. In recent years, the same bowls have been used as holders of holy water in Anglican and Catholic churches, in which the congregation dip their fingers when crossing themselves. In each situation, the bowl itself retains its physical form, but is said to become another thing, defined mainly by its effects: a Chinese bowl, a *gawai* bowl, a Christian bowl. These are not simply "biographical" phases that a single object moves through.[46] Each thing is

---

[46] Igor Kopytoff, "The Cultural Biographies of Objects: Commoditization as Process," in *The Social Life of Things: Commodities in Cultural Perspective*, ed. Arjun Appadurai (Cambridge: Cambridge University Press, 1986).

distinct, produced by the integration of various elements: a *gawai* bowl equally comprises bowl, tapping knife, sound, and chant, while a Christian bowl consists of bowl, holy water, and often fingers and actions. Like "powerful powder," these are irreducible entities.

The lighting of the Paschal candle at a Holy Saturday service.
Photo by Liana Chua, 2010

Contemporary Bidayuh Christianity is filled with similarly constitutive packages. Apart from being used in church, holy water—itself an irreducible combination of water and sanctification—is collected by Anglicans and Catholics in small plastic bottles on their household altars. Merely accumulating it, however, is pointless, for its ability to do good must be activated for particular purposes in combination with words, actions, and other elements: through making the sign of the cross, anointing the infirm, or in baptism, for instance. On a larger scale, such packages are also found on specific liturgical occasions, such as Holy Saturday, which my village friends describe as *simayang di-an* (literally, prayers with/of candlès). *Simayang di-an* refers to the opening rite—observed by churches worldwide—of lighting a Paschal candle in the darkness outside, and distributing the flame to members of the congregation, who hold candles, as they process into church. While few of the Bidayuhs with whom I spoke can explain why this is done, all agree that candles are essential to the correct observance of Holy Saturday. Throughout the service, people ensure that their and their neighbours' flames are not extinguished: in that hour, person, spoken prayer, and candle form a single whole.

In order to bring effects into being, then, Bidayuh religious practices are not only performative but combinatory: words, actions, and material objects go hand-in-hand, often coalescing to reemerge as momentarily distinct entities, which confound the original distinctions among these components. Each component brings its specific properties to bear on the resultant bundle: Chinese porcelain bowls, for example, emit a unique sound when tapped with a metal knife, which could not be reproduced by any other material. In these moments, persons, actions, words, and objects constitute a "field of forces set up through [their] active and sensuous engagement";[47] they are acknowledged as co-constitutors, united not by what they are but by what they *do*. For one to be elevated above the others—or worse, for the others to be dispensed with—would probably render these practices both incomplete and ineffective.

This principle may account for why Bidayuhs often pay as much attention to materiality and mechanistic actions as they do to the verbal and doctrinal aspects of both *adat gawai* and Christianity. The twist, however, is that for those who observe these *adat*, the most compelling and convenient focal points are often material and performative, simply because of their tangibility. It is easier, for example, to encapsulate a specific process of summoning spirits by reference to a *gawai* bowl, and to describe Holy Saturday services through candles, than to expound on the combinations of different elements involved in them.. In a curious paradox, this strategy thus verbally and conceptually obviates the very multiplicity of heterogeneous elements that people acknowledge is critical to the performance of ritual. For in talking about that bowl or those candles, they are not simply referring to the objects per se, but acting and working *through* them as the material facets of a larger constitutive sequence.

CHRISTIAN THINGS: TRANSCENDENCE OR TRANSFORMATION?

Unlike their Anglican and Catholic neighbors, who are content to watch *gawai* rituals and receive the practitioners' annual blessings, SIB adherents unequivocally shun any contact with the old ways. Instead, like their brethren elsewhere,[48] they depict themselves as having broken away from an ignorant, sinful past. Fueling their rejection is a pronounced version of a long-standing transcendental impulse within Protestant Christianity: a propensity to locate "'authentic' … religious practice in disdain for material culture" and external accoutrements.[49] Instead, members of the SIB strive to cultivate a direct connection with god, mediated only by words, songs, and "text Bible": for them, "spiritual immediacy is a near-"immaterial quality."[50]

---

[47] See Tim Ingold, *The Perception of the Environment: Essays in Livelihood, Dwelling, and Skill* (London: Routledge, 2000), p. 342. Although Ingold's is an ontological point about how humans "dwell" within the world, this aptly articulates my informants' understanding of the constitutive mechanism explored in this chapter.

[48] Amster, "Community, Ethnicity, and Modes of Association among the Kelabit," p. 283.

[49] Simon Coleman, "The Charismatic Gift," *Journal of the Royal Anthropological Institute* 10,2 (2004): 421-42, especially p. 424.

[50] Matthew Engelke, *A Problem of Presence: Beyond Scripture in an African Church* (Berkeley, CA, and London: University of California Press, 2007), p. 7.

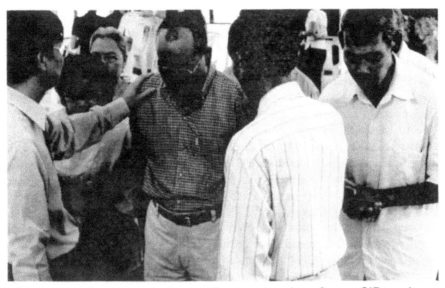

Pastors praying over members of the congregation after an SIB service.
Photo by Liana Chua, 2010

The incursion of the SIB's relatively ascetic mode of prayer has thrown into relief the features of ritual that many other villagers most value, as I discovered during my conversation with my Catholic friend. The "empty cross" that she invoked was not a hollow material vessel needing to be infused with words, meanings, or divinity. In fact, it did not even exist, for the very space in which the SIBs prayed was empty—devoid of the pictures, objects, candles, substances, and verbal and physical protocols that characterized her experience of Christianity. As nearly all my Anglican and Catholic acquaintances pointed out whenever I mentioned attending SIB services, "they don't even make the *sign* of the cross." For them, I suggest, such tangible elements are critical *aspects of* rather than mere supplements to the human performances that bring about religious effects. Christianity does not dwell in words, actions, and objects; it arises at the point of their conjunction. Put differently, materiality and performativity need not be transcended to access the divine, because they are the very things that give rise to, and, indeed, instantiate, its presence and reality.

These constitutive sequences are thus transformative—or, as some Bidayuhs might put it, a continuous sequence of becoming (*jadi*). In *gawai* and Christian practices, things are constantly on the move: a blue-and-white bowl becomes an heirloom, then a *gawai* bowl, then a Christian bowl. Each is an effect-producing form that fleetingly holds together or transforms different elements within a particular context. This notion of "becoming" is perhaps exemplified by the consumption of the Eucharist as interpreted by Anglicans and Catholics. Opinions within both congregations vary over whether a communion wafer is or merely stands for the body of Christ. However, it is often said by members of both denominations that consuming communion is akin to consuming rice: it is a process by which a life-giving spirit (*simangi padi* or *simangi Jesus*) *becomes* a thing (rice grain or wafer) that is simultaneously spirit and corporeality, which when consumed becomes the *simangi* of humans, enabling their bodies to grow safely and healthily.[51]

This example leads to a final, crucial point. Procedures such as the taking of communion and lighting of the Paschal candle are not Bidayuh inventions or "localized" appropriations, but have their historical, official, and often doctrinal roots in Christianity itself—or rather, various incarnations of the Christian church. Such occurrences underscore the fact that prescribed action and materiality have long been inescapable and often problematic features of Christian practice, mediating but also potentially hindering relations with the divine.[52] As Fenella Cannell points out, these concerns are encapsulated by the fundamental paradox that "[a]lthough ... Christian teaching tends to elevate the spirit above the flesh, Christian doctrine in fact always also has this other aspect, in which the flesh is an essential part of redemption."[53] Consequently, "encounters between Christianity and local cultures cannot ... be adequately typified [as is often the case] as encounters between transcendent and nontranscendent religious conceptions."[54]

Put differently, Bidayuhs have not "domesticated" Christianity by turning it into a "thingy" religion. Instead, I would argue that the deep-rooted *non*-transcendental predilections and institutional conventions of Anglicanism and Catholicism have converged—or at least found common ground—with those of *adat gawai* and other forms of Bidayuh sociality. This has resulted in the establishment of a set of object- and protocol-centered practices and discourses at the core of much contemporary Bidayuh Christianity, which onlookers have interpreted in various ways: as signs of a fetishistic pagan mentality, the laudable observance of institutional prescriptions, or perhaps the workings of a contiguous object-centered cultural logic.

CONCLUSION

Unlike the interpretations outlined above, my aim has not been to account for why (im)materiality is important to Bidayuh religious practices, but to describe how the very practices to which it is central are understood to work. Thinking through the sorts of objects, substances, and performances that missionaries saw as evidence of fetishism reveals what we might call a constitutive, combinatory "model" of action, characterized by forces rather than static entities and "becoming" rather than "being," at the core of both *adat gawai* and Christianity. Using this model as the conceptual basis of my analysis, I have suggested that, rather than mistakenly investing their faith in materiality, Bidayuhs are more interested in how they can act through **it** in order to make things happen. In this respect, my analytical and methodological strategy is analogous to the way my acquaintances try to generate effects through things: instead of being ends in themselves, these things have become the necessary constituents of the next step along.

In the process, my analysis has illuminated some of the issues at stake in the problematic subject of "empty crosses." Although SIB Christianity remains a minority denomination in the village I studied, its mere presence has generated

---

[51] Cited from Harris, "Growing Gods," p. 176.

[52] Cannell, *Anthropology of Christianity*; Engelke, *Problem of Presence*; and Keane, *Christian Moderns.*

[53] Cannell, *Anthropology of Christianity*, p. 7.

[54] Ibid., p. 44.

questions over what constitutes proper or efficacious forms of prayer and the place of objects, images, and substances in religious practices. In this regard, the diverse and often fragmentary opinions expressed by Anglicans and Catholics on SIB religiosity may be seen as belated, if inadvertent, responses to the criticisms of Bidayuhs' "fetishistic" behavior leveled by earlier generations of missionaries, scholars, and officials. The problem they are addressing, however, is not that of the muddied Cartesian boundaries that preoccupied their observers, but the ongoing challenge of how to bring *adat* and its effects into being. And it is this concern that this chapter has sought to draw out from the tangle of materiality, performativity, theory, and history in which Bidayuh religious practices are caught up. In this regard, the problem of "empty crosses" reminds us that a key challenge in analyzing material religion is not simply "trying to determine how other people think about the world," but in working out "how we must think in order to conceive a world the way they do."[55]

---

[55] Henare et al., *Thinking Through Things*, p. 15.

CHAPTER 8

DRESSING FOR MODERN WAR IN OLD-FASHIONED MAGIC: TRADITIONAL PROTECTIVE CHARMS OF THAILAND'S FORCES IN THE VIETNAM WAR

Richard A. Ruth

When Thailand's troops went to fight in South Vietnam in the late 1960s, they arrived armored in twin layers of magic. They were adorned in the symbols of the Thai state's recent efforts to promote Buddhism as a defensive weapon against ideological enemies and in the remnants of the esoteric folk traditions of their rural native villages. Before setting off to battle the Viet Cong, nearly every one of Thailand's 37,000 troops acquired a protective suit of magical charms speedily cobbled together from spiritual-themed gifts offered by their commanding officers, families, community elders, and *bhikkhu* (Buddhist monk) mentors.

Initially, many Thai soldiers were skeptical about the power of these traditional defense charms. They accepted the state-sponsored Buddhist amulets out of military protocol, and took the village charms out of filial piety and simple good manners. The soldiers dressed themselves in these objects at a time when the meaning and purpose of both were undergoing dramatic changes in the domestic context. But it was during their time in the war zones of South Vietnam and in the company of foreign soldiers who admired the Thais' mystical adornments that these troops most profoundly reassessed the value of their traditional magic. The movement of these amulets into the international arena of multiple armies, from many nations, assembled for war encouraged the Thais to attach hitherto unconsidered values to these quintessentially Thai objects. The soldiers returned convinced that these devices were not only efficacious and necessary but superior to any form of spiritual protection produced by either allied or enemy troops. They also came back with a new pride in these Thai religious objects born out of the reverence that foreign troops demonstrated for them. Their eclectic collections of charms, mementos, and magical formulae not only gave them the confidence that they could evade the destructive intentions of their communist Vietnamese foes, they also encouraged them to believe that such objects had transformed them into envied and respected warriors in the eyes of their American and Australian allies.

These Thai troops traveled to South Vietnam to fight alongside the United States military as members of the "Free World" forces there. According to the Thai government's rhetoric, they were all civilian volunteers who had come forward to halt communism's advance before it could spread from South Vietnam into Thailand's provinces. In reality, all of the volunteers were or had been soldiers in the Royal Thai Army before joining the special unit created, in part, out of pressure from the United States. Their mission was to protect South Vietnam from communist aggression—to fight the Viet Cong in the villages and forests of Bien Hoa province—and to discourage Hanoi from supporting Thailand's domestic communist insurgency. Thailand's political–military leadership created these combat units in an atmosphere of acute patriotic fervor that stressed the combined themes of an enduring Thai warrior tradition along with the Thai government's recent push for American-inspired economic models. The offensive weapons and defensive magic that these soldiers acquired for service in South Vietnam mirrored these sometimes contradictory themes.

This chapter examines the change in attitudes toward traditional religious protective devices—Buddhist amulets and other protective charms—that many soldiers underwent while in the international environment of wartime South Vietnam. It analyzes the circumstances under which educated military men fighting in the Second Indochina War reassessed traditional Thai protective charms while in contact with American, Australian, and Vietnamese troops in South Vietnam. Most of the sixty men I interviewed for this project indicated that they had been skeptical or dismissive of these spiritual devices before fighting in the Vietnam War. My goal is to identify the specifically international social and cultural factors that encouraged the more doubtful among them to alter their initial casual regard for these protective devices. Did their survival as Thai soldiers in a foreign and spiritually perplexing war zone, in contests against the "godless" armies of global communism, encourage them to view their charms as particularly efficacious? How much did the admiration of Thai amulets by Western soldiers from technologically advanced armies contribute to the Thai soldiers' newfound regard for their own traditional protective charms? Did foreign testimonials regarding the effectiveness of the amulets suggest objective, or non-chauvinistic, confirmation of the charms' worth? And, finally, and more broadly, did the reports of foreign admiration that appeared in official wartime press accounts and in postwar recollections of Thai veterans contribute to the increased popularity of Buddhist amulets in Thailand in the latter half of the twentieth century?

In recruiting Thai men to fight in the Vietnam War, the Thai government stressed modernity. It repeatedly assured potential recruits that they would be armed with state-of-the-art weapons supplied by the United States.[1] Its focus on the modern had been a cornerstone of Thailand's military adventure in South Vietnam since its inception. In its negotiations with the United States, the Thai government had demanded that its forces receive the most up-to-date personal weapons and access to the same support systems serving US forces in South Vietnam. This condition would ensure that the Thai troops went to war with the most advanced weapons available, a benefit not shared by America's other allies—the South Koreans, Taiwanese, and even the South Vietnamese—fighting there.[2] Beyond the

---

[1] "VN-bound Thai Troops Get Top Grade Weapons," *Bangkok Post*, June 3, 1967, p. 1.

[2] "S-VN Troops Use Inferior Weapons," *Bangkok Post*, September 15, 1968, p. 3.

military efficacy of these new weapons, the prestige of the Thai troops in the realm of domestic and international opinion was important to Thai military leaders and the volunteers themselves. Thailand's human contribution to the defense of South Vietnam had to appear to the world as a modern, professional, Asian fighting force.[3]

The Thai men who responded to these recruiting drives were similarly focused on the modern. In recalling their motivations to join, many Thai soldiers cited an ambition to go to war equipped with modern weapons and their related systems. They described a desire to fly into battlefields in America's newest helicopters, to call in air support from circling AC-47 "Spooky" gunships, and to return home in the high-altitude luxury of Boeing 707s.[4] And more than anything, they desired access to the M-16 assault rifle that all American combat soldiers had recently acquired. The arrival of the miraculously lightweight and powerful rifle into the region's battlefields made these Thai soldiers chafe at the memory of their now antiquated bolt-action M-2s, a weapon that dated to the Second World War.[5] For most of these recruits, the M-16 itself was nearly magical in its promise of awesome firepower from a seemingly insubstantial source.

ACQUIRING DEFENSIVE MAGIC

At the time of the Vietnam War, the objects addressed in this article were divided into two categories: Buddhist and *sayasat* (related to esoteric arts). Generally, in the dichotomy of the period, those objects created and sacralized by Buddhist monks within a Buddhist *wat* (temple complex) reside in the Buddhist category. All others—the animal parts, teeth, magic flora, and defensive tattoos—were considered *sayasat*. But as several anthropologists of Thailand have demonstrated, there is considerable overlap between categories.[6] Many of the objects and practices labeled *sayasat* are older than Thailand's recorded history. They have roots in the pre-Buddhist rituals that some have termed as "magico-animism."[7] And they have always been associated chiefly with marshal prowess and personal protection.[8] Sri Lankan Buddhist monks conveyed their own esoteric elements attached to their Theravada practices when they journeyed to mainland Southeast Asia beginning in the sixth century CE. As the various polities of the Chaophraya valley embraced

---

[3] *Prawatsat Khong Thahan Thai Nai Songkhram Wietnam* (Bangkok: Amrin Publishing and Printing, 1998), pp. 84, 140.

[4] Khamron Mahaban, interview with author, Kanchanaburi, September 20, 2003; Noi (pseudonym), interview with author, Chiang Mai, March 20, 2003.

[5] "Our own weapons weren't good," Private First Class Suwit Kaeokhlaitha explained, "Whenever [Thai communist insurgents] attacked us, we would get completely wiped out … [Our guns] fired one round at a time. We didn't have M-16s." Attracted by the new weapons that the US military had promised to give the Thai troops in South Vietnam, Suwit applied to go abroad. He described his desire to use an M-16 in combat as a youthful "goal." Suwit Kaeokhlaitha, interview with author, Udon Thani, October 15, 2003.

[6] Stanley Jeyaraja Tambiah, *The Buddhist Saints of the Forest and the Cult of Amulets* (Cambridge: Cambridge University Press, 1984), p. 199; Andrew Turton, "Invulnerability and Local Knowledge," in *Thai Constructions of Knowledge,* ed. Manas Chitakasem and Andrew Turton (London: School of Oriental and African Studies, University of London, 1991), p. 170.

[7] The anthropologist B. J. Terwiel coined this term. See B. J. Terwiel, *Monks and Magic: An Analysis of Religious Ceremonies in Central Thailand* (London: Curzon Press, 1979).

[8] Chris Baker and Pasuk Phongpaichit, *The Tale of Khun Chang Khun Phaen* (Chiang Mai: Silkworm Books, 2010), p. 940.

Buddhism as the official faith in the thirteenth and fourteenth centuries, these older religious practices were blended with the more formal and scripture-based practices of Buddhism. For centuries, the indigenous and imported traditions existed within a syncretic Buddhist blend that few questioned or sought to separate, even within the Buddhist order itself. It was not until King Mongkut (r. 1854–68) sought to reform Siamese Buddhism in the mid-nineteenth century by ridding it of its magico-animistic elements that Thai Buddhists began to consider where Buddhist practice ended and *sayasat* began. In the years leading up to 1957, the 2,500[th] anniversary of the Buddha's birth, official discomfort with these enduring esoteric practices increased. Although the Thai state and its related religious institutions did not formerly ban non-Buddhist elements, Buddhist leaders tried to discourage the celebration of mystical monks and associated practices within the grounds of *wat*. Only partially successful, the state's Buddhist order stripped many of the *sayasat* elements from the temples' purview and pushed these traditional practices into the control of devoted laypeople. The Thai state's efforts to impose a more orthodox, or logical, framework on Buddhism in the American-dominated Cold War period would have resonated with other modernist themes to which these soldiers responded.

The extent to which *sayasat* traditions had faded by the mid-twentieth century is demonstrated by the insignificant role they played in the lives of the Thai men whose age and education qualified them for the special units being put together for South Vietnam. Many of the non-Buddhist charms were in the process of being delegitimized by Thailand's *sangha* (Buddhist ecclesiastical order) in the period of these soldiers' youths. Although nearly all of these *sayasat* devices had formerly been associated with Buddhism in the period before Thailand's rulers had encouraged the rationalization of Buddhism, only a few remained within the Thai Buddhist establishment's body of accepted practices by the mid-twentieth century. The "magical" protective qualities attributed to the specifically Buddhist amulets are reminders of the lingering *sayasat* components remaining in Thailand's Buddhism.

In his work on Thai Buddhist practices in the 1960s, anthropologist B. J. Terwiel describes the importance of amulets in the religious and social life of Thai adolescents in central Thailand.[9] In my research on education-minded males who came of age a few decades earlier in the 1940s and 1950s, however, the amulets appeared to be less significant. Of the Thai veterans who qualified for service in South Vietnam, I found only a few who recalled a profound attachment to these magical devices prior to their deployment. On the contrary, many had largely rejected these spiritual objects as emblematic of the superstitions and conservatism of the rural societies they had abandoned prior to joining the military. While aware of the charms' existence, and of the previous generations' attachments to them, few soldiers possessed any amulets before volunteering to fight in South Vietnam. The young soldiers considered these objects to be at odds with the evermore rational—and thus more modern, in the logic of the day—Buddhism of their youth; they saw charms as the fixations of their older and less educated kin. One reason for this difference might be education. Terwiel's informants had largely eschewed secondary education as unnecessary or impractical within the agricultural communities in which they lived.[10] My interviewees, conversely, all stressed the importance of

---

[9] Terwiel, *Monks and Magic*, pp. 71–95.

[10] Terwiel, *Monks and Magic*, pp. 72–73.

advanced education as a means of transcending the socio-economic class of their childhoods. Although proud of their rural roots, these soldiers had consciously committed themselves to a program of self-improvement designed to elevate them out of the embrace of the traditional and into the arms of the modern.[11] All had graduated from secondary school—a condition for recruits to the all-volunteer forces being sent to South Vietnam—and many had left their native villages to seek jobs within the apparatuses of Thailand's state institutions, as bureaucrats, teachers, and policemen. Having failed in these ambitions, they sought positions in Thailand's expanding national army. As a result of their separation from their parents' milieu, few could explain in detail the magical logic behind the objects they had been given to protect themselves. They took them only because their immediate elders had offered them along with their farewell blessings. And they accepted claims of their efficacy with respectful skepticism. To the Thai soldiers who set off for Vietnam, Buddhist amulets, talismans, and esoteric magical paraphernalia were nearly as alien to their experiences as were the ArmaLite rifles, Claymore mines, and Starlight Scopes offered by the US Army.

SOURCES OF PROTECTIVE MAGIC

In general, all Thai soldiers acquired their collections of protective magical objects in the same manner and during the same phase of their training. There were two sources, one for amulets and another for esoteric charms. Most received their Buddhist amulets in military–religious ceremonies conducted by their commanding officers in the Royal Thai Army's camp at Lad Ya in Kanchanaburi and during farewell ceremonies on the Sanam Luang parade grounds outside of the former Grand Palace. An amulet (*phra phim* or *phra khruang rang*) was usually a small brass frame containing a sacred natural or manmade object, including stones, metals (sometimes mercury), plant roots, wood, bark, seeds, antlers, teeth, inscribed cloth, carved wooden phalluses, and other sacred talismans.[12] The most common amulet in these military ceremonies was a Buddhist image pressed in clay or metal, usually a tiny reproduction of a celebrated Thai Buddha statue. The collection and display of these charms evolved out of the ancient practice of acquiring votive tablets to mark pilgrimages or make merit. The images were—and are—designed, minted, and sacralized by teams of monks within the grounds of a *wat*. Lay jewelers and metal smiths form the casings. Monks distribute them to their students and other adherents in religious ceremonies. Once in the possession of laypeople, the amulets are frequently sold or traded in markets and shops. The amulets that the South Vietnam-bound troops received had been produced at Buddhist *wat* celebrated for their long histories or well known because they were patronized by high-ranking officers in the Royal Thai Army. Even while *sayasat* objects were enduring official disfavor for their esoteric and specifically non-Buddhist associations, these temple-produced Buddhist statuette amulets were being promoted as important symbols of Thailand's national

---

[11] Rungrit Aphichai, interview with author, Chiang Mai, June 13, 2003; Bandit Sinamthieng, interview with author, Udon Thani, October 14, 2003, pp. 2–3; Thawat (pseudonym), interview with author, Chiang Mai, August 18, 2003; Wanchai Klinbun, interview with author, Udon Thani, October 16, 2003.

[12] Philip Cornwel-Smith, "Amulet Collectors: Lucky Charms as a Lifestyle," in Philip Cornwel-Smith, *Very Thai: Everyday Popular Culture* (Bangkok: River Books, 2005), p. 142.

faith. As a result, the veneration of (and trade in) these ancient Buddhist objects was becoming increasingly popular throughout Thai society in the late 1960s.[13]

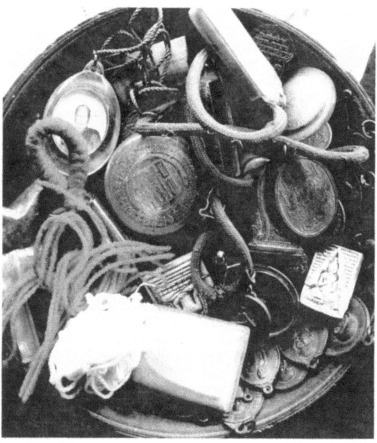

A collection of Buddhist amulets, medallions, and talismans taken to South Vietnam by one Thai soldier. Photo by Richard A. Ruth

The *sayasat* charms—those non-Buddhist defensive objects—came from unofficial sources. Most soldiers received their esoteric devices from their families while at home for a final visit before shipping off to South Vietnam. In accepting these unofficial sources of defensive magic, most of the Thai volunteer soldiers were uncertain about what they should choose to take with them. Almost all confessed that they had only the vaguest ideas of the invulnerability charms still used by the elders of their native villages and in their parents' homes.

The soldiers' general ignorance of these traditions was not entirely a result of their fixation on the modern or a rejection of the traditional; most had not deemed them necessary. Few soldiers recalled as young men being afraid of dying. Many said they had not considered their mortality in anything but the most abstract terms prior to their volunteering for service in South Vietnam. In the course of their spiritual education—and despite Buddhism's focus on impermanence and

---

[13] Marlane Guelden, *Thailand: Into the Spirit World* (Singapore: Times Editions, 1995), p. 132.

reincarnation—the soldiers overlooked the reality of their vulnerability. But when faced with the prospect of physical harm or death in South Vietnam, they entered into a local process that had traditionally preceded the dispatch of young Siamese men into the ranks of campaigning armies, raiding parties, or local defensive forces. This process of accumulating protective charms relied as much on the knowledge and energies of family or community members as it did on those of the departing soldier. These soldiers of the 1960s, for their part, were expected to seek those objects that would best guarantee their return. Their elders would then pass on their most efficacious talismans along with testimonial accounts of their powers. What started out as a polite indulgence of one's elders' beliefs turned into a more sincere search for magic protection as the date of departure approached. Bandit Srinamthieng, a typist clerk for the headquarters of the Royal Thai Army's Volunteer Force who served in South Vietnam in 1968–69, described the process as an individual quest:

> Each person had to search for good luck talismans. We searched for the charms of old that people had said were efficacious; we searched for them wherever they might be. When the grandchildren were preparing to go [to war], the old people would go find these things for them. They would take these old things and give them to [their grandchildren]. For example, if they had an old charm they wouldn't hold on to it. They would tell their grandchildren to take it to protect them.[14]

And they took all that was offered. In most cases, every object offered by a loved one found its way into the Thai uniforms, rucksacks, and helmets.[15] They donned a rich chainmail of protective objects drawn directly from their kinfolk's bodies, clothes, homes, and biographies. They girded their chests with the preserved teeth and thighbone fragments of their deceased fathers. Some soldiers received white cloths onto which their parents had pressed footprints and handprints using turmeric to create the images.[16] In an imitation of ancient kings who went to battle with images of the Buddha's footprint in their headgear, they affixed these parental footprints into their helmet liners. They also packed their helmets with the ragged strips of their mothers' *phasin* (wrap skirts) and undergarments. They lined their US Army-issued flak jackets with boar fangs, snake skins, and tiger claws. Around their necks they dangled satchels of soil scraped from the time-tinctured dirt found beneath their family homes. They borrowed beautiful *ta-krut* tubes—rolled metal amulets with ancient Khmer incantations scratched upon them—from compelling advocates.

---

[14] Bandit Sinamthieng, interview with author, Udon Thani, October 14, 2003.

[15] Soldiers preparing for war were uncertain about what they should seek out for protection and whether they should accept every bit of defensive magic offered to them. As the scheduled date of their departure grew nearer, they were increasingly less discriminating about what they should take. By the end of their home leaves, most soldiers found themselves accepting whatever was offered to them.

[16] Si Sichaimun, interview with author, Udon Thani, October 15, 2003; Chatchai Methulin, interview with author, Kanchanaburi, September 20, 2003, p. 3; others used ink to make the images. Siwon Kawiwon, interview with author, Chiang Mai, Thailand, August 17, 2003. One soldier wrote, simply, "mother" and "father" on his helmet. Khamron Mahaban, interview with author, Kanchanaburi, September 20, 2003.

The troops' native communities also provided Buddhist charms. At village temples, the soldiers added to their military-sponsored Buddhist amulets by acquiring *phayan* and *suayan*—colored cloths imprinted with *yantra* (mystical Brahmanical diagrams)—from the rural monks who had taught them in their youths. In a spiritual and literal sense, they entrusted their physical safety to the power of their families, their temples, and village traditions. Thus fitted out, the departing Thai soldiers left for South Vietnam encased in two layers of magic. They displayed the officially sanctioned Buddhist amulets in their open collars as visible testaments of their faith in Buddhism and the Thai state that promoted it. Meanwhile, they secreted the many and varied *sayasat* devices—mysterious in their origins and activation methods—in the dark folds and pockets of their fatigues and battle armor.

Buddhist amulets became increasingly popular in Thailand in the 1960s for several reasons. On a national level, the ideological basis of the Cold War—with the "Free World" side warning of the atheistic hostility of their communist rivals—encouraged Thailand to combat local and regional opponents with its globally recognized national religion. Buddhism—not the disorganized practices of *sayasat*—provided an instantly recognizable and unified set of symbols for Thailand's religiously tinged opposition to communism. Likewise, on the local level, the proliferation of small arms in rural areas and the escalation of violence—developments related to the war in neighboring Laos and to the domestic insurgencies in Thailand's northeast and south—sparked an increased demand for Buddhist amulets in the 1960s.[17]

In this atmosphere of clashing global ideologies, many came to believe that only a properly blessed, Thai-produced Buddhist amulet could render its wearer impervious to bullets fired by communists. As more Thai defense forces entered into combat in the border provinces, senior police and military commanders became increasingly vocal advocates of Buddhist amulets. Their public declarations about the efficacy of Buddhist charms to protect soldiers in combat contributed to the talismans' growing popularity among the lower ranks and civilians. A newspaper profile of an important general involved in Thailand's expeditionary forces, for example, described his amulets as being "among his most treasured possessions." The feature on Major-General Chalard Hiranyasiri ran in the *Bangkok Post*, in June 1967, while Thailand's volunteers were training for South Vietnam, and described the "veteran of three wars" as a "brilliant strategist" who nonetheless had to rely on the amulets to rescue him from harm while in combat.[18] Even Thailand's mainstream papers carried sensational articles about amulets. But unlike the tabloids and specialty magazines, these news sources often undermined claims about the invulnerability granted by these talismans. With headlines such as "His Amulet Failed," the papers conveyed tales of overly zealous amulet enthusiasts who ended their own lives while attempting to demonstrate the power of their charms to deflect bullets at close range.[19] When a Bangkok sign maker offered to sell an amulet for 300,000 baht (US$15,000), the skeptical *Bangkok Post* proposed testing the amulet's

---

[17] For an analysis of this historical development, see Chalong Soontravanich, "Small Arms, Romance, and Crime and Violence in Post-WWII Thai Society," *Southeast Asian Studies* 43,1 (June 2005): 26–46; and Christopher E. Goscha, *Thailand and the Southeast Asian Networks of the Vietnamese Revolution, 1885–1954* (Surrey: Curzon Press, 1999), p. 184.

[18] Anond Bunnag, "Chalard: Veteran of Three Wars," *Bangkok Post*, June 5, 1967, p. 2.

[19] "His Amulet Failed," *Bangkok Post*, July 29, 1968, p. 5.

alleged powers by draping it over a duck. A marksman shot the creature with a 9mm Luger in a field near Kitthikachorn Stadium. The resulting mess prompted one observer to declare the amulet-adorned fowl "the deadest duck I ever saw." Three chickens tested during the same session fared no better against a shotgun's blast. The *Post*'s triumphant headline declared "Magic Fails, Duck Dies."[20]

Amulet enthusiasts were not deterred by media efforts to debunk their claims. The magic in these charms, as many believers will argue, cannot be tested in staged circumstances using farm animals as trial subjects. Amulet enthusiasts contend that such experiments—with their intention to harm the animal test subjects—are un-Buddhist anyway. In the markets and temples, in the newspapers and drinking spots, debates raged about the relative power of amulets. And in this atmosphere of increasing rural violence, of competing claims and counterclaims of amulet efficacy, the amulets became increasingly important parts of the departing Thai soldiers' identity as that identity was portrayed in the newspaper articles and photos that described their preparation for deployment.

The increased visibility of the amulets was at odds with their ancient origins. In the distant past, the metal amulets were often concealed within the plaster or bronze bodies of Buddha images. They were often buried in the arm or body of Buddha statues of all sizes. The art historian A. B. Griswold points out that the famed sixteenth-century Mangalapabitra Buddha image at Ayutthaya contained numerous tiny bronze statues in its left arm.[21] The buried statuettes provided concentrated but invisible power to the principal Buddha images venerated upon the main platform of an *ubosot* (ordination hall) or *wihan* (lecture hall).

In Thailand of the 1960s, these very same Buddha statuettes were meant to be seen. Former prohibitions about wearing amulets during sexual encounters, while defecating or urinating, or while sleeping were increasingly ignored. It became common to display them in public and non-religious settings. Today all but the smallest provincial markets include at least one dealer in Buddhist amulets and other magic charms; the display of magical amulets is always a source of keen and steady interest from collectors. The amulets are scrutinized with magnifying glasses and jewelers' loupes like precious stones or fine art masterpieces. The devout do not "sell" or "buy" amulets, for these commercial terms are considered inappropriately crass or blasphemous in the context of such refined spiritual power; instead, they "rent" or "loan" them to others, and accept an agreed-upon donation in return. The display is extended through publications of glossy magazines and bound catalogs dedicated to the collection and study of amulets, many of which were first published in the final years of the Vietnam War. The monthly magazines contain profiles of famous amulets, of their origins and histories of ownership. A popular feature is the testimonials. Stories of the amulets' amazing power in protecting the owner fascinate readers and contribute to amulets' reputations and potential selling prices. The amulets that traveled to South Vietnam were featured in these magazines accompanied by the stories of their miraculous powers.

In secreting multiple tiny images around their torso, head, and arms, Thailand's soldiers mirrored the ancient practice of bodily concealment. On combat missions,

---

[20] David M. Knapp, "Magic Fails, Duck Dies," *Bangkok Post*, July 22, 1968, p. 12.

[21] Griswold makes these observations in A. B. Griswold, *What is a Buddhist Image?*, Thai Culture, New Series, No. 19 (Bangkok: Fine Arts Department, 1968), p. 3; the excerpts of Griswold's essay that I used come from Tambiah, *The Buddhist Saints*, pp. 195–96.

they hid most of their Buddha images within the folds of their uniforms, under their flak jackets, and inside their helmets. Often, they displayed only a few images while patrolling the forests and countryside and while fighting. Away from combat, they tended to show off their amulets in sometimes ostentatious displays of dozens or more amulets. A small minority of particularly devout soldiers, however, chose to entrust their safety to a single amulet, especially if they believed it to be a powerful one. Their reasoning betrays both strains of Buddhist logic and military practicality. Somchin Changklud, a driver in a combat support company, was told by a monk that multiple amulets bound to various respective charms would shirk their duty in times of crisis. As Somchin recalled:

> It's like this: if you filled up your neck with them ... and then something happened, they would all pass the responsibility [to protect you] to the other ones.[22]

The monk told Somchin that he would be just as safe under the protection of a single amulet or, at most, two. Somchin acknowledged the wisdom of this senior monk, and brought two amulets. But his spiritual thrift was exceptional.

It was common for Thai soldiers to depart with more than one hundred *phra khruang rang* objects. Some carried more. The portability of the amulets made them ideal for infantrymen. In taking them on patrol, the Thai troops were extending the original function of the amulets as votive tablets and potent religious symbols designed for easy transportation over great distances and difficult terrain. The small size of these earlier efficacious objects allowed pilgrims to carry them afar at a time when most pilgrimages were conducted on foot over rural roads and trails or by hand-paddled vessels on Siam's intricate waterways. During the Vietnam War, the amulets' smallness and portability seemed to encourage this tendency toward excess common among the volunteer soldiers. Few were satisfied with one or two holy images. It was far more common for Thai soldiers to carry more than ten charms on them, as if to surround themselves in a protective force equal in total to that of a rifle squad. Many soldiers liked to carry thirty, or roughly the number of members in a platoon. Strung together in protective rings, the amulets provided a sense of protection without being overly heavy or noisy. But some soldiers were only satisfied with a hundred or more amulets, enough to match the number of fighters in an entire infantry company. There was a saying popular among the volunteers that went: For every division of Thai soldiers sent to fight in Vietnam, there were at least ten divisions of Buddhist amulets sent along with them.[23]

The amulets became the Thai soldiers' distinctive emblem. The talismans marked the soldiers as devout Buddhist warriors. In official and personal photographs, the amulets are often the central focus. The Thai soldiers in South Vietnam displayed these amulets in Saigon and Bearcat Camp, the US-built facility they shared with some Americans and Australians. And it was within their encounters with their *farang* (Caucasian, or people of European descent) allies in the international

---

[22] Somchin Changklud, interview with author, Kanchanaburi, Thailand, September 25, 2003, p. 4.

[23] Pa-nua (pseudonym), interview with author, Chiang Mai, Thailand, August 18, 2003; Siwon Kawiwon, interview with author, Chiang Mai, Thailand, August 17, 2003.

environment of Bearcat Camp that the Thai volunteers came to reassess their initial passivity and indifference toward these quintessentially Thai protective devices.

AMULETS IN THE WAR ZONE[24]

During their tours of duty in South Vietnam, the Thai soldiers became increasingly strong promoters of the amulets. Experiential and anecdotal evidence turned the formerly passive recipients of these charms into staunch and vocal believers in the efficacy of the amulets' powers to protect the lives of those who wore them. The soldiers treated the small charms with a reverence that left a strong impression on outside observers. Or they displayed them with élan that was arresting.

A Buddhist amulet is evident above the dog tags of a Thai infantryman (right) as his unit assembles for a combat mission in Bien Hoa province, South Vietnam.
Photo courtesy of the National Archives of Thailand

For example, some wore twin strings of amulets crossed at their chest like bandoliers, the arrangement generating a striking analog to those American soldiers who wore twin strings of 60mm bullets crisscrossing their chests. Others looped

---

[24] Some of the passages in the following section appear in Richard A. Ruth, *In Buddha's Company: Thai Soldiers in the Vietnam War* (Honolulu, HI: University of Hawaii Press, 2011).

multiple necklaces of varying lengths around their necks so that the tiny images draped like loosely woven chainmail armor over the top half of their chests.

In recalling their use of these Buddhist amulets during combat, some soldiers stressed the power of the amulet to focus their minds on the example of the Buddha and his teachings on karma. Some asserted that a powerful amulet helped facilitate mindfulness in the wearer while he walked among booby traps and landmines.[25] Others described the power of the amulets flowing into them in important situations, a sensation evocative of the fiery brilliance of the Buddha at the moment of his enlightenment.[26] The amulets also focused their minds on karmic matters during firefights. Sergeant Khamma, for example, recalls the extraordinary thoughts that flashed through his mind as he aimed his M-16 at an enemy guerrilla:

> I would close my eyes for an instant and think, "If I have never done anything against you in [a previous life], may the bullet that I fire not hit you. And if you have never had karma with me in the past, may your own shot not hit me." And then I would fire. Sometimes when I fired I could see them, sometimes I couldn't see them. Sometimes I saw them running away, thud, thud, thud. I had to fire. When I fired I tried to have compassion in my heart. For instance, [I said to myself], "If it isn't your time to die, or if we didn't have any conflict in our previous lives, don't let anything happen to you. You don't have to be hit."[27]

A close call with death encouraged the soldiers to increase their reverence toward the amulets and other talismans. Sergeant Ben Air's unit, for example, was attacked on their first day patrolling the forests of Long Thanh district. "After that we had a joke: I would ask my men, 'Did you pray to your amulets today? Because if you haven't, we will certainly be shot to death.'"[28]

The Thai volunteers spoke passionately about the protective power they gained from the amulets. According to several Thai soldiers, their display of amulets and their willingness to talk about them with allied soldiers helped encourage open-minded Americans to adopt them. They suggested that those GIs searching for extra measures of protection found the amulets especially compelling. What may have appeared as a kind of Buddhist dog tag around a foreign soldier's neck quickly became a sought-after commodity for desperate Americans. Most of the time, the Thais and the Americans, and all the other "Free World" forces working in the camp, did not come in contact with each other. Their joint missions were coordinated by liaison officers from each side who passed on information and instructions through translators and radiomen. For the common soldiers of each army, their interaction in the field was limited to friendly gestures made from afar; a wave, a smile, or a shouted "hello" sufficed when the two units passed nearby each other.[29] Most Thai soldiers only interacted with those GIs searching for drugs, Thai liquor, and amulets. Only in these encounters did the Thais engage in any long or meaningful

---

[25] Siwon Kawiwon, interview with author, Chiang Mai, Thailand, August 17, 2003; Pa-nua (pseudonym), interview with author, Chiang Mai, Thailand, August 18, 2003;

[26] Tambiah, *The Buddhist Saints*, p. 203.

[27] Khamma (pseudonym), interview with author, Chiang Mai, June 13, 2003.

[28] Ben Air (pseudonym), interview with author, Chiang Mai, June 10, 2003.

[29] Thanin Yensong, interview with author, Lopburi, Thailand, June 18, 2003.

conversations with Americans. And it was only in the relationships built around amulets that the Thai troops expressed any pride or sense of accomplishment.

A Thai infantryman displays dozens of amulets and charms while cleaning his M-16 rifle in Bearcat Camp. Photo courtesy of the National Archives of Thailand

In the underground economy of illicit trade that developed between the Americans and the Thais, amulets took their place among other commodities being exchanged out of sight. Interest in acquiring Buddhist amulets often increased in the aftermath of an attack on the camp. As the Thais explained to these open-minded Americans, a Christian cross was inadequate protection against the Viet Cong's 82mm mortar rounds; in circumstances like these, the Thais maintained, only a properly blessed Buddhist amulet could do the job. Ta Khamla, an infantryman from Chiang Mai who served in South Vietnam in 1970, said:

> In Bearcat camp, whenever a shell or rocket came in, I usually saw twenty to thirty Americans go to the hospital, but only two or three Thais were injured. [The Americans would say,] "Buddha Thai number one!" If we needed a tape player or a camera, [we'd offer] an old amulet or a new amulet, [and] they would throw away their [Christian] crosses. We exchanged [amulets]

for their things. They took the amulets and wore them around their necks. They were safe and happy. "Buddha Thai number one!"[30]

Sometimes the amulets were free for the asking. Thai soldiers who wore one hundred or more of the charms commonly gave extra amulets to their newly made acquaintances. The momentary sense of camaraderie gained in the transaction, several soldiers suggested, was more valuable to the Thai amulet giver than any tape recorder or camera could have ever been. Inthon Monison, who served in a combat support company, recalled:

> There were some *farangs* [Caucasians] who came and asked me for amulets. They said, "Thailand number one Buddha!" So I gave them some. There were some black Americans and some white Americans who would do this. I gave amulets to more than ten of them. When we had nothing to do we would sit around and drink beer together. We'd meet in the PX and shake hands, and they'd ask for Buddha amulets. We'd give them the amulets and tell them that they had to *wai* [press palms together in reverence] the Buddha image. We were devout. We didn't know if the guys who took the amulets remained safe or not because we were soon separated. I can't remember who they were because there were so many of them.[31]

Most of these acquaintances were short lived. But some soldiers managed to stay in touch with their American friends for years after the war. After striking up a friendship over the gift of an amulet, one Thai soldier continued to exchange Christmas cards for years with an American whose religion he did not understand.[32]

Over time, the monolingual American soldiers even formulated a silent and somewhat reverential gesture to indicate their desire for a Buddha image. Staring at the line of Buddha images around a Thai soldier's neck, they would hold their right hand open while flashing a two-fingered peace sign with their left.[33] After a while, the Thai soldiers began to appreciate the power that these cultural artifacts had over some foreign soldiers. Private First Class Singthalesai, for example, remembers one American soldier who collapsed in tears when he discovered he had lost his Buddhist amulet.[34] Incidents like these with American amulet fanciers were often moments of revelation to the Thai troops. Far from still believing that the Americans had everything, the Thai volunteers came to understand that the GIs—these soldiers who appeared to "fight like kings," as the Thais often said—came up deficient in matters of spiritual power.[35] Montri Rasri met one American long-range reconnaissance patrol soldier who talked with great passion about how his Thai Buddhist amulet had saved his life during a recent enemy attack. Montri was impressed by the way the American dropped to his knees in extreme reverence when

---

[30] Ta Khamla, interview with author, Chiang Mai, June 20, 2003; Khamron Mahaban also talks about exchanging amulets for stereos. See Khamron Mahaban, interview with author, Kanchanaburi, September 20, 2003.

[31] Inthon Manison, interview with author, Chiang Mai, Thailand, June 13, 2003.

[32] Fluk (pseudonym), interview with author, Chiang Mai, June 12, 2003.

[33] Singthalesai (pseudonym), interview with author, Chiang Mai, July 16, 2003.

[34] Ibid.

[35] Wad Kaeokalong, interview with author, Udon Thani, October 14, 2003.

he bowed to *wai* the Buddhist charm. Montri even snapped a photograph of the American kneeling before the amulet to show his friends and family back in Thailand. Before the two men went their separate ways, the GI asked Montri if he had any extra amulets he could spare to give away.[36] Montri, who carried nearly forty amulets on him, was generous to his new American friend.[37]

The form of the amulet was important in advancing the belief in its superiority over Christian crosses. The size and shape of some amulets seemed to promote their efficacy in stopping a bullet. The formerly tiny terra cotta amulets had seemingly grown in size as a result of the surge in enthusiasm for them. Some were as large as hand mirrors. Others amulets were in the shape and approximate radius of the human heart. These large-scale amulets, especially when worn outside the uniform, boasted visually of their potential to *physically* halt the flight a bullet.

A Thai soldier in the field poses for a photo wearing protective amulets of various sizes. Photo courtesy of Narong Wonggasem

Such was the foreigners' interest in Thai amulets that even the Thai ranking officer in South Vietnam reported the phenomenon to the press back in Bangkok. Colonel

---

[36] Montri Rasi, interview with author, Kanchanaburi, September 22, 2003.

[37] Ibid.

Sanan Yuthasarnprasith, field commander of the regiment-sized Queen's Cobra unit, relayed an anecdote describing ten American radio operators working alongside the Thai forces who requested their own Buddhist amulets to wear on operations. "They really seem to believe in their power," Sanan told the *Bangkok Post*. "Some who had them were shot at while on patrol, but only their uniform was torn."[38]

Nevertheless, among the Thai soldiers, some skeptics remained. Chamlong Srimuang—a devout Buddhist and career army officer who would leave his mark on Thailand's modern history as a pivotal political figure in several significant public escapades in the decades after his return from Vietnam—sought verification of the increasingly fanatical claims made by his fellow soldiers. His test site was the Thai army's morgue. Chamlong asked the grave's registration personnel if any corpses had come in wearing amulets. The answer was yes.[39] Chamlong's demand for proof that the amulets could physically protect their wearers echoed the more rational strain of Buddhism being promoted by the Sangha in his lifetime.[40] Other soldiers who, like Chamlong, remained skeptical of the more fanatical claims did still acknowledge that the amulets provided psychological reassurance to their owners.

The US military—one office, at least—seemed to acknowledge the psychological benefit that these protective amulets afforded. In 1967, the year that Thailand first committed troops, a team from the Joint United States Public Affairs Office (JUSPAO) in South Vietnam studied the psychological effects of the magical charms on allied troops as part of a broader psychological operations program. Their observations and recommendations appeared in a short report titled "The Use of Superstitions in Psychological Operations in Vietnam."[41] JUSPAO became interested in the amulets during a study designed firstly to manipulate "superstition as an enemy vulnerability" and secondly to "accommodate superstitions of friendly forces" during military operations. According to the psychological operations officers who prepared the report, "Tampering with deeply held beliefs, seeking to turn them to your advantage[,] means in effect playing God, and it should only be attempted if one can get away with it."[42] Their research into ways to exploit matters of faith turned up amulet-related problems encountered by American troops serving alongside Southeast Asian troops. These allied forces were not Thai, but were most likely drawn from the upland groups of South Vietnam's western provinces.[43]

---

[38] Banyat Tasaneeyavej, "GIs Want Cobra Talisman," *Bangkok Post*, January 18, 1968, p. 1.

[39] Duncan McCargo, *Chamlong Srimuang and the New Thai Politics* (New York, NY: St. Martin's Press, 1997), p. 80.

[40] Chamlong's skepticism in spiritual matters endured throughout his decades in the military and in public service. As governor of Bangkok in the 1980s, Chamlong ordered city workers to remove the dilapidated spirit shrines obstructing the city's footpaths and to remove the colored ribbons from trees believed to be inhabited by spirits. The municipal workers refused, citing their fear of retribution from the *phi* (spirits) they would anger and render homeless when throwing away the shrines. See Marlane Guelden, *Thailand: Into the Spirit World* (Singapore: Times Editions, 1995), p. 89.

[41] JUSPAO, Saigon, "The Use of Superstitions in Psychological Operations in Vietnam," Psyops Policy, Policy Number 36, May 10, 1967.

[42] Ibid., p. 2.

[43] A study of the religious beliefs of the upland peoples of South Vietnam's western provinces prepared by the Special Operations Research Office at American University for the US Army in 1966 includes descriptions of amulets and other charms. See "Customs and Taboos of Selected Tribes Residing along the Western Border of the Republic of Vietnam," available through Texas Tech's online Vietnam War Archives, available at http://www.virtual.

Quoting a US Army after-action report written by an American officer, the report described practical and psychological impediments posed by the amulets:

> As we started on the patrol, we heard a lot of noise as the men walked. The advisor, who was brand new, stopped them and found hanging around their necks, dangling from their belt[s] or in their pockets, objects of stone, wood, and metal. The noise would have surely revealed our position, so the advisor collected all of the amulets and sent them back to the camp area. This proved to be a bad mistake.[44]

The troops would not fight without amulets. Half of the men deserted before the unit had moved deep into the forest. "The other half," the report concluded, "would have been better off lost, because they believed it was their time to die."[45] The fatalism and defeatism that overcame the troops prompted JUSPAO to recommend steps be taken to accommodate those allied troops who relied on Buddhist amulets and esoteric charms to protect them. The report recommended that US advisors make their foreign troops wrap the amulets in sound-absorbing material before setting out on patrol. And while the report framed the matter in terms of morale, it nonetheless had to conclude that troops who wore amulets performed better and stayed alive longer. The sixth and final recommendation of the report called for psychological operations officers to teach American commanders unfamiliar with local beliefs about the amulets and to counsel "respect for and sensitivity to" these belief systems.

There is no evidence, however, to suggest that the Americans drawn to the Thai soldiers' amulets had ever been counseled by psychological operations officers. In fact, their fascination seemed genuine and spontaneous. The enthusiasm with which the American soldiers sought out amulets and, less commonly, the *sayasat* devices became a source of enormous pride for the Thai soldiers in Bearcat Camp. It seemed to demonstrate to the Thais that in matters of spiritual power, Thai culture was superior to that of the United States. American and Australian testimonials to the efficacy of the amulets and charms convinced many Thais that their own belief in the objects' power was being confirmed by foreign and objective sources in an international setting. Unlike the duck test in Bangkok and Chamlong's inquiries at the morgue, the American testimonials in South Vietnam were entirely positive. This shared belief in the apparent efficacy of the protective devices encouraged many Thai soldiers to question the limits of American power. They concluded that all of the technological innovations and material comforts of modern America were inadequate for protecting the souls of its fighting men in Asia. In this Thai conception of the situation, the absence of these necessary defensive devices, these spiritually charged protective objects that would become so basic to the Thai warrior mentality while fighting in South Vietnam, put the American fighting man in a state of vulnerability.

This deficiency surprised the Thais who served with the Americans. They admired the Americans for their logistics, firepower, and medical technology, but

---

vietnam.ttu.edu/cgi-bin/starfetch.exe?dC0pDrlVW3Fgj2aW8AsvluGNBqX8Icm6.cJylVZOvIA KU2HG0InKcsvBxbZw0qk6FPizvTeVCYYEQOwK7YdjT1nad1N2vLWXGFf2zREh8YU/10712 19001a.pdf, accessed May 2, 2012.

[44] JUSPAO, "The Use of Superstitions in Psychological Operations in Vietnam," p. 2.

[45] Ibid.

wondered why the US military was grossly negligent in providing the means to protect individual bodies (and their attached psyches) from harm. This lack of protective charms among the American forces, many Thai soldiers decided, was one of the superpower's shortcomings. They became convinced that only an Asian culture, one that was as ancient, powerful, and refined as that of Thailand, could protect its soldiers adequately in this Asian theater of war. The devotion with which the GIs collected amulets and others charms, and the testimonials that they passed on to the Thai troops regarding their effectiveness, suggested to the Thai troops that the individual soldiers of the world's greatest army recognized this deficiency, even if their commanding officers and political leaders failed to do so.

Their physical survival and military success in South Vietnam assured many Thai soldiers of the amulets' efficacy and utility, especially when matched against the powers of an atheistic enemy fighting on behalf of a godless ideology. The Thai soldiers did not abandon their fixation on the modern—in fact, it appears to have been intensified during their time living within the American-built war infrastructure—but their Vietnam War experiences compelled many to reassess the value of traditional magic in matters of personal security and spiritual wellbeing. And they came away far more enthusiastic than they had been while first collecting these objects in their home villages and army bases. Based on the recollections of these soldiers, I would argue that Thai involvement in the Vietnam War played a role in boosting popular attitudes toward Buddhist amulets and those charms now labeled as *sayasat*. In the most direct manner, the returning veterans promoted the power and value of these objects by relaying the foreign testimonials to the people of the very same villages in which they had acquired the objects. In an age when many Thais were eagerly embracing the government's mantra of national development wrought through American aid and American-style capitalism, these Thai volunteers brought back stories of American appreciation for the rural cultures and traditions they themselves had initially ignored or spurned. Even as they pursued this American-inspired economic and political agenda, they applied the apparent lessons of Thai spiritual superiority that they had absorbed while fighting in South Vietnam. For many Thai soldiers, this revelation was their most significant and memorable experience in the war.

CHAPTER 9

CONCENTRATING PEOPLE AND ENDOGENOUS POTENCY AT THE SOUTHEAST ASIAN PERIPHERY: THE CASE OF THE *LONGAN* HOUSE ALTAR OF THE BENTIAN OF INDONESIAN BORNEO[1]

Kenneth Sillander

This chapter analyzes religious materiality among the Bentian,[2] a small group of shifting cultivators who live in a relatively remote and thinly populated upriver area of Indonesian Borneo and still largely follow traditional rituals and beliefs. The chapter explores the twofold importance of the Bentian house altar—the *longan*—and some associated ritual objects for concentrating people and potency, and the nature and rationale of the pervasive use of material objects in Bentian rituals.

A common and much studied function of religious rituals, and objects used in them, is to move people, or, alternatively, to immobilize them, either temporarily, for the duration of the rituals, or more permanently, for a period extending beyond them. Among other things, rituals function to gather people, and thereby to mobilize audiences, followers, constituencies, allies, and others. In Southeast Asia, this purpose has been most famously attributed to the grand ceremonial spectacles

[1] The fieldwork for this chapter was conducted under the auspices of Universitas Indonesia and Lembaga Ilmu Pengetahuan Indonesia, in cooperation with Isabell Herrmans from the University of Helsinki. It was funded by the Academy of Finland, The Ella and Georg Ehrnrooth Foundation, The Finnish Ministry of Education, The Nordic Institute of Asian Studies, The Nordenskiöld Society, The Swedish School of Social Science at the University of Helsinki, and The Oskar Öflund Foundation. My participation in the Asia Research Institute conference on "New Directions in the Study of Material Religion" in 2008 was enabled by a grant from the Finnish Society of Science and Letters, and the writing of this chapter by a three-year postdoctoral research project funded by the Academy of Finland (2008–10).

[2] The Bentian number about 3,500 people, who live in the province of East Kalimantan in Indonesian Borneo, close to the Central Kalimantan border. They inhabit twelve villages, most of which are located in the subdistrict of Bentian Besar in West Kutai district. My eighteen months of fieldwork among the Bentian were conducted in 1993 and 1996–97, primarily in upriver non-Christian (Kaharingan) villages.

performed in the traditional Indic kingdoms of the region, the so-called "theater states," or "galactic polities."[3] But similar political purposes are also commonly associated with ceremony in small-scale societies in the political peripheries of the region.[4] The prevalence of such political rituals in Southeast Asia may be understood against the background of demographic and social-organizational factors—low population density, frequent migration, non-ascriptive identities, absence of corporate descent groups—which traditionally made Southeast Asian social capital scarce and contested, and "control over men," as opposed to control over less scarce land, "the key to Southeast Asian social systems."[5]

Central in such Southeast Asian rituals serving to mobilize collectivities of variable size is often a category of potent material objects, which are used to promote the well-being of the organizing collectivity. In the centralized polities, such objects typically form the regalia of the ruler, while among tribal populations in the hinterlands they may be ancestral heirlooms, valuables obtained in exchange, peculiar natural objects, or severed heads. These objects often represent "inalienable possessions,"[6] and, more specifically, a subcategory of such possessions, described as "inalienable and unalienated" by Maurice Godelier.[7] In many Austronesian societies, the potent object may be a stationary object that forms part of the structure of the house.[8] Whatever their specific form, these objects are typically a principal source of potency and reproductive power in society, and connect the groups acting as their custodians to an ancestral or historical source of identity. Mediating "an authority that transcends present social and political action," they are simultaneously vested with, and invest society with, "cosmological authentication."[9]

---

[3] Clifford Geertz, *Negara: The Theatre State in Nineteenth-Century Bali* (Princeton, NJ: Princeton University Press, 1980); Stanley J. Tambiah, "The Galactic Polity in Southeast Asia," in *Culture, Thought, and Social Action: An Anthropological Perspective* (Cambridge, MA: Harvard University Press, 1985).

[4] For example, Jane Monnig Atkinson, *The Art and Politics of Wana Shamanship* (Berkeley, CA: University of California Press, 1989); Clive S. Kessler, "Conflict and Sovereignty in Kelantanese Malay Spirit Seances," in *Case Studies of Spirit Possession*, ed. Vincent Crapanzano and Vivian Garrison (New York, NY: John Wiley and Sons, 1977); Thomas A Kirsch, *Feasting and Social Oscillation: Religion and Society in Upland Southeast Asia*, Data Paper 92 (Ithaca, NY: Cornell Southeast Asia Program Publications, 1973); Anna Lowenhaupt Tsing, *In the Realm of the Diamond Queen: Marginality in an Out-of-the-Way Place* (Princeton, NJ: Princeton University Press, 1993); and Toby Alice Volkman, *Feasts of Honor: Ritual and Change in the Toraja Highlands* (Urbana, IL: University of Illinois Press, 1985).

[5] Anthony Reid, *Southeast Asia in the Age of Commerce. Volume Two: Expansion and Crisis, 1450–1680* (New Haven, CT: Yale University Press, 1993), p. 8; cf. Carter G. Bentley, "Indigenous States of Southeast Asia," *Annual Review of Anthropology* 15 (1986): 275–305; Oliver Wolters, *History, Culture, and Region in Southeast Asian Perspectives* (Singapore: Institute of Southeast Asian Studies, 1982).

[6] Annette Weiner, *Inalienable Possessions: The Paradox of Keeping while Giving* (Berkeley, CA: University of California Press, 1992).

[7] Maurice Godelier, "Some Things You Give, Some Things You Sell, but Some Things You Must Keep for Yourselves: What Mauss Did Not Say about Sacred Objects," in *The Enigma of Gift and Sacrifice*, ed. Edith Wyschogrod, Jean-Joseph Goux, and Eric Boynton (New York, NY: Fordham University Press, 2002).

[8] James Fox, "Introduction," in *Inside Austronesian Houses: Perspectives on Domestic Designs for Living*, ed. James Fox (Canberra: Australian National University, 1993).

[9] Weiner, *Inalienable Possessions*, p. 45.

This chapter analyzes a particular category of such objects in a peripheral Southeast Asian society, and the dual endeavor of acquiring potency and organizing people through them. It charts the continuities and discontinuities between the metaphysics and politics of potency at the Southeast Asian center and periphery, with special reference to how potency is mediated and constituted by material objects. The focus of the analysis is on the *longan*, along with some other objects and valuables inherited from the ancestors that are stored on or near it. I describe how the *longan* forms a multi-dimensional center of centripetal rituals of concentration, and how its ritual use testifies to a "centrist" orientation identified by Shelly Errington as characteristic for western insular Southeast Asia.[10] However, my analysis contests Errington's view that "the political geography that potency constructs for [Southeast Asian] hill tribe people is an outward-looking one."[11] Contrary to this view, I argue that Bentian potency is principally endogenous, and that the Bentian possess centers of their own at which it is sourced. Furthermore, I argue that the ritual efficacy of the *longan* and associated material objects does not so much reflect inherent potency or association with an accumulable, quasi-physical soul-substance. Instead, the efficacy of the *longan* reflects its symbolic-performative capacity to represent and enact negotiation with the spirits, and invoke the authority of what Maurice Godelier calls "the sacred," understood as "a relationship humans entertain with origins, with the origins of themselves as well as of everything around them."[12]

THE *LONGAN:* PHYSICAL DESCRIPTION AND ASSOCIATION WITH THE HOUSE

There are actually a variety of ritual objects referred to by the Bentian as *longan* (e.g., *longan bungo, longan tou, longan biowo, longan nansang, longan teraran*). The one discussed here is more specifically known as *longan teluyen*, the "ironwood *longan*," although it is also referred to as "the *longan*" for short, a vernacular usage that I will follow. All *longan* are upright, vertical structures, sometimes likened to trees. The *longan teluyen* is a roughly two-meters-tall, somewhat ungainly, cone-shaped construction consisting of some four to eight anthropomorphically carved poles (depicting *naiyu* spirits), which are connected at the base where they are inserted in holes in a rectangular or zoomorphic piece of wood (see photo on next page). The poles, which lean outwards as they reach higher, hold up a small shelf on which potent objects inherited from the ancestors are kept, such as pearls, tiger teeth, small wooden figurines, and unusually shaped stones and pieces of wood. Just above it, in a separate, lower bamboo section of the rafters to which the whole structure is fastened through rattan cords, the skulls of prominent ancestors are stored in a wooden box. At the foot of the *longan*, one or several old ceramic jars are typically stored. The *longan* is thus *associated* with some other important objects—indicating this, the ancestor skulls are referred to as *utek tuha longan*, "ancestor (or elder) skulls of the *longan*"—together with which it forms what I will call the "*longan* complex." In

---

[10] Shelly Errington, "Incestuous Twins and the House Societies of Island Southeast Asia," *Cultural Anthropology* 2,4 (1987): 403–44; Shelly Errington, *Meaning and Power in a Southeast Asian Realm* (Princeton, NJ: Princeton University Press, 1989).

[11] Errington, *Meaning and Power,* p. 292.

[12] Maurice Godelier, *The Enigma of the Gift* (Cambridge: Polity Press, 1999), p. 179.

the collective rituals in which the *longan* is used, these objects, generically designated *pusaka* (heirlooms), are used along with it. The *longan* additionally becomes a place where much of the ritual paraphernalia temporarily constructed for the event is arranged, and where a large portion of the spirits invited to the ritual are negotiated with, and said to rest (*tehur*) in between ritual activities. The *longan* thus forms a center in these rituals, in which the congregation of spirits, and human ritual participants, represents an elementary, generalized goal, as well as a means through which the participants' more ultimate goal of securing the well-being of the organizing collectivity is sought.

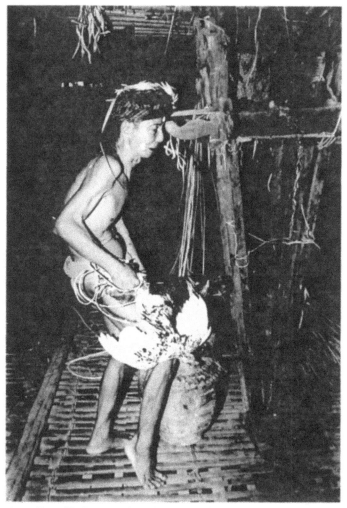

A *belian* devoting offerings to the protecting spirits at the ironwood *longan* of Sembulan village during a *buntang* ritual. Photo by Kenneth Sillander

A *longan* used to be found in most Bentian extended family houses (*lou*) and village longhouses (*lou solai*), and it is still found in a limited number of them. In these houses, it permanently occupies a particular spot, typically next to a wall somewhere in the middle of the single, unpartitioned, rectangular room, about 15 to 40 meters long, which constitutes most of these longhouses (unlike most Bornean longhouses, which are divided into family compartments). Unlike the other *longan*, and most other Bentian ritual objects, the *longan teluyen* is a permanent structure, not discarded after use and rebuilt upon the performance of new rituals, but left standing in its place.[13] As its name indicates, it is made of ironwood (*Eusideroxylon zwageri*), a tree species uniquely resistant to rot, which is identified as superior to other materials in terms of "magical power" (*kekuasaan, pengewasa*). The typical *longan* is, indeed, remarkably enduring and old—often over a hundred years— qualities that contribute to its perceived ritual efficacy, as does a commonly proposed claim that its initial construction demanded offerings of human blood. As a ritual object, it has unusually high status, being used only in rituals involving water buffalo sacrifice, in which the most powerful and authoritative beings of the Bentian spirit universe are contacted. Unlike lesser-ranking rituals, these rituals are sponsored not by households but by extended families (*buhan*), house groups (*lou*), or entire villages (*benua, desa*), and involve considerable expenditures. An important feature of the *longan*, as an example of the rich variety of worship structures used by Southeast Asian peoples, is that it organizes the enterprise of acquiring potency at the very center of society and makes it into a major collective enterprise.[14]

In terms of its basic functions and relationship with the house, in which it permanently occupies a particular location, the *longan* can be seen as the principal "ritual attractor" of the Bentian, to use a term coined by James Fox for a variable object (e.g., a house post, ladder, hearth, platform, altar) that often forms part of the structure of Austronesian houses and functions as their ritual center. Like other ritual attractors, the *longan* "represents, in a concentrated form, the house as a whole," meaning that it metonymically and symbolically stands for it, and by way of this association, provides a focus for the collective identity of its inhabitants.[15]

As Claude Lévi-Strauss[16] and a number of edited volumes on the subject[17] have demonstrated, the house in many Southeast Asian societies represents a social unit of

---

[13] Besides the *longan*, the most significant and conspicuous examples of enduring Bentian ritual objects are probably the sacrificial poles (*blontang*) and bone repositories (*temla, keriring*) erected during secondary mortuary rituals (*gombok*) and left standing as monuments of the events in open spaces in the villages or the nearby graveyards. Like the *longan*, they are also made of ironwood, but unlike it, they are not continually reused in ritual, and since they belong to the realm of death rituals (*warah*) as opposed to life rituals (*belian*), they are not a source of potency. However, like the *longan*, they are typically owned by extended families (*buhan*) or Houses (*lou*), as are most other durable Bentian ritual objects, including the soul house (*blai juus*), soul search ship (*sampan benawa*), fortune tree (*kayun tueh*), and great heavenly assembly hall (*langit balei solai*), all of which are, like the *longan*, used in *buntang* and *nalin taun* rituals.

[14] Compare, for example, the temporary *tapo'* outdoor "prayer stations" of the Berawan of northern Borneo. See Peter Metcalf, *Where Are You, Spirits: Style and Theme in Berawan Prayer* (Washington, DC: Smithsonian Institution Press, 1989).

[15] Fox, "Introduction," p. 1.

[16] Claude Lévi-Strauss, *The Way of the Masks* (London: Jonathan Cape, 1983); Claude Lévi-Strauss, *Anthropology and Myth: Lectures 1951–1982* (Oxford: Blackwell, 1987); Claude Lévi-Strauss, "Maison," in *Dictionnaire de l'ethnologie et de l'anthropologie*, ed. P. Bonte and M. Izard (Paris: Presses Universitaires de France, 1991).

[17] Charles Macdonald, ed., *De la hutte au palais: Sociétés à maisons en Asie du Sud-Est insulaire* (Paris: Editions du CNRS, 1987); James Fox, ed., *Inside Austronesian Houses: Perspectives on Domestic Designs for Living* (Canberra: Australian National University, 1993); Janet Carsten and Stephen Hugh-Jones, eds., *About the House: Lévi-Strauss and Beyond* (Cambridge: Cambridge University Press, 1995); Susan Gillespie and Rosemary Joyce, *Beyond Kinship: Social and*

the same order as kinship categories, and, as I have shown, the Bentian, too, until recently, constituted a "house society" (*société á maison*) in Lévi-Strauss's terms.[18] This means that "Houses," in the sense of social categories, as opposed to just buildings, formerly represented—and to a lesser extent still represent—important structural categories in Bentian society. Until settlement in nucleated villages was imposed upon the populace by the Sultan of Kutai and the Dutch colonial government in the late nineteenth century, most *lou*, which were then "scattered in the forest" (*sentebar saang laang*), had a *longan* that was used during the house group rituals (*buntang*) that prescribed it; the *longan* was seen as a mark and defining characteristic of a *lou*, and its autonomy and equal standing *vis-à-vis* other houses. (Any *lou* without a *longan* and ancestor skulls was, theoretically at least, not yet *lou* in a full sense, and ritually dependent on other *lou*.)[19]

The *lou* at this time represented the largest residential grouping of the Bentian. As such, it represented a largely autonomous entity, associated with a particular territory and named after some feature of the landscape in it. It formed a "minimal community" consisting of a small number of internally related conjugal families—whose core members were often related as siblings—that would periodically gather in the *lou*, while at other times staying dispersed in single-family farmhouses (*blai ume*). Even though the buildings that accommodated their gatherings, which were built of perishable materials, would be frequently rebuilt and moved, the *lou* constituted a relatively enduring social category—lasting several decades—whose endurance and continuity was symbolized by the *longan*, which would be moved and reinstalled in new houses when old ones were abandoned. The members of a *lou* identified as "one family" (*erai aben, erai buhan*), and were led by a house leader (*manti lou*) who acted as their spokesperson and controlled much of the house group's material and reproductive resources.[20] In many ways, these *lou* represented examples of "centrist" social formations, as Errington understood them, including in the sense of being preferentially endogamous, "wishfully complete and autonomous as in the Indic States," and "centered on an Ego or a set of full siblings."[21] The leaders of these *lou*, who typically belonged to or had married with their core members, also exemplified this centrist pattern of organization, since these prototypical "men of prowess" represented what one might call centers of social gravity around whom Houses and, later, village communities were formed. Through the agency of these "men of prowess," the different *lou* were able to attract members in competition with

Material Reproduction in House Societies (Philadelphia, PA: University of Pennsylvania Press, 2000); and Stephen Sparkes and Signe Howell, *The House in Southeast Asia* (London: Curzon Press, 2003).

[18] Sillander, "Houses and Social Organization among the Bentian of East Kalimantan," *Borneo Research Bulletin* 33 (2002): 82–99; Lévi-Strauss, *The Way of the Masks*, p. 174.

[19] The *longan teluyen* is, in fact, not used in all *buntang* rituals, but only those that last eight days or longer and feature water buffalo sacrifice. Four- and six-day *buntang* rituals, which only involve sacrifice of domestic chickens and pigs, instead employ the *longan teraran*, a temporary structure resembling the *longan teluyen* made of the stems of the *teraran* palm. However, when a ritual of the latter sort is performed in a house that has a *longan teluyen*, the *longan teraran* is typically erected next to the former. Thus, despite that fact that it is not used in most of the ritual activities, the *longan teluyen*, along with the rest of the *longan* complex, still receives *ngulas*, blood lustration.

[20] Sillander, "Houses and Social Organization among the Bentian of East Kalimantan."

[21] Errington,"Incestuous Twins," p. 405.

other, neighboring *lou*, with which their members could potentially also affiliate on the basis of their widely ramifying bilateral kindreds and affinal connections.[22]

The *longan* thus formed a symbol of identity and continuity of these Bentian house groups, and contributed, through its ritual use, to their integration in practice. Essential to the *longan*'s symbolical importance was its quality, shared by other ritual attractors discussed by Fox, of manifesting a concrete connection to the ancestral origins and predecessor houses of the house, from which it, along with the ancestral objects associated with it, typically had been moved. Through this connection, manifested perhaps most patently by the ancestor skulls that had belonged to the founders or other prominent members of the house group (leaders, shamans, warriors), the *longan* complex embodied the origins and social history of the house. Another crucial factor, in this respect, was that these objects endowed it with the presence of protecting spirits, attracted to it through the lustration with blood from the animals sacrificed during the rituals when the house group came together.

Bentian village longhouse (*lou solai*) surrounded by "development houses" (Sambung village). Photo by Kenneth Sillander

Hence, the *longan* complex, according to a pattern that Errington[23] identifies as characteristic for Austronesian Houses, established the *lou* as a "worship community." That is to say that the *longan* established the *lou* as a social unit constituted primarily through ritual (as opposed to structural) integration focused on sacred inherited objects (*pusaka*), while providing a motive—spirit protection and blessing—for its continuous reproduction. In this regard, it exemplified a pattern

---

[22] Wolters, *History, Culture, and Region.*

[23] Errington, "Incestuous Twins," p. 406.

characterizing both the ritual attractors of small-scale Austronesian house societies and the *pusaka* of traditional Southeast Asian polities.[24] All these objects typically index the identity and origins of socio-political units and promote their social cohesion through rituals. They are able to do so by providing, in Errington's words, "a spiritual and metaphysical *raison d'être*" for this endeavor. Achieving concentration is not just expedient for political purposes but it also involves attaining what Errington calls "centeredness," a state which is "ultimately moral as well as practical and beneficial, for to be close to the center is to be close to the ancestral potency that brings peace, fertility, safety, and effectiveness to the world."[25]

LONGAN IN VILLAGE LONGHOUSES AND COMMUNITY RITUALS

When the Bentian began to settle in nucleated villages around the turn of the twentieth century, this pattern of house organization and use of the *longan* initially persisted, but, after some time, it was partly replaced with a new pattern. This transformation was paralleled by other changes in the wider social system of the Bentian, brought about by roughly the same factors. Basically, these factors consisted of various aspects of external influence, which occasioned their increasing regional and local integration, and, for a period, increasing social hierarchy.

In the late nineteenth century, some particularly influential leaders who paid tribute to, traded with, and received honorary titles from the Sultan of Kutai led the construction of some particularly large *lou*, for which, for the first time, ironwood was used as a construction material. These buildings were intended to serve as "grand longhouses" (*lou solai*) or "community assembly halls" (*lamin adat*) of permanent villages, into which the sultanate ordered the dispersed Bentian population to congregate in order to facilitate more efficient trade and administration. Specifically, these more durable longhouses served to accommodate the entire population of village communities for the duration of a newly introduced community ritual, the *nalin taun*. This very costly ritual, typically lasting several weeks, or even months, could only be initiated by aspiring community leaders who, during tributary visits to the sultanate capital, had received small yellow pouches of unhusked red and white rice (*boias mea lemit*), a necessary ingredient in the ritual required to invoke the spirits.

In the *nalin taun*, as in the rather similar house group rituals held in extended family *lou* out of which it developed, the *longan* represented a focal point, although, in the case of *nalin taun*, the event was for entire villages, not just for house groups. This expansion of the group of participants promoted social integration on a higher structural level than before, and helped raise the status of the leaders initiating the ritual over other house group leaders and turning them into community leaders. This development was consistent with a government expectation, supported especially by these leaders, that all members of a village, encompassing several house groups, should be united and should recognize the overarching authority of a single leader holding a government title and position. Besides entailing socio-political integration and a more nucleated form of settlement, this development and the associated use of

---

[24] See, for example, Suryakenchana Omar, "Sacred Objects and the Absence of God: Ideas of *Pusaka* in Contemporary Java," paper presented at the "New Directions in the Study of Material Religion in Southeast Asia Conference," Singapore, August 14–16, 2008.

[25] Errington, *Meaning and Power*, p. 139.

the *longan* complex thus also promoted the authority and ascendancy of Bentian community leaders, another example of how this general move toward consolidation entailed employing religion in the service of politics in a way typical for *pusaka* in centralized Southeast Asian polities.

The *nalin taun* indeed formed a typical example of what Deborah Tooker refers to as "rituals of aggregation," as a designation for a form of ritual identified by Tambiah in Southeast Asian societies organized according to a "galactic polity" model.[26] These are rituals that incorporate the constituent social units (e.g., households, Houses) of a social domain (such as a village) and "recognize the protective power and status of its exemplary center and its leader."[27] In fact, the *nalin taun* served this purpose on several levels simultaneously, since it also entailed the incorporation of the local social domain within the realm of the sultanate; this incorporation was accomplished through the tributary recognition of the sultan's authority, an act necessary for obtaining the sultan's recognition of the village's official status and its leader's authority (through the deferring of titles), as well as through the use of the red-and-white rice necessary to initiate the ritual.[28] In addition, the *longan* complex supported the authority of early Bentian village leaders through a notion that the welfare of the realm was contingent upon the agency of the protecting spirits associated with its center (i.e., the *longan*). These spirits could be appeased and attracted to it principally through the performance of *nalin taun*. Thus, the ritual compounded the leaders' social authority with spiritual authority. In addition, the ritual's spiritual aspects could increase a leader's social authority, for some of the objects associated with the *longan* complex (especially the ancestor skulls and tiger teeth) played an important role as paraphernalia in the administration of customary law, the enforcement of which was a basic task of the leaders.[29]

---

[26] Deborah. E. Tooker, "Putting the Mandala in Its Place: A Practice-Based Approach to the Spatialization of Power on the Southeast Asian Periphery—The Case of the Akha," *Journal of Asian Studies* 55,2 (1996): 323–58; Tambiah, *The Galactic Polity.*

[27] Tooker, "Putting the Mandala in Its Place," p. 334.

[28] The full significance of the *nalin taun* as a ritual of aggregation and vehicle of local and regional integration cannot be discussed here. Of special interest, however, illuminating how the *nalin taun* promoted the symbolical cohesion of both the royal and the upriver realm, is the fact that the ritual was performed both in the sultanate capital of Tenggarong, for the benefit of the royal realm, and, as a perceived replica, in Bentian and other Dayak communities, for the benefit of the local realm. (The rice brought home by the tribute-paying leaders to be used in the ritual performed upriver had first been used in the *nalin taun* performed in the capital.) The performance of the ritual in the capital also provided the occasion through which the Bentian came to know about the *nalin taun*, which they would later study by observing their closely related Benuaq Dayak neighbors, who were the ones that performed it in the capital on behalf of the sultan. As all of this shows, the ritual entailed complex two-way influences and dependence between the upriver and downriver realms. Southeast Asian traffic in potency and cultural innovations between coastal/lowland "Indic States" and inland/upland tribal societies was by no means always unilateral. For a detailed analysis of the *nalin taun*, see Kenneth Sillander, "Local Integration and Coastal Connections in Interior Kalimantan: The Case of the *Nalin Taun* Ritual among the Bentian," *Journal of Southeast Asian Studies* 37,2 (2006): 315–34.

[29] Ibid., pp. 278–79. The objects stored on the *longan* exhibit a striking resemblance to the sacred *gaukang* (*gaukeng*) that legitimized the authority of the rulers and served as sources of potency in early Bugis and Makassar communities in South Sulawesi. Like those objects associated with the *longan*, these were typically strange objects, such as unusual pieces of wood or stones that had been found under mysterious circumstances by some ancestor of the communities that acted as the custodians of the objects. *Gaukang* functioned in ways similar to

For a number of decades, most house groups that settled in villages maintained lesser village *lou* and *longan*—used in House rituals of their own—and their leaders and constituencies typically only reluctantly and partially relinquished their autonomy and status. However, in response to another government instruction, especially strongly promulgated in the postcolonial era, decreeing that the population should take up residence in small and "modern," single-family village houses (*rumah pembangunan*), these independent *lou* became rarer, while the house groups affiliated with them became residentially fragmented, and lost much, albeit not all, of their importance as social units functioning on an intermediate level between the village and the domestic family. (This development would increase the autonomy of the family, as the titles and privileges held by the title-holding leaders were abolished after Indonesian independence.)

At the same time, many *longan teluyen* were discarded, so that in many Bentian villages there is just one remaining, typically located in its *lou solai*, although in other villages one or several house groups retain a *longan* of their own.[30] The *longan's* loss of importance has been especially apparent in villages where all or most of the population has converted to Christianity, a process beginning in the late 1930s, which for many people has deprived the *longan* of ritual significance or even made it into a stigmatized object associated with evil forces, thus occasioning its loss or sale.[31]

Nevertheless, in many cases house groups continue to gather in large modern-styled buildings (referred to and effectively functioning as *lou*), or in one of the few remaining traditional *lou*, and some house groups until quite recently retained forest *lou* and did not, in practice, take up village residence. All or most of the remaining *longan*, a few of which are not on continuous display but, rather, disassembled in-between rituals, are also still regularly used in ritual ceremonies, which remain, along with public speeches and collective work, a principal vehicle for the congregation and symbolical manifestation of groups that extend beyond the domestic family in Bentian society. In this usage, the *longan* represents a symbol and vehicle of publicly celebrated, but difficultly achievable, ideals—the ideals of being united with one's relatives and of maintaining a connection with one's origins. It

the regalia of the kingdoms that later developed in this area, regalia that consisted of valuables associated with royal ancestors believed to have descended from heaven. See Leonard Andaya, "Kingship-*Adat* Rivalry and Islam," *Journal of Southeast Asian Studies* 15,1 (1984): 22–42; and Thomas Gibson, *And the Sun Pursued the Moon: Symbolic Knowledge and Traditional Authority among the Makassar* (Honolulu, HI: University of Hawaii Press, 2005). This, along with the fact that all of these objects were anointed with blood, illustrates the continuum between the ancestral objects of tribal communities and the regalia of Southeast Asia kingdoms, while also suggesting that there was often considerable overlap between the ritual traditions of the Southeast Asian centers and peripheries. For some other examples of this overlap, see Ian W. Mabbett and David Chandler, *The Khmers* (Oxford: Blackwell, 1995); and Sillander, "Local Integration and Coastal Connections in Interior Kalimantan."

[30] There is now a total of some ten to fifteen traditional *lou*, and *longan*, remaining in the twelve present Bentian villages.

[31] Since the indigenous religious tradition, referred to as Kaharingan, is not officially recognized in the province of East Kalimantan—unlike in Central Kalimantan, where it is accepted as a religion (*agama*)—most Bentians are officially Christians (mostly Protestant). However, in actual practice, only about 50 percent of the Bentian population identified as true Christians in the 1990s, and of these, many occasionally took part in Kaharingan rituals, except in the two communities that were situated the farthest downriver and whose residents had first been converted to Christianity, and in which few Kaharingan followers remained.

thus forms, as I have argued elsewhere, a "node of spatio-temporal unification."[32] Religious beliefs sanction these ideals by equating social harmony and affirmation of social relationships with cosmic harmony and an ensuing state of health, fertility, and general well-being. In the face of severe crisis, such as widespread illness, extensive collective misfortune, or disturbances in the natural cycles (e.g., draught, excessive rains), the belief system postulates collective ritual, featuring symbolical reconnection with social and cosmic origins through the *longan* and other house group or community *sacra*, as the principal and most powerful means of achieving redress and revitalization.

RITUAL USE OF THE *LONGAN* AND ITS ASSOCIATION WITH POTENCY

An overview of the physical and symbolical association of the *longan* with houses and social categories suggests that a pursuit of *social integration* and *power* (especially for house group or community leaders) is closely connected with a pursuit of *potency*, understood here in a broad sense to encompass health, vitality, fertility, and prosperity. Potency, often identified with an immaterial but quasi-physical substance or energy, has been regarded as the principal good sought in Southeast Asian ritual, as well as a principal measure of social status enabling the establishment of hierarchies distinguishing between individuals, households, and social strata.[33] Focusing on the ritual use of the *longan* as my main example, I will now turn to an exploration of Bentian potency to give a picture of its nature, acquisition, origination, and association with material objects. Given that the *longan* represents the center of the supposedly most efficacious and powerful rituals—or means of any kind—available to the Bentian for overcoming collective and severe individual crises and promoting well-being, how then are the *longan*, the activities surrounding it, and these rituals in general, perceived to enable these goals? What represents potency in this connection? What are the mediating, ritually invoked forces perceived to be instrumental in generating well-being?

When we pursue answers to these questions, it is essential to focus on the *longan*'s ritual use, because when it is not involved in a ceremony, it is not the subject of much attention, or reverence—raw meat or wet clothes may be hung on it, for example. Even though it is perceived to provide protection for Houses and communities on a permanent basis because of its association with protecting spirits, Bentians rarely seek potency from a *longan* outside ritual ceremonies; this is, in fact, generally true for material objects, and potency, in Bentian society. The acquisition of spiritual potency is almost exclusively a ritual and collectively organized endeavor, generally less esoteric in character, and much less of a constant, individual

---

[32] Kenneth Sillander, *Acting Authoritatively: How Authority is Expressed through Social Action among the Bentian of Indonesian Borneo*, PhD Dissertation, University of Helsinki, Swedish School of Social Science Publications No. 17 (Helsinki: University of Helsinki Press, 2004), p. 23.

[33] See, for example, Benedict R. O'G. Anderson, "The Idea of Power in Javanese Culture," in *Culture and Politics in Indonesia*, ed. Claire Holt (Ithaca, NY: Cornell University Press, 1972); Errington, *Meaning and Power*; Ward Keeler, *Javanese Shadow Plays, Javanese Selves* (Princeton, NJ: Princeton University Press, 1987); Thomas A. Kirsch, *Feasting and Social Oscillation*; Tooker, "Putting the Mandala in Its Place"; and Wolters, *History, Culture, and Region*.

preoccupation, than the search for potency appears to be in the hierarchic state societies of the so-called centers of Southeast Asia.[34]

How, then, is the *longan* used in Bentian rituals? Even though the *longan* is, in some ways, a rather exceptional ritual object (i.e., a permanent structure used only in the most high-ranking Bentian rituals), its basic purpose is simple and shared by most ritual objects. It is meant to facilitate communication with spirits, to provide a place and object enabling spirits to become present, and to enable the transmission of offerings and rewards in exchange for blessings or other assistance. In one sense, the *longan* is but an example of the wide range of variously sized worship structures, including spirit houses (*kesali*), offering trays (*ansak, kelangkang, sangar*), "altars" (*longan*), and shrines (*balei*), which in Bentian rituals function as dwelling places or receptacles for specific spirits or offerings dedicated to them, and which together make ritual objects a conspicuous feature of Bentian rituals.

The *longan*, as an informant expressed it to me, is a "place for demonstrating devotion and making prayers" (*antai beresinta berdua*). It is a place where protecting spirits (*pengiring*), and spirit familiars assisting in the ritual activities (*mulung*), are "devoted respect and offerings" (*besemah*) and asked to provide assistance and well-being. These acts of devotion take place during *buntang* house-group and *nalin taun* community rituals. These collective rituals, which represent complex multiprogram events, are held for a variety of reasons, such as to inaugurate new houses, villages, leaders, or land opened up for cultivation, or to remedy severe illness, prolonged misfortune, or disadvantageous conditions, such as drought, epidemics, and the hot state of "listlessness" (*utas*) associated with death. In most cases, these ceremonies are held in fulfillment of a vow (*niat*) made to the spirits during an earlier, lesser-ranking ritual, and they always feature both thanksgiving and supplication to spirits.

The *longan* is of central importance in these rituals, as suggested by the fact that the expression "to raise the *longan*" (*nerek longan*) is used as a metaphor for performing them. On the first day of such an event, the *longan* is consecrated for use in the ceremony (*muat longan*, an activity involving sacrifice of a chicken), and thereafter it plays a role in a number of different program activities. Besides enabling the use of the *longan* for these subsequent activities, the act of consecration also serves to indicate that the house or village is in a liminal state of heightened connection with the spirit world for the duration of the ritual (and a subsequent period of a few days).

One such ritual activity that involves use of the *longan*, which lasts over several days, is the drawn-out recitation of origin myths (*tempuun*) recounting the origins of the sacrificial animals and plants used as construction materials for the ritual paraphernalia, and, in the case of the *nalin taun*, of the origins of mankind, the world, and much of what is important in it. This activity, performed by the ritual experts (*belian*) at the base of the *longan* to a slow and monotonous drum beat, reflects the fundamental cultural notion that the origins (*asar*) of things and practices must be recognized and ideally traced back step-by-step to enable their legitimate and efficient appropriation. Closely associated with this notion is the concept of *puun*. This word, from which *tempuun*, the word for origin myths, is derived, means "trunk" or "source," and designates, as in many Austronesian languages, individuals, groups, and houses positioned relative to others as trunks are to branches (*pakaak*) or tips (*lai*), that is, in a position as founders, initiators, leaders, or

---

[34] See Anderson, *The Idea of Power*; and Errington, *Meaning and Power*.

"owners." In this position, we find, for example, certain elders with a special, personal responsibility over particular people who can turn to them with requests for support and guidance, and the mythological and ancestral originators and "owners" of current ritual tradition, whose heritage is honored by their heirs through the *tempuun*.

Fundamentally, the recitation of *tempuun* at the base of the *longan* acknowledges the community's debt to the predecessors, "the elders who came before" (*ulun tuha one*), and it invokes the cosmological and cultural foundations of the Bentian world and society. Thereby this activity serves not only to express gratitude but also to make present-day ritual action efficacious by tapping the potency of original, exemplary acts and events, which are regarded as infinitely superior to present-day instantiations of them, in accordance with a widespread Austronesian view of the past as an unsurpassable glorious age, and subsequent history as beset with cultural and moral decline.[35] For example, the recitation of *tempuun* is seen, in a rather concrete sense, to activate or charge the ritual objects sung about with this potency, without which, I was told, they would have little or no ritual efficacy. In this context, the *longan*, together with the incense (*jemu*) burnt at its foot, serves as a pathway enabling connection with the unseen spirits being addressed—said to gather at and descend into the house along it—thus performing the same function as the twined *sarong* cloth (*penyenlenteng*) that hangs down from the ceiling during lesser-ranking curing rituals (or a spear in some other ritual contexts).

Besides a symbol of particular, proximate social origins of Houses and communities, the *longan* is thus, also, a symbol and means of connection with the original, generative forces of the world more generally, from which potency is seen ultimately to derive, including the ancestors who established the social order and engendered the people and social units that exist today, and various autochthonous and primordial spirits who created or regulate the natural and cosmic order. As we shall see, the central activities in the rituals involving use of the *longan* address these agencies, demonstrating that these rituals represent what Robert Horton labeled "rites of recreation," rituals designed to achieve revitalization through celebration and symbolic reenactment of original events and an earlier era of greater powers.[36]

The *longan* also basically functions to serve as a means and symbol of connection when the spirits at several points are "told the news" (*matek berita*) at the *longan*, an activity informing them about the purpose and progress of the rituals. In this case, a range of different spirits are addressed, including the "refined ancestor spirits" (*kelelungan*), various ambiguously human- and animal-like protecting spirits (*naiyu, timang, juwata,* and others), and different kinds of ancestral and other spirit helpers (*mulung*) that assist the ritual experts. *Matek berita* is essentially a preparatory activity, as well as an obligation; one must perform it in order to carry out the ritual, but it does not by itself generate the expected benefits of the ritual. This is basically true also for another important activity, the *besemah*, the deferential ceremonial presentation of offerings and respect, during which the same spirits are addressed at

---

[35] See, for example, Geertz, *Negara*, pp. 15–18; James Hagen, *Community in the Balance: Morality and Social Change in an Indonesian Society* (Boulder, CO: Paradigm Publishers, 2006), p. 12; Webb Keane, *Signs of Recognition: Powers and Hazards of Representation in an Indonesian Society* (Berkeley, CA: University of California Press, 1997), p. 99; and Atkinson, *The Art and Politics of Wana Shamanship*, pp. 53, 314.

[36] Robin Horton, "African Traditional Thought and Western Science," in *Rationality*, ed. Bryan R. Wilson (New York, NY: Harper & Row, 1970), pp. 167–68.

the *longan*. However, during *besemah*, the ritual experts extend requests for well-being, fertility, and prosperity from the spirits. Both *besemah* and "telling the news" are, in fact, indispensable ritual elements, without which the spirits could not be contacted or assumed to be receptive. Indeed, all the offerings, and the rituals in their entirety, are regarded as services and prestations to the spirits, and there is a general assumption that the greater the animal sacrifices, overall ritual expenditures, and human participation in the rituals, the greater will the desired spiritual rewards be.

This assumption goes some way toward explaining the general importance attributed by Bentians to *ruye*, material objects used as paraphernalia or offerings, and the fact that whenever even a small ritual is to be initiated, several forms of offerings have to be prepared; at the least, there must be incense (*jemu*) and bowls of uncooked glutinous and ordinary rice with coconut leaf decorations (*ringit*). The basic purpose of the diverse objects used in Bentian rituals is to enable an exchange relationship with the spirits for the purpose of obtaining or restoring human well-being. At least most of these objects, such as the crudely made anthropomorphic *ganti diri* figurines given to spirits in exchange for people's souls, are *means* of acquiring well-being rather than *sources* of well-being in their own right. Regarding this particular category of ritual objects, Bentians often told me that they do not, as outsiders sometimes claim, represent primitive *objects of worship*, but, rather, represent plain, utilitarian instruments of communication, as demonstrated by the fact that the participants in the rituals even spit on them (so as to connect them metonymically to the people they represent) and discard them after the ceremony has been completed.

An important reason why material objects are seen as indispensable in Bentian rituals is precisely that they have a special capacity to index social *relationships*, in which some of the actors represent givers, others receivers. This capacity is partly a function of their sensate substantiality and autonomy with respect to people (and spirits), which makes them well-adapted to serve simultaneously as extensions of and mediators between them.[37] Furthermore, the perceived indispensability of ritual objects probably also reflects an understanding that in Bentian society it is difficult for people to maintain an important lasting relationship with others if they do not exchange anything substantial—that is, objects or services (in contrast to just words). The same principle evidently applies to Bentian relations with spirits. Material objects are also perceived as essential complements to ritual speech, as they provide a base for it to rest on, a perception shared by the Anakalangese of the Indonesian island of Sumba.[38] Significantly, the two principal Bentian strategies of negotiation with spirits—"offering payment" (*sentous*) and "providing respect and offerings" (*besemah*)—which feature as distinct program activities in most Bentian rituals, correspond to the two principal forms of interaction—trade and tribute—that the Bentian have historically pursued with outsiders. Interactions with spirits, in many ways, resemble social interaction, particularly with outsiders, and the fact that this activity, mediated by sacrifice, is a central, constitutive aspect of Bentian religion indicates that the religion is essentially molded on the model of human society and that the unseen forces it identifies are predominantly conceived in an anthropomorphic idiom.

---

[37] Keane, *Signs of Recognition*, p. 92.

[38] Ibid., p. 66.

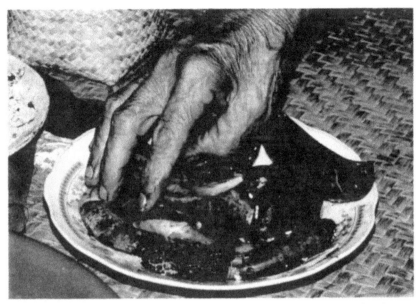

Ngulas ("blood lustration"): Anointing ancestral objects (including large feline canine teeth, stones, and an unidentified object described as spirit tongue) in the village of Sembulan during a *buntang* ritual. Photo by Kenneth Sillander

Arguably the most important activity involving use of the *longan* and the objects associated with it is *ngulas*, "blood lustration." The purpose of this all-important ritual activity—a feature of most Bentian rituals—is said to be to create "coolness" (*rengin meroe*), a pleasant and safe state involving health, fertility, and prosperity, which is opposed to one of "heat" (*layeng lihang*), associated with illness, misfortune, and death. Lustrating the *longan*, the ancestor skulls, and the ancestral valuables is variably said to have this effect or to be aimed at attracting protecting spirits to these objects, or this action can be meant to feed (*makan*) the protecting spirits already associated with the objects and the house, village, and local environment, and thus ensure that these spirits continue to provide protection and blessings. Lustration is also said to harden the souls (*petokeng juus*) of the sponsors (*dali puun awing*) and other ritual participants. Retrieving the sponsors' and other participants' souls (*pekuli juus*) from a wide range of spirits that might potentially have stolen them is, indeed, an important activity in these and most Bentian rituals. However, rather than being envisioned as "soul stuff" or an all-pervading "cosmic energy" of the kind described by Errington and Benedict Anderson, the potency sought in these rituals mainly comes in the form of spirits, and rather endless numbers of them, at that.[39] But just as with the "regalia" (*arajang*) in South Sulawesi, where, according to Errington, the concentration of potency, in the form of *sumange'* ("*soul*"), is densest in society, the concentration of potency in Bentian society, in the form of spirits, is strongest at the *longan*, at least for the duration of the rituals during which it is used. Demonstrating further correspondence with the geography of potency in "centrist" Southeast Asian societies, Bentian *ngulas* and other activities associated with the *longan* exemplify what Deborah Tooker refers to as a "center-out movement of potency," whereby

---

[39] Albert C. Kruyt, *Het Animisme in den Indischen Archipel* (Den Haag: Martinus Nijhoff, 1906).

potency (e.g., "coolness," spirit protection) is sourced at the center of a domain and from there disseminated for the benefit of its members.[40]

During *ngulas,* which together with the principal animal sacrifices preceding it represents the climax of these rituals, numerous individually named *naiyu,* the most important subgroup of the protecting spirits, are "fed" and presented requests for well-being, which participants expect will be delivered in return for the offering. The *naiyu* are a heterogeneous category of variously human- and animal-like beings— prominently characterized by a desire for blood offerings—some of which are specifically associated with the *longan* and act as house or community protecting spirits (*naiyu lou, naiyu benua*), while others are associated with the ancestor skulls (a kind of transformed ancestral spirits) and other ancestral *sacra.* The *naiyu* include, as well, a large number of autochthonous guardian spirits of the local natural environment, and some ancient primordial beings that preceded mankind.[41] Potency for the Bentian is intimately associated with the *naiyu,* to the extent that the word *naiyu* may be used metaphorically as a general designation for potency. In further testimony of this association, the *naiyu* are associated with thunder, and with heavy rains and floods (which are often interpreted as signs of their disapproval of human behavior, generally involving the violation of basic moral rules or authorized ancestral tradition). After *ngulas* has been carried out, during *makan aning,* "feeding the clean ones," cooked meat is offered to the celestial *seniang,* the most god-like spirits of the Bentian pantheon, the ultimate guardians of cosmos, nature, and society, along with the heavenly collectivity of refined ancestor spirits (*kelelungan*). These offerings, too, are accompanied by requests for well-being. Together, these activities—*ngulas* and *makan aning*—are perceived to be the most immediately efficacious activities in these rituals.

As this suggests, the state of well-being sought by the Bentian in rituals is seen to come about through the agency of spirits—or indirectly, as the result of human action influencing the actions of the spirits. The same is true for misfortune and other untoward developments, which are believed to be, typically, induced by spirits in response to violations of tradition-sanctioned, socio-moral behavior (although sometimes spirits cause misfortunes out of plain, motiveless, wickedness). According to the Bentians' world view, the blessings and misfortunes that befall people in exceptional measure, or for indeterminable reasons, are caused by the spirits. Conditions beyond the control of man are controlled by the spirits, and people's

---

[40] Tooker, "Putting the Mandala in Its Place," p. 343.

[41] See Sillander, *Acting Authoritatively,* p. 221. *Naiyu*-like spirits are referred to by cognates of the word throughout south Borneo. They exhibit intriguing resemblances with various other Southeast Asian spirit categories, including the "superhumans" of the Orang Asli peoples of peninsular Malaysia, and the *dhanyang* guardian spirits of Java. See Kirk Endicott, *Batek Negrito Religion: The World-View and Rituals of a Hunting and Gathering People of Peninsular Malaysia* (Oxford: Clarendon Press, 1979); Signe Howell, *Society and Cosmos: Chewong of Penisular Malaysia* (Chicago, IL: University of Chicago Press, 1989); and Robert Wessing, "A Community of Spirits: People, Ancestors, and Nature Spirits in Java" *Crossroads* 18,1 (2006): 11–111. Sometimes associated with aquatic snakes, the *naiyu* also resemble the widely recognized *naga,* or water dragon, spirit (although many south Borneans also recognize another sprit, known as *juata* by the Bentian, which even more closely resembles the *naga*). The association of *naiyu* with pythons and thunder echoes widespread beliefs found throughout Southeast Asia and parts of Melanesia. See Andrew Strathern and Pamela Stewart, *The Python's Back: Pathways of Comparison between Indonesia and Melanesia* (Westport, CT: Bergin & Garvey, 2000).

means of influencing these conditions primarily involve negotiation with the spirits, or behaving in ways that do not offend them in the first place.

Exactly how the spirits go about generating well-being is not clear, however, and generally not a matter of great concern. Bentians claim ignorance of the process and emphasize that spirits are invisible, impossible to know completely. Potency is mainly known through its effects, metaphorically described in terms of "coolness." Unlike in Sulawesi and various other Austronesian and Polynesian societies, there is no developed notion of a unitary, transmissible spiritual substance in the Bentian cosmology that would explain how potency is *transmitted* (in Roger Keesing's words, a "metaphycis of *mana*" has not developed here).[42] Health, fertility, prosperity, and so on may be obtained, but as the indigenous explanations of how potency is obtained through headhunting suggest, as discussed by Rodney Needham, potency is perceived as the work of the spirits—or, alternatively, as the direct outcome of ritual action (especially *ngulas*)—not as the result of the operation of a mystical force.[43]

CONCLUSION

In this chapter I have explored the symbolism, ritual use, and sociological significance of the *longan* house altar of the Bentian, a small-scale society of shifting cultivators of interior Indonesian Borneo. These aspects of the *longan* illustrate similarities in politics and religion across different societal types in Southeast Asia. The *longan* exemplifies a widely encountered category of diverse, but functionally similar, objects that index the center and origins of social domains of different scale— families, Houses, villages, polities—and serve a double function of concentrating people and potency in rituals. Such objects include the royal regalia of the former Indic States and sultanates, and the ancestral heirlooms and ritual attractors of tribal communities and Austronesian Houses. They testify to the prominence in Southeast Asian rituals of material objects as mediators of relations with non-human agencies and among people.

Formerly a defining characteristic of Bentian extended family longhouses (*lou*) and village longhouses (*lou solai*), the *longan* symbolizes house groups and village communities, and their connections with their origins, both their short-term historical origins from predecessor houses, from which the *longan* was typically moved, and generic long-term mythological origins, acknowledged through the recitation of origin myths at its base. Through its tangible form, evoking an image of growth and the origination of a clump of plants from a single source, and through its location within multi-family houses, the *longan* stands as a permanent reminder of this constitutive and derivative relationship of the house's inhabitants with their past. Like the remarkably similar Tanimbarese house altar (*tavu*) described by Susan McKinnon, it forms a symbolic representation both of the past as a "source of life" and of "the group of descendants who have issued forth from this source."[44]

The *longan* testifies to the existence of a centrist pattern of social organization and potency acquisition among the Bentian. According to the pattern identified by

---

[42] Roger Keesing, "Rethinking *Mana*," *Journal of Anthropological Research* 40,1 (1984): 137–56.

[43] Rodney Needham, "Skulls and Causality," *Man* (n.s.) 11,1 (1976): 76, 80.

[44] Susan McKinnon, *From a Shattered Sun: Hierarchy, Gender, and Alliance in the Tanimbar Islands* (Madison, WI: University of Wisconsin Press, 1991), pp. 92–94.

Errington for what she calls the "centrist archipelago"—Western insular Southeast Asia—"social and symbolic forms tend to emphasize centers."[45] My analysis confirms other observers' findings that this pattern is not restricted to the centralized polities in the coastal and lowland centers of the region.[46] At the same time, the Bentian pattern of organizing potency in space challenges Errington's somewhat contradictory idea that the ritual space of the egalitarian, noncentralized tribal communities of Southeast Asia is undifferentiated—uncentered and unhierarchical— comparable to "an egg ... composed of all white without a yolk," an idea reflecting her understanding that "the source of potency is outside it, not within it."[47]

Refuting this proposition, the Bentian have social and ritual centers—extended family and village longhouses—that represent sources of regenerative potency. These centers are marked by the *longan*, and become activated as such through what Tooker calls "rituals of aggregation," which simultaneously amount to the symbolic manifestation and concrete congregation of the social units associated with them, and the concentration of spiritual potency for the benefit of these social units.[48] "Raising the longan" (*nerek longan*), in the sense of holding a House or community ritual, entails establishing extended family and village longhouses as temporary centers of ritual activity, where invited people and spirits gather. Within this ritual space, the *longan* represents the inner center, the place where the most central ritual activities occur, and where the most potent assembled spirits are contacted to ensure fertility, prosperity, and general well-being. These spirits include the ritual officiants' ancestral spirit familiars, the protecting spirits of the house or village and its sacra, the guardian spirits of the local environment, and god-like celestial spirits charged with regulating different aspects of the social, natural, or cosmic order.

This means that the *longan* is not just a site where potency is concentrated, but a source of potency in its own right, and hence that there exists *within* Bentian society locations where endogenous potency may be directly accessed. The *longan* is both a center and a source. This contests Errington's idea that "the movement of potency in ... [Southeast Asian hill tribe] societies can be conceptualized as *lateral*, moving directionally *from the outside to the inside*."[49] The Bentian occasionally seek potency also outside society—from the forest and the downriver realm—but to access the most powerful sources of potency, they turn inward to address the originative forces of their world.

---

[45] Errington, *Meaning and Power*, p. 207.

[46] Atkinson, *Art and Politics of Wana;* and Tooker, "Putting the Mandala in its Place."

[47] Errington, *Meaning and Power*, p. 294.

[48] Tooker, "Putting the Mandala in its Place."

[49] Errington, *Meaning and Power*, p. 291 (original italics).

CHAPTER 10

BECOMING ACTIVE / ACTIVE BECOMING: PRINCE VESSANTARA SCROLLS AND THE CREATION OF A MORAL COMMUNITY

Sandra Cate and Leedom Lefferts[1]

Scholars have had much to say about *Bun Phra Wet*—the temple-based festival celebrating the life of Prince Vessantara, the penultimate incarnation of the Buddha, before the Buddha's birth as Siddharta Gautama.[2] The most ethnographically rich and detailed accounts of this festival from Northeastern Thailand (Isan) and Laos depict monks reciting or singing the prince's story (*Thet Mahachat*) throughout the night to laypeople, seated before them on the floor of the temple's meeting hall, or *sala*.[3] Patrice Ladwig characterizes the reception of the participants as far beyond merely passive listening, for the monks' dramatic song-like chanting (*thet lae*) encourages participants' emotional engagement with the moral dilemmas of this story, translatable by listeners into everyday family drama. The event shapes what Ladwig calls an "ethical subjectivity" out of the "dialogic exchange" between an "idealized moral system and the requirements of the quotidian."[4] As many have noted, listening to the recitation of the Prince Vessantara story gains great merit for the listener and increases the possibility that she or he will be reborn in the time of the future Buddha.[5]

---

[1] We thank the James H. Thompson Foundation for generously supporting our research. We are grateful also to the participants in the conference "New Directions in Material Religion," Singapore, August 14–16, 2008, for their theoretical reframing of the issues.

[2] This essay concerns Bun Phra Wet, the Northeastern Thai-Lao and Lao festival of Prince Wet (short for *Wetsandorn*, the local translation of *Vessantara*).

[3] See Stanley Jeyaraja Tambiah, *Buddhism and the Spirit Cults in North-east Thailand* (Cambridge: Cambridge University Press, 1970); and Patrice Ladwig, "Narrative Ethics: The Excess of Giving and Moral Ambiguity in the Lao Vessantara-Jataka," in *The Anthropology of Moralities*, ed. M. Heintz and J. Rasanayagam (Oxford: Berghahn/EASA, 2007).

[4] Ladwig, "Narrative Ethics," p. 2.

[5] Bonnie Pacala Brereton, *Thai Tellings of Phra Malai: Texts and Rituals Concerning a Popular Buddhist Saint* (Tempe, AZ: Program for Southeast Asian Studies, Arizona State University, 1995); and Tambiah, *Buddhism and the Spirit Cults*.

Procession with scroll, Khon Kaen, Thailand. Photograph by Leedom Lefferts

Instead of emphasizing the recitation, co-author Lefferts's earliest fieldwork notes from the *Bun Phra Wet* festival highlight instead the haunting sound of a deep gong, which grew steadily louder as a group of villagers, carrying a long scroll painted with the Vessantara story, approached the temple *(wat)* prior to the recitation. The scroll was then circumambulated around the *sala* and hung on the inside, enclosing the space of the recitation. Where did the villagers come from? Why carry the scroll instead of just hanging it? As one Isaner said, "the scrolls present the news *(khaaw)* which the people are interested in." What news?

The scroll and other material aspects of the festival remain lightly described and largely unexamined in the literature on the *Bun Phra Wet*.[6] Examining these scrolls in detail has led us to rethink how we see the *Bun Phra Wet* and what people do during the recitation and the festival as a whole.

---

[6] Brereton, *Thai Tellings*; Steven Collins, *Nirvana and Other Buddhist Felicities* (Cambridge: Cambridge University Press, 1998); Margaret Cone and Richard F. Gombrich, *The Perfect Generosity of Prince Vessantara* (Oxford: Clarendon Press, 1977); Georges Condominas, *Le bouddhisme au village: Notes ethnographiques sur les pratiques religieuses dans la société rurale lao (plaine de Vientiane)* (Vientiane: Éditions des Cahiers de France, 1998); Bernard Formoso, "Le Bun Pha Wet des Lao du Nord-est de la Thaïlande," *BEFEO* 79,2 (1992): 233–60; William J. Klausner, "Ceremonies and Festivals in a Northeastern Thai Village," in *Reflections on Thai Culture, Collected Writings of William J. Klausner* (Bangkok: The Siam Society, 2509/1960 [Reprinted 1993]), pp. 37–52; William J. Klausner, *Reflections: One Year in an Isaan Village Circa 1955* (Bangkok: Siam Reflections Publications Co., Ltd, 2005); Suriya Smutkupt, Pattana Kitiarsa, Kanokpon Diiburii, Sathapon Undaeng, and Priichaa Sriichai, *Kaan Muang Watthanathaam nay Bun Phawet Roi-et* [Cultural Politics and the Secularization of the Bun Phawes in Roi-et Market Town] (Nakhon Ratchasima Province: Suranarii Technology University, 2543/2000); Melford Spiro, *Buddhism and Society: A Great Tradition and its Burmese Vicissitudes* (Berkeley, CA: University of California Press, 1970); and Tambiah, *Buddhism and the Spirit Cults.*

Nakhon procession on *phaa yao Phra Wet* (cloth scroll), Paxong, Lao PDR.
Photograph by the authors

The scroll and its journey from the "forest" (any area outside the *wat* designated as such) to the temple offer a different, but complementary, framework for understanding this story in different performative modes. The lengthy preparations of offerings and the transformation of the temple space culminating in the installation of the narrative *Phra Wet* scroll—*phaa yao Phra Wet*—require the physical engagement of the lay congregants in cooperative activities over several weeks. The formation of subjectivities that we examine here, resulting from carrying the scroll and other preparatory activities, refocus our attention from individual states of being, states implied in and through the recitation, to the communal processes of actively becoming participants in a merit-making community. This essay thus shifts attention from the aurality of the Vessantara text in recitation to the visuality and materiality of "textual practices," processes of objectification that bring teachings and doctrine to life in the present moment in particular Buddhist communities.[7]

---

[7] Anne M. Blackburn, "Theravada Buddhism: Strategies of Knowledge and Authority," presentation at the annual meeting, Association of Asian Studies, March 14, 1999, Chicago, IL; and Daniel Miller, *Material Culture and Mass Consumption* (Oxford and New York, NY: Basil Blackwell, 1987). In her presentation, Blackburn defined textual practices as "the activities of composition, redaction, and interpretive reception that draw the contents of texts and the social values attached to texts, into the lives of particular Buddhist communities."

The teachings of Theravada Buddhism—specifically the *Dhammacakkappavatta-sutta*—set forth a conditioned relationship between humans and the sense-pleasures of the material worlds they inhabit: their bodies, relations with others, and the objects they create. This relationship of attachment or desire gives rise to *dukkha*, simply translated as "suffering,"[8] and has been posed in both Hindu and Buddhist contexts as a theological "critique of materiality."[9] In Southeast Asian Theravada Buddhist societies, the giving (*dana*) of things and of the self effects renunciation of the material world, a path to end suffering.[10] The practical and often ambiguous challenges of overcoming material attachments and of renunciation pose contradictions in the selfless, yet also selfish, nature of giving. They find widespread popular expression in the *Vessantara Jataka* (birth story) commemorating the Buddha-to-be's act of perfecting the virtue of generosity (some say "excessive generosity") and the great merit he attains through giving his wealth away. As Vessantara, he offers his kingdom's sacred elephant, his riches, his children, and, finally, his wife, all as gifts that others have requested. Tambiah says, "For all Buddhists this [story] is preeminent for its moral implications of selfless giving and its deeply moving drama that leads from tragedy to final vindication and triumph."[11]

Merit accrued through gifting thus unites materiality and sociality in a single conceptual frame, one in which people evaluate their own and others' ethical subjectivity largely though material means. The political subjectivities of the inhabitants of Northeast Thailand and Laos may be at stake as well. If we consider these processes from ethnographic and theoretical perspectives on materiality that refuse primacy to either objects or subjects, the *Phra Wet* scroll and the merit it activates reveal how "the things that people make, make people."[12]

This paper draws on ethnographic observations, interviews, and scroll documentations conducted at over two hundred *wat* during the period 2007–11. Our survey represents a small, non-scientific sample of the thousands of urban and rural *wat* in Northeast Thailand and lowland Laos. Regardless of whether a *wat* possessed or borrowed a scroll, we found tremendous variation in the timing, rituals, and sequencing of the festivals' events. While the *Vessantara Jataka* suffuses popular and religious culture throughout mainland Southeast Asia, the scrolls we examine here are concentrated in the ethnic Lao areas of the region. Some temples celebrate the *Bun Phra Wet* every three to four years, some annually or biannually, some perform the recitation of the narrative in association with other major *wat* rites, e.g., the consecration of a Buddha image and Songkhran, the Thai-Lao New Year. Some hang the scroll for the festival but do not carry it to the "forest" first. But our observations—built on decades of our research on Buddhist practices in the region—are generalizable in terms of what could be found at almost any *wat* throughout the region.

---

[8] Walpola Rahula, *What the Buddha Taught* (New York, NY: Grove Press, 1974 [1959]); and Spiro, *Buddhism and Society.*

[9] Daniel Miller, ed. *Materiality* (Durham, NC, and London: Duke University Press, 2005), p. 1.

[10] Ladwig, "Narrative Ethics," fn 6.

[11] Tambiah, *Buddhism and the Spirit Cults,* p. 160.

[12] Miller, *Materiality,* p. 38; see also A. Henare, M. Holbraad, and S. Wastell, "Introduction," in *Thinking through Things: Theorizing Artefacts Ethnographically,* ed. A. Henare, M. Holbraad, and S. Wastell (London: Routledge, 2007).

JOURNEYS AND GIFTS

Ritual in general, as anthropologists have long proposed, entails participants' movement from one social state to another.[13] The *Bun Phra Wet* involves a journey that merges one spacio-temporal state into another, one cognitive "world" into another. In an earlier effort to account for ontological, as well as practical and ritual, concerns of the Thai-Lao peoples of Isan, Lefferts observed "two alternating evocative constructions of the world before Buddhism."[14] One of these worlds, identified in narratives as the time of the creation of the very landscape inhabited by its residents, is that of *Phadaeng Nang Ai*. In a procession connected with the *Bun Bung Fai,* or rocket festival, parade contingents (*krabuang*) (re)enact key moments of the story, including the escape of the two lovers, Pha Daeng and Nang Ai, on a white horse. To speed the escape, the princess discards her jewelry and other precious objects across the landscape, and in so doing creates the topographical features and even villages that carry the couple's names today. The act of discarding or giving away precious material goods reappears in the other pre-Buddhist text, the Prince Vessantara story we consider here. Both stories construct the Isan "natural" and "cultural" worlds; both align the present with the past, in anticipation of the future. And both festivals demonstrate local notions of "agency" extending from the mind of the subjects into their environments and the objects positioned there.[15] As Lefferts observed, "The power of this event is that the people relive the origins of the context in which they live their daily lives."[16]

The movement or journey of things and people in the *Bun Phra Wet* festival—of gifts from householders to monks, of objects from outside to inside, of the scroll from "forest" to *wat*—reconfigures the space and time of celebrants who accompany Prince Vessantara and his family from the forest of their exile, long conceptualized locally as a pre-Buddhist, dangerous space, to the Buddhist space of the *sala*, where the monks will recite the story. To make the prince, his family, and his subjects "present" in the ritual, the *sala* must be transformed into the spaces of the *Phra Wet* narrative—simultaneously the prince's forest hermitage and the royal palace—acts requiring communal organization and participation. When we observe participants "becoming active" with things and the social formations by which this is accomplished, it allows us to see that, at least in this part of the Theravada Buddhist world, the entire ritual—from preparation and procession through recitation—effects a process of "active becoming," binding individual participants into a collective as the prince's subjects. One Lao fellow proclaimed *Bun Phra Wet* the most important festival of the year because "the whole village is owner of the festival."

Carrying their festival scroll dramatizes the ways in which Thai-Lao villagers "think through things."[17] Attention to the material aspects of the festival draws us into the particular contexts in which they "*act* through things" as a means of

---

[13] See, for example, Victor Turner, *The Ritual Process: Structure and Anti-Structure* (Chicago, IL: Aldine Publishing Co., 1969).

[14] H. Leedom Lefferts, Jr., "Village as Stage: Imaginative Space and Time in Rural Northeast Thai Lives," *Journal of the Siam Society* 92 (2004): 129–44.

[15] See Alfred Gell, *Art and Agency: An Anthropological Theory* (Oxford: Clarendon Press, 1998).

[16] Lefferts, *Village as Stage*, p. 134.

[17] Henare, et al., *Thinking through Things*.

achieving specific ontologies, or how they come to *"be* through things."[18] Bringing the scroll from the "forest" back to the temple, or even merely hanging the scroll around the *sala,* effects an ontological shift of participants in space and time—from the present of this community to the past of the prince's subjects who exiled him, and from the present into the future as a karmic community, born and reborn together.

THE SCROLLS' OBJECTHOOD

Phaa yao Phra Wet are routinely a meter wide and approximately twenty-five to forty-five meters in length (82 to 150 feet). While one might see a scroll as a long, potentially awkward object, the people of Northeastern Thailand and Laos have taken these bolts of cloth, embellished them with painted stories, and invented new ways to perform with them.[19] The performances we analyze here are distinctive in the collective effort required in carrying the scroll and the enactment, rather than telling, of the story through that effort. The oral recitation comes later, with the visual story enclosing the performance space either as painted murals or the scroll itself, temporarily hung around the *sala.* These long bolts have also enabled rural *wat* to install the visual equivalent of mural paintings in their small open-walled structures, similar to those in larger, more prosperous urban temples.

One of the oldest extant scrolls, now on display in the Ubon Ratchathani museum, exhibits the same painting style as the "classical" era of Thai mural painting.[20] However, nearly all the scrolls we looked at are painted in what might be deemed "folk style" by local painters or monks who, for the most part, did not have formal art school training. In addition to individual painters who specialize in painting the *pha yao Phra Wet,* several villages in northeastern Thailand now specialize in scroll production; one village produces scrolls using stencils, with finishing touches to the figures' facial features or elephants' toenails added with a black marker. Those we spoke with at the *wat* often treasure their scrolls, not for their beauty but for their age or because the scroll was their "first." That said, some shop owners indicated preferences for certain workshops' scrolls over others, proclaiming many as *mai suay* or "not beautiful." *Wat* that have not yet been able to afford a scroll simply borrow one. Some *wat* personnel made clear that the entire festival could not take place without a scroll, indicating its critical position in the festival.

As objects, scrolls move readily in and out of commodity contexts.[21] That is, they

---

[18] Morten Axel Pedersen, "Talismans of Thought: Shamanist Ontologies and Extended Cognition in Northern Mongolia," in *Thinking through Things*, pp. 141–66; and Martin Holbraad, reply to Daniel Miller posting on Material World blog, March 4, 2007, at http://blogs.nyu.edu/projects/materialworld/2006/12/thinking_through_things.html, accessed October 2008.

[19] The association of religious oral story-telling with narrative scrolls, painted banners, and leather puppets has a long history in China, India, and Southeast Asia; see Victor H. Mair, *Painting and Performance: Chinese Picture Recitation and its Indian Genesis* (Honolulu, HI: University of Hawaii Press, 1988).

[20] Jean Boisselier, *Thai Painting* (Tokyo, New York, NY, and San Francisco, CA: Kodansha, 1976).

[21] See I. Kopytoff, "The Cultural Biographies of Objects: Commoditization as Process," in *The Social Life of Things: Commodities in Cultural Perspective,* ed. A. Appadurai (Cambridge: Cambridge University Press, 1986); and Laurel Kendall, Vũ Thị Thanh Tâm, and Nguyễn Thị Thu Hương Thi, "Icon, Iconoclasm, Art Commodity: Are Objects still Agents in Vietnam?" in this volume.

are bought with and sold for money, or commissioned for a price. One Lao artist monk painted scrolls for nine million kip (about US$950). Scrolls produced quickly and nearly identically by the workshops near Mahasarakham and Ubon Ratchathani in northeastern Thailand sell for about 5000 baht (US$150) in local stores selling Buddhist paraphernalia.

Monks and laypeople do not appear to regard scrolls as "sacred" items subject to the positioning and handling taboos accorded Buddha images, although for safekeeping they are often kept securely under lock and key at rural *wat*. However, an artist's painting a story of the Buddha or a donor's commissioning such a painting are actions that generate merit, in part because representations of the stories serve to teach and extend the life of the religion, of Buddhism itself.[22] In the making of a Buddha image or the painting of a Buddha story, the material object (matter) and its meaning (merit) emerge simultaneously in processes of production.[23] The donation of the scroll or Buddha image to the temple enacts the morality proposed by the *Vessantara* narrative: selfless generosity. Thus, embodied within these objects (and locals understand this) are the scrolls' production, exchange, and festival use; people make merit "real" through these processes. Making and using the object implies merit, constituting a "process of objectification."[24]

A layperson donating a scroll or the money to purchase one also accrues merit— with the donation often noted on a colophon at the beginning or end of the scroll itself. Therefore, that the scroll takes part in monetary exchange has no effect whatsoever on its "religious place" in the field of ceremonial objects since the exchange involving the movement of scroll from layperson to *wat* is always framed as merit-making.

SPACE AND TIME TRANSFORMED

As is often the case with Buddhist narrative in general, complex structures of time appear on the scroll and in its performative use.[25] While an extended comparative visual analysis of the *phaa yao Phra Wet* is beyond the scope of this paper, all the scrolls we surveyed include at least one scene of each *kan*, or chapter, usually captioned. In newer scrolls, these scenes are divided by either frames or landscape elements; in older scrolls, scenes flow together as a continuous narrative. Our interviews with scroll painters suggest that the number of scenes and elaborative details relate directly to the length of the scroll commissioned by the patron/donor; artists often include an additional scene of the Buddha meditating throughout the night of his Enlightenment, recalling his past life as Prince Vessantara. With this additional scene, the scroll's painted narrative recapitulates the structure of the Jataka tales themselves, in which the Buddha begins with a "story of the present," the situation that has prompted the retelling of the tale, then narrates the story itself, and finally elucidates its moral and the congruence of the past situation with the present one. That is, a narration of a past event is merged with the

---

[22] Donald K. Swearer, *Becoming the Buddha: The Ritual of Image Consecration in Thailand* (Princeton, NJ: Princeton University Press, 2004), pp. 14–19.

[23] Henare, et al., *Thinking through Things*.

[24] Miller, *Materiality*.

[25] Collins, *Nirvana and Other Buddhist Felicities*.

event or moment of the narration, a performative act.[26] Some artists highlight sections that emphasize community participation and include graphic, bawdy, or localized details to appeal to a mass audience and to relocate a story of long ago into the here and now.

One scroll in Thailand includes local rock bands, one named "Rock Phu Thai," clearly identifying the celebrants in the scroll with those carrying or otherwise viewing the scroll.[27] Additional scenes of Phra Malai visiting heaven and hell, sometimes appearing at the beginning and/or end of the scroll, project the witnessing of this story into the future.

An analysis of the narrative as depicted on the scrolls, versus the narrative as recited, provides some evidence for our assertion that villagers "see" the story differently than it is rendered textually. Briefly told, the story details Prince Vessantara giving away so much of the city's wealth, especially the white elephant that symbolized the kingdom and brought rain essential for growing crops, that the citizens of the Kingdom of Sivi ask his father, the king, to exile Vessantara. The prince then decides to become a hermit; his wife, Matsi, goes with him because she loves him. Their children, a boy and a girl, go with their mother because they are attached to her. The family eventually arrives in the Himalayan forest and settles there. The citizens of Sivi become reconciled to their profligate donor when they recognize that he gives things away because it is not only in his best interests, but also in theirs. Eventually, the king and queen, Vessantara's parents, and their subject-citizens, make their way to the forest, the prince's hermitage, to beg him to return.

The text is divided into thirteen *kan*, with a total of 1,000 verses (*khathaa*).[28] Scrolls include scenes of each *kan* in variable lengths—sometimes framed by decorative borders, sometimes divided by landscape elements. A comparative analysis of five scrolls—three in Baltimore's Walters Art Museum and two from the Khon Kaen area examined in the field—explores the relative emphasis given specific events in numbers of textual verses or visual length. The largest number of verses in written or recited texts concern the prince and his acts of generosity (e.g., giving away his white elephants, other treasures of his kingdom, and his children). The scrolls make a different point. The *Nakhon*, in which the procession returns to the prince's home city, receives by far the most space. One scroll devotes almost 35 percent of its length to this one section. The panel showing the children's reunion with their royal grandparents and Chuchok eating himself to death is the second longest section on the scrolls. Significantly, the panels concerning Vessantara's gift of the children and Matsi's return to the hermitage—which Patrice Ladwig and Steven Collins pose as the emotional climax of the story-in-recitation—are only of middling importance, visually.[29]

---

[26] Sandra Cate, *Making Merit, Making Art: A Thai Temple in Wimbledon* (Honolulu, HI: University of Hawaii Press, 2003), p. 73.

[27] Ibid. Cate analyzes the narrative strategy of Thai muralists who insert genre scenes and details of their viewers' "everyday" existence as a means of drawing viewers into the action; scroll painters likewise engage their viewers.

[28] Cone and Gombrich, *The Perfect Generosity*.

[29] Ladwig, *Narrative Ethics*; and Collins, *Nirvana and Other Buddhist Felicities*.

Local band on scroll from Nakhon Phanom, Thailand. The accompanying caption reads: "(the people) working to take care of, to give (things) to the Brahmin, Old Man Chuchok." Photograph by the authors

"SOEN PHRA WET KHAW NAY MUANG": (INVITING VESSANTARA TO RETURN TO THE CITY)

The scroll makes its appearance for each festival not on the wall of the *sala wat*, but in the "forest." Why? The forest is a strange and wonderful place that resonates with Thai-Lao rural villagers because this natural world is full of strange and fearsome things.[30] The forest is the opposite of the way humans live, and no normal human would want to go live there. Before villagers install the scroll in the *sala*, they carry it to an area outside the temple grounds they have chosen as "forest," the site of the prince's exile. There monks ceremonially bless the scroll. The communicants gather and perform the usual ceremony to receive from the monks the basic commitments that fulfill Buddhist ethics. Then one of their number, usually the lay head of the *wat* committee, asks Vessantara, often played by a monk (or some other appropriate individual, i.e., a virtuous layman), to return to the city from which he has been exiled. Agreeing, and sometimes only reluctantly, Vessantara joins his wife, children, and parents—community members dressed as the story's characters. In the visual story, the royal family returns, riding on elephants. For the reenactment, some communities rent real elephants, or construct bamboo and cloth replicas that go to the forest and return by pickup truck. Finally, the participants unroll the scroll, grasp its upper edge, and carry it in procession back to the *wat*, collectively connecting with

---

[30] See Lefferts, "The *Bun Phra Wet* Painted Scrolls of Northeastern Thailand in the Walters Art Museum," *Journal, Walters Art Museum* 64/65 (2006–7): 149–70.

the *saksit*, or spiritual power, of the blessed scroll and "touching" the spirit of the prince.

Cloth, and the thread from which it is woven, figures large in the material life of Theravada Buddhist communities in this part of the world.[31] That so many people in the procession eagerly hold onto the cloth scroll (as the procession moves through the village, more people join in and take a place along the scroll) reinforces the definition of a merit-making community bounded by thread, a conduit for sacred power. In the *Kathin*, or robes-giving ceremony, we observed in Southeast Laos while conducting this research, long lengths of twisted thread (*sai sin*) were held by celebrants who in turn were encircled by those same threads to signify the boundary of the merit being accrued through the *kathin* ceremony.[32] After the monks' initial chanting, the temple-goers removed all their offerings from the central ceremonial structures (*khabuan*), went outside, and, collectively holding onto the *sai sin*, circumambulated the *sala* prior to the final act of donating their gifts to the monk. Once back inside, another length of *sai sin* was passed around to encircle the entire group of several hundred worshippers prior to the monk's acknowledging the gifts, again reinforcing the participants' sense that collective, rather than individual, merit was involved in the giving. Establishing congruence between the *Vessantara* scroll and *sai sin*, one monk in Vientiane told the congregants at his urban temple not to process with the scroll due to traffic, but rather hold a length of thread as they walk back from a beach area along the Mekong River, their "forest."[33]

To bring the cloth back is, literally, to bring the prince back, since the spirit of the prince is "in the cloth."[34] This notion of cloth embodying sacred power and the prince was rearticulated at another Lao temple, where we were told (in English) that the procession often speeds up as it nears the *wat*. Why? "Because *Phra Wet* is anxious and happy to get home." Drums, music, and people dancing complete the procession, attracting more and more people as the scroll travels through the village. From the point of view of these participants, the scroll becomes far more than a representation, a mere visual depiction, of the story; it provides the means by which the community transforms itself into the subjects of the prince. For unlike the murals or framed lithographs of this popular narrative that adorn many *sala* throughout Theravada Buddhist Southeast Asia, Thai-Lao and Lao scrolls are "murals on the move," rather than static visual representations on temple walls.[35]

---

[31] See Mattiebelle Gittinger and H. Leedom Lefferts, Jr., *Textiles and the Tai experience in Southeast Asia* (Washington, DC: The Textile Museum, 1992).

[32] Cited from Tambiah, *Buddhism and the Spirit Cults*; and Phya Anuman Rajadhon, *Life and Ritual in Old Siam: Three Studies of Thai Life and Customs* (New Haven, CT: HRAF Press, 1961).

[33] Personal communication with monk, Vat Chieng Yun, Vientiane, 2008.

[34] Cited from Margaret Chan, "Bodies for the Gods: Image Worship in Chinese Popular Religion," in this volume.

[35] Cate, *Making Merit*.

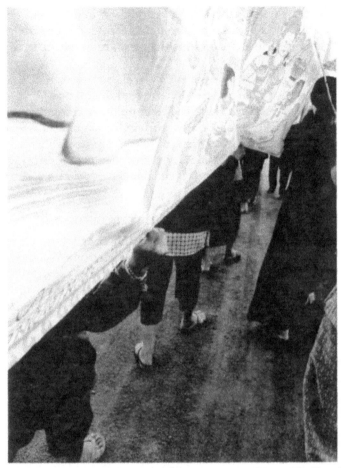

Bun Phra Wet procession in Nong Bua Lam Phuu, Thailand.
Photograph by Sandra Cate

After their arrival and circumambulation of the *sala* three times, the celebrants enter and hang the scroll inside, bringing the spirit of the prince and his family into the ritual space where the remainder of the festival will take place. Through these movements, subjects unite with objects; objects—here, the scroll—create subjects, the kingdom celebrating the return of the Buddha-to-be.

Paradoxically, when set within the larger material context of the *Bun Phra Wet*, the procession with the scroll presents the conclusion of the story before it has been recited, enacting the twelfth and thirteenth *kan*. This conundrum is best posed on one of the oldest extant scrolls, from Wat Luang in Ubon City, now installed in the National Museum in Ubon Ratchathani. On this scroll, the story line runs from left to right. The scroll ends at the right, with a scene of the people asking Prince Vessantara and his family to return. In the upper left hand corner of this final panel, an elephant is shown heading back the other way. The procession has turned back into and above the story line of the scroll. Members of the procession are repeated across the top of the scroll, going from right to left. Finally, as we return to the palace where the story began, while Phra Wet is shown giving the white elephant to the Brahmins, the returning procession enters the palace gate. In this visual performance, the *Vessantara* story resists a linear telling; it lacks a beginning, a middle, and an end where it is possible to escape. The story and the scroll, but especially the scroll, returns us to the beginning. The people in the story, just like us, are involved in coping with life in this world.[36]

The procession not only "re-locates" festival celebrants, it also "re-temporalizes" them by conflating two time periods: the pre-Buddhist time of Prince Vessantara and our time, denoted as Buddhist time. The contemporary community thus defines itself as a group of merit-making consociates, born in Vessantara's lifetime, now reborn in their contemporary community. Through collective preparations and listening to the recitation, the members of the community increase their potential to be reborn in a better, future time, through the merit they all make during the festival.

NARRATIVE AND PERFORMANCE: "A DISCOURSE ON BECOMING"

While the scroll provides the focus for the congregation's engagement with Vessantara's success, the people have also constructed the festival's physical environment to convey the immediacy of the story and conflate it with its ultimate conclusion, the coming of the Buddha. The arduous journey to the forest to ask Prince Vessantara to return to the *muang* (city) is sometimes actualized as a labyrinth constructed on the *wat* grounds. The *sala* and the *wat* are decorated so as to welcome royalty, with mats for them to walk on and the necessary royal trappings of nine-tiered umbrellas, fly whisks, and flags. The interior of the *sala* is transformed into Vessantara's hermitage and its surrounding forest. A bamboo fence demarcates the central space made royal (*parimonthon/rajawat*) and closely encompasses the *thammat*, or preaching chair. Wasps' nests, flowers made from wood, and other "forest" items hang from the ceiling, contrasting the foreignness of the family's life in exile with daily community life. The *parimonthon/rajawat* usually contains one or two pots of water with lotus buds and leaves, fish, turtles, and mud, recalling the pond where Vessantara's two children hide to escape from becoming the greedy Chuchok's servants. The scroll, now hanging around the inside of the *sala*, reinforces and provides a reference for the transformation of this physical space into that narrative space. Finally, telegraphing the coming of the Buddha, the preaching chair is garlanded with flowers, branches, and other decorations, merging Vessantara's forest hermitage with the Buddha's perfumed chamber.[37]

Producing the festival requires weeks of preparation: coordination with other local temples for monks to come to chant, construction of the forest and the palace in the *sala*, and the preparation of the many kinds of "1,000 things" that the villagers offer during the festival (e.g., cigarettes, betel chews, small paper flags, candles, incense sticks, and balls of sticky rice). When a fair accompanies the festival, villagers must make arrangements with vendors and performers and, in order to increase the merit they will receive, produce things and donate money for the "wishing tree." This coordinated, collective action of community members, materialized by plates of offerings representing the participation of each household, indexes their mobilization in the community of past, present, and future reborn communicants.[38]

---

[36] Collins, *Nirvana and Other Buddhist Felicities*, pp. 254–81.

[37] John Strong, "*Gandhakuti*: The Perfumed Chamber of the Buddha," *History of Religions* 16,4 (1977): 390–406.

[38] Cited from Tambiah, *Buddhism and the Spirit Cults*, p. 156.

The next day's recitation can be anti-climatic, with numerous distractions. The people have already participated in the merit-making aspect of the story when they made their household offerings, prepared the *wat* spaces, and processed with the scroll. Indeed, at many festivals, far fewer people actually attend the hours-long recitation than participate in its preparations and the procession. Monks reciting the story must compete with noisy processions of household members, followed by drummers, dancers, and now battery-powered music machines, bringing their *ton ngoen* or money trees as gifts to the *wat*.

Bun Phra Wet Semiotic Ideologies

The transformations of time and community effected by the ritual use of the *Phra Wet* scroll constitute a parallel to the long-studied dynamics of consecrating a Buddha image, analyzed by Donald Swearer. The "programming" of the Buddha image with his story "charges" it with the power of the Buddha's enlightenment, and endows the image with the living presence of the Buddha.[39] Both actions, consecrating a Buddha image and performing with the scroll in the *Bun Phra Wet* festival, actualize what is potentially present; they are part of the process by which the image becomes the person and the story (or stories) of the Buddha, thereby overcoming the barriers of time.[40] This actualization may in part derive from an agency attributed to both Buddha statues and Vessantara images on the scroll. With Buddha images, the locus of the activated relationship is through the eyes.[41] The *Vessantara* scroll, first painted by its artist and later blessed in the *soen Phra Wet* ceremony in the forest, manifests its agency through collective touch. The relationship here follows Alfred Gell's theory of the agency of "idols," which he conceptualizes as social others engaged in intersubjective relations with their worshippers and as alive in some sense. Worshippers do not necessarily think of idols as independent living things in the biological sense, but rather as "passive agents" with an "intentional psychology" attributed to them in the form of a "spirit, soul, and ego."[42]

This relationship between the object (the Buddha statue or the painted *Vessantara Jataka* on a scroll) and the subject reveals something about the semiotic ideology of the Thai/Lao and, indeed, Theravada Buddhists throughout Southeast Asia.[43] While it is tempting to speak of these "things" as visual representations or signs of the person or story, ethnographic observations suggest that our informants ascribe greater qualities, human-like qualities to the things. As we have tried to argue, a performative perspective applied to the *Phra Wet* scroll would overcome any distinction between the story and its depiction. The image is not merely a "sign" of the story, the signified; it *is* the story performed visually, just as the *Bun Phra Wet* procession *becomes* the story, performed kinesthetically. If we do resort to semiology

---

[39] Swearer, *Becoming the Buddha,* p. 109.

[40] Strong, "*Gandhakuti.*"

[41] Swearer, *Becoming the Buddha.*

[42] Gell, *Art and Agency,* p. 129; see also Alexandra de Mersan, "'The Land of the Great Image' and the Test of Time: The Making of Buddha Images in Arakan (Burma/Myanmar)," in this volume.

[43] Webb Keane, *Christian Moderns: Freedom and Fetish in the Mission Encounter* (Berkeley and Los Angeles, CA, and London: University of California Press, 2007).

in order to comprehend relationships among the many instances of these stories, the performances (in many genres) could be called indexical—they *are* the story and they resemble, with varying degrees of congruency, other versions in textual, aural, and visual forms.

As for the significance of these particular enactments of the story in Isan and Laos, the elaborations of the *Bun Phra Wet* festival suggest, in some ways, that Prince Vessantara is more "realistic" than the Buddha, more "human-like," with his family still around him as he succeeds. One basis for the popularity of Vessantara is the story's strong appeal to laity and its strengthening of family and community patterns, obvious in the festival preparations and the scroll's procession. In addition, the *Phra Wet* festival allows an annual community performance, whereas a Buddha image's consecration ritual happens much more infrequently.

As does the consecrated Buddha image for the viewer who beholds him, the *phaa yao Phra Wet* brings festival participants into "ontological communion" with the villagers of Vessantara's kingdom, celebrating the prince's return and the reunification of his family.[44] This ontological communion is achieved in two dimensions. First, the cloth scroll mediates social relations based on the constitutive merit exchanges between community and *wat*.[45] Patrons donate money to purchase a scroll or to commission its painting. In several instances in Northeast Thailand, schoolchildren painted a *Phra Wet* scroll for the local *wat* as an exercise in group merit-making.

Second, the scroll mediates spiritual relations. Carrying the scroll collectively activates socio-karmic relationships, ensuring that the group that makes merit together in this life will be reborn together in a next life, in a group transmigration. In his typology of socio-karma, Walters notes that all karma occurs in a social setting. Socio-karma thus represents joint acts of merit—as in the cooperative activities of the *Bun Phra Wet*. Processing with the scroll—that is, celebrants *actively becoming subjects of the Prince and accompanying his return*—explicitly reenacts the events of the narrative and suggests that the underlying intention is a "co-transmigration of the social unit."[46] The key move from the one type of socio-karma to the other is the "active production" of the group through meritorious activities that, given the workings of karma, will result in the group's future rebirth.

The *Bun Phra Wet* is also a festival of allegiance: the people have acquiesced and accepted this prince as their future king. But in Northeast Thailand, this procession also demonstrates that today's citizens now come to agree with today's ruler and his kingdom. Flags—both the Thai national flag and the yellow flag of Buddhism—are ubiquitous during this festival along the route of the procession.

---

[44] The term "ontological communion" is used by Kinnard, cited in Swearer, *Becoming the Buddha,* p. 110. Katherine Bowie has been helpful in clarifying the emphasis on family reunification in this region.

[45] Stanley J. Tambiah, *The Buddhist Saints of the Forest and the Cult of Amulets* (Cambridge: Cambridge University Press, 1984).

[46] Jonathan S. Walters, "Communal Karma and Karmic Community in Theravada Buddhist History," in *Constituting Communities: Theravada Buddhism and the Religious Culture of South and Southeast Asia,* ed. J. C. Holt, J. N. Kinnard, and J. S. Walters (Albany, NY: State University of New York [SUNY] Press, 2003), pp. 9–39, especially p. 21.

นครกัณฑ์ ๔๐ ทาวา

Procession on scroll, including Thai national flag. Photograph by the authors

Phra Wet processions in the Lao PDR also raise, but do not necessarily resolve, issues of just and righteous governance.[47]

The relationship between king, Buddhism, and subjects has undergone revision in Thai history. Patrick Jory has written that various Thai monarchs attempted to suppress the messianic readings of the *Vessantara Jataka* that were taking place in the late 1800s and early 1900s throughout Siam.[48] These attempts to displace the centrality of the *Vessantara Jataka* were intended, in part, to mute direct associations of the monarchy with *bodhisattvas*, or future Buddhas, and, in part, to keep attitudes towards state authority centralized upon the king rather than local rulers. However, while the *Bun Phra Wet* may have become a minor ceremony in central Thailand, it flourishes still in Isan and lowland Laos. Isan residents have devised a means by which they can continue to perform their preferred story—*Phra Wet*, instead of the Life of the Buddha—while still being loyal subjects.[49]

---

[47] Ladwig, *Narrative Ethics.*

[48] Patrick Jory, "The *Vessantara Jataka, Barami,* and the *Bodhissattva*-Kings: The Origin and Spread of a Thai Concept of Power," *Crossroads* 16,2 (2002): 36–78.

[49] Leedom Lefferts and Sandra Cate, "The 'Routinization of Millennialism': Impacts of Colonialism on the Ethnic Lao Festival of the Observance of the Life of Prince Vessantara," a

CONCLUSION

Through visual representation, physical enactment, and listening to the recitation of the one-thousand verses of the *Vessantara* story in a setting that recreates the story, celebrants re-engage with the immediacy and explanatory power of the narrative. These events enable them to make sense of or, at least, reconsider the struggles of their own lives—tensions in marriages, children leaving home, the economic necessities of migration and movement, the moral complexities of giving, and the obligations of family that press upon an individual's desire to follow the religious path. In addition, the procession, the activities in the *wat*, the scroll, and the story's telling all move believers from the position of observers/spectators to direct participants in the reunification of family and the ultimate triumph of the Buddha-to-be.

The festival—the preparations and the act of collectively carrying the *phaa yao Phra Wet*—accrue merit for each and merit for all, promising a better rebirth in the future. The Vessantara story lies close to the lives of the peoples of this region as it articulates the struggles of perfecting virtue, not the attainment of perfection achieved by the Buddha in his historical life. The *Phra Wet* story offers participants a modest, yet realistic and attainable, step towards becoming the Buddha. An unresolved question here would be the degree to which individual celebrants in the festival identify or take up the subject-position of the prince or Buddha-to-be.[50] It is the prince's community that appears most prominently on the *Phra Wet* scroll and in murals of the story; it is this community that the celebrants create in and through the material aspects of the event. The festival participants use the scroll to create and recreate new Buddhist subjectivities, through the performance of an alternative time and space in this world. The *Phra Wet* scrolls, and the ancillary environments they help to construct, thus provide the ultimate resource for people to believe in the Buddhist mysteries of rebirth and betterment of their karma, binding a community of believers together in the past, present, and possible future.

These ontological concerns, the creation and re-creation of moral beings, suffuse performances of the *Bun Phra Wet* and other festivals in Thai-Lao regions, but these performances resist any claim that they reassert the "tyranny of the subject" or merely reify the social formation of the laity of the temples in socio-karmic relations.[51] Why? The subjectivities that emerge out of these performances are ultimately shaped by humans interacting with objects—physically, mentally, and morally. One can easily pose a conceptual separation between subject and object, as in the case of a woman carrying her bowl of offerings to the temple, rolling hundreds of balls of sticky rice, or unrolling a scroll. Yet the meritorious production and movement of those objects through time and space, on a daily basis during alms rounds or through the heightened and materially elaborated performances of the

paper presented at the "Conference on Theravada Buddhism Under Colonialism: Adaption and Response," Institute of Southeast Asian Studies, Singapore, May 24–25, 2010.

[50] Walters poses a similar question in his analysis of communal karma, arguing that few Theravadins achieve the status of a Bodhisattva, but rather strive to become *arahants*, participants in his intimate community. See Walters, "Communal Karma," p. 26.

[51] Henare, et al., *Thinking through Things*, p. 27.

Bun Phra Wet, suggest analytic inseparability.[52] These objects, crucial to the *Bun Phra Wet,* establish particular modes of materiality, framed by Theravada Buddhist concepts of merit, as adherents think and act through things.

---

[52] Ibid., p. 1.

CHAPTER 11

THE POTENCY OF *POON*: RELIGIOUS SCULPTURE, PERFORMATIVITY, AND THE *MAHAL NA SENYOR* OF LUCBAN

Cecilia De La Paz

This chapter is an attempt to give new directions to the study of religious sculptural images in the Philippines called *poon* that are venerated in Lucban, Quezon.[1] In particular, the image of the Dead Christ called *Mahal na Senyor* ("beloved lord") will be examined in terms of how the concept of potency can be linked with the materiality of the sculpture, while its clothing and various decorations, which figure as ritualistic objects, are transformed into amulets for healing. I am interested in exploring the various ways in which people have constructed notions of "sacred" objects through the performance of rituals focused on the image of the Dead Christ. Collective community rituals (called *pag-uusong*) concerned with the fulfillment of vows, expressed through street processions by the male devotees, and rituals performed as worshippers change the clothes of the sculpture (called *pagbibihis*), are performative discourses that reveal the conflicting social relationships in the town based on social class and gender constructions. Moreover, the settings where these rituals occur also highlight the transformation of secular spaces, such as homes and town streets, into sacred spaces as liminal sites of meaning-making during the traditional Holy Week celebrations carried out by members of the Catholic faith.

While popular Catholic images that abound in the Philippine cultural landscape are dominated by the Catholic Church, this paper argues that the presence and significance of these sculptures do not just remain inside the churches. Catholic religious sculptures can be found in many private residences in almost every town and city. In many cases, community identity is built around rituals that Filipinos have practiced in caring for these private images, and, by extension, the meanings and value of these religious images, for members of the faith, have been based on these everyday experiences, rather than being influenced by the institutional Catholic Church. It is for this reason that this study seeks a better understanding of the ways Philippine religious sculptures function by considering the relevance of appropriation and performativity, thereby examining the negotiated and contested

---

[1] Lucban is located in the southeastern part of the Luzon island in the Philippines, at the foot of the "mystical" mountain called Mt. Banahaw.

meaning of culture as it is played out in everyday life in the contemporary Philippines.

FROM *SANTO* TO *POON*: THE APPROPRIATION OF RELIGIOUS IMAGES

An analysis of the *Mahal na Senyor* can be situated within the larger context of cultural and religious understandings associated with the *poon,* or privately owned religious icons. Such religious sculptures were first introduced to Filipinos, and these transactions negotiated by them, during the Spanish colonization of the islands, and these images are found in most provinces throughout the archipelago that underwent Christianization, and specifically, Catholicization. Four kinds of religious sculpture may be noted here: first are the popular icon-saints brought into the country by the colonizers, which nevertheless came to be widely venerated and important in the national psyche;[2] second are the Western-looking icons that usually represent the patron saints of various towns, and are therefore under the control of the respective local church; third are the images that are owned by rich families in the various towns in the province, which are valued as "antique" and are usually life-size and Caucasian in iconography; and fourth are the small images, considered family heirlooms, that are treasured by both rich and poor families, images characterized by an eclectic and unclear iconography.[3]

Although the Spanish colonizers introduced the concept and physical images of saints upon their arrival in the sixteenth century, the mode of reception, or how the inhabitants accepted these icons, was largely undocumented and remains unclear. We can only see glimpses of the past by reading between the lines in historical documents written by Spanish chroniclers bemoaning the fact that early Filipinos were prone to idolatry, as evidenced by the way they would sing, dance, and drink large amounts of liquor in front of wooden sculptures called *licha* during various festivities, including burials for the dead. While the chroniclers variously acknowledge that the Catholic Filipinos observe the rituals of the faith, attend masses, or even confess their "sins," the Spanish observers express bewilderment regarding the practice of Filipinos who hide or bury their traditional wooden gods in their backyards. In the lowlands, where colonial towns were built, the transition from belief in the traditional *licha* to veneration of the Catholic *santo* became inevitable as the church imposed its influence on the daily life of the settlers.

By the nineteenth century, a social class called the *mestizo,* or creole, emerged from the intermarriages between the Chinese migrants and the native population, and over time this class gained social and economic prominence. The rich *mestizo* families acquired their wealth through extensive land holdings and lucrative trading in Mexico and China. To proclaim and display their newfound wealth, they established huge ancestral houses, commissioned formal family portraits, and purchased life-size religious icons for processional purposes, as status symbols in a colonial society. Borrowing from Pierre Bourdieu's theory of the field of cultural production, we can argue that these elite families accumulated prestige through their

---

[2] Examples of these icons are the Nazareno of Quiapo, Santo Niño de Cebu, the Virgin of Antipolo, and the Virgin of Manauag, among others, which are believed to possess miraculous powers and have been appropriated to represent local and national meanings through tourism and festivals.

[3] Esperanza Gatbonton, *A Heritage of Saints* (Manila: Editorial Associates Ltd., 1979), p. 101.

ownership of religious icons, which figured as symbolic capital, in which the habitus of Catholic colonial culture was manifested as a "system of predispositions."[4] By identifying the field of cultural production as "sites of struggles in which what is at stake is the power to impose the dominant definition," Bourdieu also maintains the role of human agency as a social force that can act to change the structured habitus and field. This notion will be useful in this study, as it invites us to consider the various roles townspeople have assigned to themselves vis-à-vis a certain religious icon and how they construct social relations through the performance of specific rituals.

The value and meaning of a religious icon did not stop inside the circumscribed world of the elite families. Land tenants and employees of the elite were conscripted to carry the families' heavy images on shoulder-borne supports called *andas* during feast days and celebrations, such as those that take place during Holy Week. In other words, the icons achieved a public life that neither the local church nor the elite families of a town could completely control. Mythical stories about the statues abound, and it is said that healing powers, related to these rituals, pass from one person to another, from one generation to another. In one sense, Filipinos have constructed an alternative faith outside the purview of the institutional Catholic church by developing various rituals centering on religious icons, such as public processions, community prayers, acts of devotion, and the celebration of feasts for town saints. In addition to myths concerned with miracles and acts of healing attributed to particular icons, Filipinos have also evolved a system of knowledge and beliefs that link to an indigenous culture not necessarily consistent with Western thought.

Images of the suffering Christ (such as "the Crucified," "the Nazarene," and "the Interred"), images of the Virgin Mary from different localities, each of which identifies its own icon by baptizing it with the town's name, and secular versions of the Santo Niño all point to different ways of making meaning in relation to the icons.[5] Many contemporary studies are currently being done that focus on the *relational* aspect of a person's interactions with saints/images, examined in the context of that person's social condition—a reciprocal order with regards to the spirit world that results in *ginhawa,* or relief, from poverty and illnesses through acts of propitiation anchored in indigenous rituals.[6] It might be that the doctrinal and ethical teachings of the church that guide believers to enter "heaven" might not be important to some devotees or have been redefined to fit the context of their lives. Rather, the motives behind people's religious actions are geared toward issues concerned with everyday, earthly ambitions and struggles—occupation, recovery from illness and disease, good harvest, education, protection from natural calamities. An example of an icon that promises mundane benefits is the Virgin of Antipolo, who is considered the patron saint for travelers, especially Filipinos seeking employment abroad who frequently fly in and out of the country. In Cebu, we can

---

[4] Pierre Bourdieu, *The Field of Cultural Production: Essays on Art and Literature* (New York, NY: Columbia University Press, 1993), pp. 70–71.

[5] For a discussion of images of the Virgin Mary and the Christ Child and their cooption into Filipino secular politics, see Julius Bautista, *Figuring Catholicism: An Ethnohistory of the Santo Niño de Cebu* (Quezon City: Ateneo de Manila University Press, 2010), chap. 6.

[6] For further discussion on these, see Fenella Cannell, *Power and Intimacy in the Christian Philippines* (New York, NY: Cambridge University Press, 1999).

find the famous Santo Niño, which is worshipped through the dance of the Sinulog, performed by old women vendors as an alternative form of prayer.[7] In many ways, religiosity and faith are not abstract concepts in such contexts, but rather have materiality and, more importantly, transformative potential. Recent studies have also suggested that these religious icons now also play a role in the process of "imagining" a nation, as in the case of the Ati-Atihan festival in Aklan, which features the image of the Santo Niño; at this festival, one can see evidence that the government exploits the economic potential of religious street spectacles as an important drawing card for state-sponsored tourism.[8]

Aside from the icons that one can easily find inside churches, many more are privately owned by families, considered among the town's elites, which, more often than not, have a long genealogical history intertwined with local history and political life. The *poon* they own have public lives and archive the family's importance through the worship, or *panata*, they attract from the ordinary townsfolk. This social relationship between the private owners and public followers of a respected icon has functioned for centuries, and exists up to the present. A *panata* may be characterized as a private vow that is inherently secret, known only by the person making it. The potency of the vow—the performance of the actions involved, its purpose, and the duration of its performance—depends on the believer. A *panata* loses potency or power if it is revealed to anyone; the state of secrecy is of prime importance. Generally, the local church turns a blind eye to this kind of devotion to a particular saint. However, a *panata* is publicly performed, so that all members of one's town actually know, because they observe, that one is undergoing such a process. While the content of one's vow is private, the realization can only be achieved in the public sphere, in spaces outside the ecclesiastical jurisdiction of institutional church authority, so that rituals and myths concerning a *poon* can potentially transform secular spaces such as home interiors and street spaces into sacred spaces. This sacralization of space facilitates the patronage of amulets, or *anting-anting*, and healing practices associated with them, which involve touching the *poon* and its clothes with the amulet. This practice is believed to make it possible for a celebrant to transmit the icon's curative power to a sick relative in another location.

The term *poon* may also be connected with the material with which it was carved and sculpted—*puno*, or tree. Almost all popular *poons* that are believed to be miraculous are linked to myths describing how they originated as mysterious pieces of wood seen to be floating on rivers, lakes, or the sea, and which would eventually be found by a fisherman, farmer, or hunter. In this characteristic myth, the wood or trunk of the tree is considered as alive and organic and displays lifelike qualities that are communicated to humans through its weight when the wood/sculpture is carried. The dynamics that join the *poon* with its devotees (called *namamanata*, literally "a religious penitent who performs a vow") are based on the tactile relationship of touching, kissing, wiping, and carrying the sculptural icon—a phenomenon that points to the heightened awareness of the body's sensory capacities and perceptions. For example, meanings are constructed if the *poon* is not easily carried (*mabigat*), because this would mean the image is communicating non-

---

[7] With regards to the Sinulog dance, see Sally Ness, *Body, Movement, and Culture: Kinesthetic and Visual Symbolism in a Philippine Community* (Philadelphia, PA: University of Pennsylvania Press, 1992), chap. 6.

[8] See Bautista, *Figuring Catholicism*, chap. 7.

approval of the intended action (to be moved). On the other hand, if the *poon* were weightless (*magaan*), then it would mean that the *poon* is willing to let itself be carried to another place and is in agreement with the intention of the believer.

The common color for a miraculous *poon* is black, which we can compare to ancient images, called *licha,* of indigenous Filipinos, who deliberately blacken the wooden images of their *anito,* or ancestor spirit. Historical documents from sixteenth-century Spanish chroniclers describe the presence of *anitos* to whom daily prayers and gifts were offered. Antonio Pigafetta, Ferdinand Magellan's chronicler, who documented the fleet's 1521 arrival in the Philippine Islands, describes the painted images that the explorers found in the island of Cebu as being "made of wood, hollow, lacking back parts, arms open, and feet turned up under their legs." More significantly, Fray Juan de Plasencia wrote in 1580 that the "Tagalogs anointed their *anitos* with fragrant perfumes such as musk, civet, the gum of the storax tree [*kamanyang*], or other aromatic wood."[9] Returning to 1565 Cebu, the Spanish colonizers found an image of the Christ Child in a large house that had survived a fire that ravaged the settlement. The icon was clothed in native attire, and many flowers, given as offerings, were found before the image, and it had been anointed with oil, just as the natives did with their *anitos.*[10] It is therefore easy to relate such indigenous practices to the veneration and appropriation of the *poon* today, with the various rituals of procession, prayers, devotion, and cleaning and dressing of the icons being meaningful to Christianized Filipinos who are experiencing poverty and social inequity. Together with the network of constructed myths recognized as narratives that make claims regarding power and truth, this system of knowledge, involving ancestral and Christian icons, was created by the devotees in a way that inverts modern-day notions of "rationality" based on Western thought. The system has constructed an alternative "rationality" through the merging of indigenous practices with alien religious forms.

The devotion to a *poon* also implies the capacity of people to determine which spaces are transformed into sacred spaces, depending on the ritualistic appropriation of the icon. The usual arenas for such activities are the street and the private home, where, in both instances, the priest and doctrinal rules are absent. The ritual veneration of *poon* was also conducted during the sixteenth century in places where structures for worship were meant for individual or family affairs. Occasionally, a large gathering would be hosted in the house of the chief, where a festival, or a *mag-aanito* (spirit-possession ceremony), would be held—a four-day celebration, with continuous light and drums. According to Plasencia, on such occasions, "the house was referred to as a *simbahan,* a place of adoration."[11] These practices have been carried into the present with the traditions of Holy Week, especially the tradition of the chanting of Christ's passion, the *pabasa,* in death rituals and in festivals for the *poon.*

For the purposes of this study, a ritual may be considered as a social construct pertaining to a "special occasion" in the life of a group of people that recognizes the imperative or compulsory nature of its performance in a space and at a time agreed

---

[9] Cited by Regalado Trota Jose in *Simbahan: Church Art in Colonial Philippines, 1565–1898* (Makati: Ayala Foundation, 1991), p. 13.

[10] Bautista, *Figuring Catholicism,* pp. 65–68.

[11] Juan de Plascencia, "Customs of the Tagalogs," in *The Philippine Islands, 1493–1898,* ed. E. Blair and J. Robertson (Mandaluyong: Cacho Hermanos, 1973), p. 185.

upon. Although this might erroneously lead us to imagine a harmonious relationship within a particular society, it must be pointed out that rituals do not have a hegemonic nature, but rather are continuously contested and negotiated by social actors having divergent interests. In many ways, "rituals create and maintain, sometimes change, the cultural identity and social relations in society."[12] It is important to determine who constructs the ritual, how this is created, and which people are meant to benefit from its efficacy. Class, gender, and even ethnic "interests" create myths, and their corresponding rituals are contested in a society because of their potential to be the sources of symbolic power. This means that social recognition is given to those who perform special rituals that would lead to the potency of the *anting-anting*, or amulets. A break in the performance of ritual would mean a failure of meaning and sacredness. Women's role in cleaning the images, and the women's continuous narration of the myths, help create such an atmosphere, in conjunction with the role performed by the men, who carry the image. Both these actions satisfy *panata*, or vows, that pertain to the performance of specific roles and, as such, the actors may also be considered to be in the state of "liminality," or "in-between states," as explained in Victor Turner's work.[13] According to this theory, liminality is a state of transformation or *rites de passage*, of the kind enacted in Lucban, on Good Fridays, by barefooted male devotees, wearing identical clothing, crowded in a massive choreography of push-and-pull as they bear the glass carriage through a sea of people vying for the chance to perform their *panata*. Such a ritual may be considered a "moment in and out of time"—where a *communitas* of devotees is created, rendering all participants temporarily equal in a moment of time.[14] Rules of normal living are also temporarily suspended, so that unusual behavior is tolerated, extraordinary shows of strength are accepted, and civil law and legal law are meaningless.

Thus the normal rules of social relations are suspended during the *Mahal na Senyor* procession, with the rationalization that the worshippers are all governed by spiritual power that must be appeased every Good Friday. The sacredness of Good Friday in the Philippines is still recognized in many towns, and the holiday interpreted as a time to forgo comfort and ease, to display solidarity with others, and to perform sacrifices in the community. This is why we can consider Christian Filipinos to be experiencing the condition of liminality during the commemoration of Good Friday—a place out of time, when "God is dead." It is widely believed by the poor that many things can happen when people act out their *panata* during this time—one may receive blessings for a good harvest, relief from sickness and disease, deliverance from natural calamities, and so much more. Thus, the status of Good Friday as a sacred time opens an avenue to power and potency through the veneration of the *poon* that is strongly associated with the funeral of Christ.

---

[12] Daniel de Coppet, ed., *Understanding Rituals* (London and New York, NY: Routledge, 1992), p. i.

[13] Victor Turner, *The Ritual Process: Structure and Anti-Structure* (Chicago, IL: Aldine Publishing Co., 1969).

[14] Ibid., p. 96.

THE DEAD CHRIST, OR *MAHAL NA SENYOR,* OF LUCBAN, QUEZON

In Lucban, Quezon, the image of the Dead Christ is called *Mahal na Senyor,* or just simply "Senyor." Most townsfolk are not actually familiar with the term *Santo Entierro* (Interred Christ); rather, they regard this miraculous image as alive—as a friend, a child, a father figure, even as a landlord. The image is six feet long, carved in hardwood, and outfitted in the gold regalia of a funerary costume for its Good Friday procession; the costume is embroidered with forty symbols of the passion of Christ done in gold thread (Figure 1). Claimed to be made of solid wood (even its joints), the only parts of the body that will be seen by the viewer on an ordinary day are the head and the blackened feet. The image owns as many as forty sets of clothes in all imaginable shades, as well as bedclothes given to it by various patrons, most of whom are well-off and, significantly, residing and working in other countries. Stories abound of people who donated clothes to the icon because they felt compelled to do so; in some cases, the Senyor appears in people's dreams.

Figure 1: The *Mahal na Senyor* (April 2003). Photo by Cecilia De La Paz

The Senyor is believed to have originated in the mid-nineteenth century, but its origins are a subject for debate and dependent on the narrator of the tale. Let us consider the perspective of the owner: the Rañola clan, owners of the icon, insists on the ambiguity of the statue's origin, claiming that it came from Mexico, presumably to connect the status of the image with foreign aesthetics and market value. According to their family history, they trace the ownership of the *poon* to the year 1840 and with their prominent patriarch, Don Juan Rañola, alive at that time; the year 1840 also marked an uprising of the millenarian movement, Cofradia de San Jose of Hermano Pule.[15] Don Juan was a Chinese *mestizo* who may have owned a big

---

[15] In terms of understanding Filipino "history from below," Reynaldo Ileto discusses the importance of millenarian movements in resisting colonial power, and how they played out in both the local and national history of the Philippines. See Reynaldo Ileto, *Pasyon and*

rice mill during this time and eventually came to own a wide swath of agricultural lands, the basis of his wealth. While the Rañolas are connected by bloodlines to political families in the Philippines, they themselves have not achieved prestige and prominence by holding public office. Rather, their symbolic capital lies in their ownership of the image of the Dead Christ. When Don Juan died in the 1920s, he bequeathed the image and the associated duties and responsibilities (called *ako*) to his nine children, along with an endowment of two hectares of land given in the name of the icon. Through a system of rotation, the nine branches of the family sequentially take on the responsibility for overseeing the material needs of the icon and supervising the ritual performances for the image, along with administering its land. In other words, the image is literally a landowner, with its property called *lupa ng poon* (land of the *poon*), aptly enough. The income from this land is used by the branch of the family that has *ako* for the year; this income is employed (and more often, supplemented) for the icon's maintenance and Holy Week rituals, such as decorating the carriage for the procession and feeding the townspeople during the annual *pabasa*, the revered chanting of the Passion of Christ.

In Lucban, the free meals served during Holy Thursday and Good Friday are important traditions that determine the current social standing of the Rañola family according to the kinds of refreshments served, as would be true if they were hosting a wake for the dead. It must be pointed out that not all the Rañola descendants live in Lucban nowadays. Some are in Metro Manila, Bicol, Baguio, the United States, and Australia. Nine-year rotations, organized through the drawing of lots, determine who will have the *ako* for the following year. An *ako* year is usually seen as a blessing on that branch of the family, a blessing for which members can prepare. Depending on who "wins" for the year, the image moves from one house to another. It must stay within the town of Lucban, however, a condition that has effectively made it into a symbol of local identity for the townspeople, as they claim that the value of the image is solely understood by a native "Lucbanin."

On Good Friday, the male devotees, or *mag-uusong*, claim that the image is really owned by the townspeople who carried it back from Manila when it was returned during the late nineteenth century, after it was pawned off by the original owners (the Rilles family). Those referring to this history intend to make the point that the Rañolas are not the sole owners of the image. In this version of the tale, a meeting was called by the town elders in order to redeem the pawned image because catastrophe could befall the townspeople if the figure did not return to the town. They were able to raise the amount of 300 pesos out of the 700 pesos needed. Then Don Juan Rañola, described as *"pala-simba"* (which literally means "always attending mass"), provided the necessary 400 pesos,[16] presumably because one of his sons started dreaming about the Senyor. As the story goes, the family of the pawnbrokers in Manila started experiencing bad luck and illness, and they were happy enough to let the image go. Borne on two large wooden beams on the shoulders of the Lucban townspeople, the Senyor triumphantly crossed mountain trails to reach Lucban at last. Since Don Juan held the largest share in the statue, he became the steward of the icon. But as some devotees insist, the contributions of their forefathers, whether these involved small amounts of money or physical labor, cannot be denied. As heirs to

---

Revolution: Popular Movements in the Philippines, 1840–1910 (Quezon City: Ateneo de Manila University Press, 1979).

[16] One US dollar is equivalent to approximately 44 Philippine pesos.

their elders, the male devotees in contemporary times perpetuate the beliefs and actions of their fathers.

Male roles are centered on the *panata* of the *usong* (to carry), a public spectacle carried out in the streets, which are turned into testing grounds of faith. Power, strength, and endurance in both body and spirit are performed by the tens of thousands of *namamanata* in a communal show of strength and determination, coordination, and cooperation (Figure 2). Such a crowd can easily turn into a rowdy mob; it is the ultimate success if a Good Friday procession is achieved with minimal injuries. It is quite common in Lucban for disagreements to arise between the owner of the image of the Dead Christ and the devotees, centering mainly on the Good Friday ritual procession. Many people remember that, before World War II, the procession was typically solemn and quiet. Male devotees were dressed in clean shirts, trousers, and shoes. There was no shouting, and only the hair-raising sound of crystal glass bouncing off the glass of the carriage could be heard, as in a funeral. However, after the war, when Lucban suffered economic hardship, the Good Friday procession changed in character: the number of barefooted male devotees increased and they became generally more boisterous.

Figure 2: The male *mag-uusong* pull the ropes attached to the *andas* during a Good Friday procession (April 2004). Photo by Cecilia De La Paz

With this development came a change in the manner of the procession itself. It became a test of endurance, noisy and boisterous, marked by the stench of sweaty bodies and alcohol. Members of the Rañolas family disappeared from the procession. There had been times in the past that the Rañolas refused to let the Senyor be part of the procession, but now if they attempted to protect the statue in this way, men would storm into their house, claiming the icon. Eventually, the owners installed wheels and handbrakes onto the carriage, eliminating the traditional wooden beams. They also attached four pieces of synthetic ropes measuring twenty meters each, which were pulled by the devotees, which results in the pushing-and-pulling motion that one sees now. This innovation gave rise to a new belief—that the rope is transformed into an *anting-anting* after every Good Friday procession.

The "rope turned amulet" is said to enhance the rice harvest if placed on the nostrils of the *carabao,* or to insure a bountiful catch if used in fishing line. Handling this rope/amulet, and wiping the carriage, are the chief performative actions through which worshippers seek to acquire the "potential power" of a Good Friday procession (Figure 3). This raises two interesting points: 1) the rope turned amulet is a recent phenomena, which started in the mid-1980s, so that even modern material, like a synthetic rope, can have potential power; and 2) the power of the *anting-anting* does not rely on the materiality of the object, but is based on people's collective performance of faith through the *panata.* A combination of sacred time (Good Friday), sacred space (streets of the town), and action (*panata*) can create a belief that addresses contemporary concerns in an everyday life based on an agricultural economy.

Figure 3: A male devotee takes pieces of the rope that were cut after the procession in the belief that it becomes an *anting-anting* or amulet.
Photo by Cecilia De La Paz, April 2004

For such a small town, the procession lasts a long time, usually four to five hours, because of the slow pace of the men pushing and pulling the carriage—a spontaneous choreography based on directionality. For instance, devotees believe that when the procession goes into a road pointing to Manila, the carriage becomes heavy. One can explain this phenomenon through the topography of the town, in which roads predictably undulate because of the mountainous terrain. But the devotees will insist that the weight of the image is determined by the image itself, not the terrain, and they revel in the hardship that they have endured.

Finally, at close to ten o'clock in the evening, the Senyor is pulled into the church interior (by now, the pews have been disarranged by the people) with triumphant shouts and clapping from the bare-chested male devotees who have taken their shirts off. Some of these men will bring their sweaty T-shirts home to wipe, and heal, sick members of the family. The Senyor will stay in the church for an hour or so, where people can view it, wipe cloth on the glass carriage, kiss and touch the glass, and pray to it, until the women take over and push the carriage to the Rañola house—a role that they have taken upon themselves as "a reenactment" of the Biblical story about the women who visited the tomb of Christ, and found it empty, after his death.

Figure 4: The women devotees perform the *pagbibihis*, which entails cleaning, perfuming, and dressing the image. Photograph by Cecilia De La Paz, April 2004

According to the *manang*, or *haripoy*, as the women devotees are called, the image emerged from a miraculous sort of wood and saved the town from Japanese snipers, sexual violence, and American bombings during World War II. The women take charge of the changing of the statue's clothes every first Friday of each month, and on Holy Tuesday they dress it in its antique regalia, in preparation for Good Friday, when the *manang*, or old women, clean the statue. This ritual is called *pagbibihis*, or dressing the image (Figure 4). With cotton balls and rose perfume, their hands reach inside the bedclothes, and not once would the wooden figure be wholly revealed to anyone. (The used cotton balls and laundry water are also distributed to the sick.) It would be a privilege to see the wounds in the chest of the Senyor, and much care and respect is given to the *poon*. It is continuously talked to like a child, during the process of cleaning, as each woman communicates what she is doing—applying perfume, cleaning the eyelashes, sewing the hem, and clasping the seatbelt found inside the bed clothes. Female roles are geared towards the maternal caring for the *poon*—dressing and cleaning—combined with their role as teachers, for women lead the prayers and narrate stories and myths of the *poon,* and they identify with the biblical women who sought to care for Christ when he visited the homes of believers. Such roles point to the private spaces of the home usually identified with women. As these tasks are limited to a circle of old women, secrecy is important for them, perhaps because they play the dual role of venerating the *poon* while maintaining their roles in official church activities. Most of the unwedded or widowed old women are the prayer leaders and teachers of small children in the town, members of the Confraternity of Christian Doctrine, an organization for religiously devout women who help in the church activities. Indeed, like the *babaylans* (priestess) in precolonial times, they are the keepers of local knowledge purveyed through healing myths and stories of the miraculous Senyor, and sometimes these women conflict with the other claimants eager to serve the *poon.* They presumably know the birth date of the Senyor, which is August 21—a secret date kept from the Rañola family and the male devotees—and celebrate it in their own way. According to their version of the figure's origin, the image of the Senyor appeared in Don Juan Rañola's dream. He ordered lumber to be brought to his house. During the night, a mysterious person or carver came and sculpted the image of the Dead Christ from the wood.

These women also tell the tale of the Senyor's displeasure when a member of the Rañola family considered selling the land belonging to Senyor, or converting his rice fields through new real-estate ventures, and pointed out that there had been mud on the hem of the Senyor's gown at these times, presumably picked up when the statue visited his *lupa,* or land, to inspect it. They point out the importance of the rice fields to the Senyor, and explain how he had forced that particular owner to withdraw his suggestion to use the land for a different purpose. The symbolical power that the women held during the festival I observed is illustrated, in part, by the stories they know and repeat, and demonstrates the continuous contestation and negotiation of meaning being played out in the reconstructed faith in Lucban, combining faith and economics. One can therefore argue that the symbolic capital, in Bourdieu's sense of the word, can be claimed by the "players in the field"—so to speak—and performed throughout the year because of the liminal power that rituals and festivals provide to various sectors of society that have "truth-claims" about the Senyor.

In general, the various ways the townspeople of Lucban have claimed the Senyor as their own anchor of their own truths have shaped and produced their particular local culture, a contested and negotiated field. While one is tempted to say that power and social hierarchy are often challenged, and even inverted, in the Good Friday ritual procession in Lucban, so that the control of the statue's owners and church is muted, we still have to acknowledge that this is not a case of subversion. Rather, social hierarchies and gender roles are still affirmed, wherein class divisions are still evident. However, the contested myths and the changing ways in which the ritual is done through the years tell us that the field of culture production and social structure are open to interpretation by social actors in Lucban.

Good Friday, as a liminal day in Philippine culture, is widely acknowledged as that one time of the year when all things are possible, such as the potencies of amulets, because, presumably, God is dead. Metaphorically, this is, of course, an insult to the Catholic Church, which actively dissuades people from believing in magical objects. However, the phenomena of the Senyor of Lucban points to a similarity with another liminal period in one's life—that of death's presence and the concomitant funeral. Everyday normal rules are suspended in such an event. But is it not interesting that the Senyor is almost akin to a dead relative who needs to be washed, dressed, and interred? One only needs look at the Rañola family picture to know the validity of this claim, for official family photos almost always include the sculpture (Figure 5).

Figure 5: Photo of the Rañola family in the 1950s.
Photo courtesy of the Rañola family

Taking off from studies of the notion of the "potent dead" in Southeast Asia, one can easily see the similarities of the Senyor rituals to other regional rituals that assign the importance to rites for the dead, as ritual veneration of the dead connects the present generation to its ancestors and establishes one's reciprocal relationship with them.[17] In the mountains of the northern Philippines, the Ifugao people have an elaborate ceremony of *sang-a-chil* that involves washing and dressing the deceased as the dead body is sung to throughout the wake, during which it sits in a chair, rather than lying down. In Tana Toraja, Indonesia, the indigenous people carve wooden sculptures to represent a deceased relative, called *tau-tau*. The sculpture is believed to represent the soul of the deceased, and thus is also integral to the funeral rites of internment in mountain caves, where the image is displayed as a reminder of the power of the ancestors to influence the living.[18] The Senyor, as *poon* of the people

---

[17] Henri Chambert-Loir and Anthony Reid, eds., *The Potent Dead: Ancestors, Saints, and Heroes in Contemporary Indonesia* (Crow's Nest, NSW, and Honolulu, HI: Allen and Unwin, and University of Hawaii Press, 2002).

[18] Eric Crystal, "Rape of the Ancestors: Discovery, Display, and Destruction of the Ancestral Statuary of Tana Toraja," in *Fragile Traditions: Indonesian Art in Jeopardy*, ed. P. Taylor (Honolulu, HI: University of Hawaii Press, 1994), pp. 29–41.

who believe and perform their *panata* to it, is a link to a Southeast Asian culture that widely acknowledges the importance of ancestors in the present life. Whether the *poon* may be employed to influence the political and economic life of the living, or to intercede for good fortune and healing, the veneration of the *poon* of Lucban reverberates with the patterns of localization that the town underwent from the Spanish colonial period until the present.

CONCLUSION

In remapping the cultural studies of the Philippines as part of Southeast Asia, the study of *poon,* and its various appropriations, points to continuous constructions of social identities in the context of performative rituals. This study also enables us to observe how a particular town has ordered its world based on how social actors have appropriated religious icons in the struggle to claim spaces, truths, and meanings in the ever-changing social environment. Religious sculptures, as material cultural icons in the Philippines and Southeast Asia, resist being merely purely visual phenomena. Rather, sculptures *move* in various spaces of a community, thereby making them potential subjects for performance studies, integrating the aesthetics of everyday life and recognizing the impetus people ascribe to tactile sensory perceptions—touching, wiping, and kissing the *poon.*

It is interesting to note that local, historical memories are embodied in the *poon.* Centering on the town's survival and continuity up to the present, social family histories become significant when one considers the *poon* as the fulcrum of socially constructed identities. Also, gendered roles assume importance in the construction of meaning with regards to the *poon* and vice versa—the *poon* creates venues for gender to be socially constructed. One recognizes the importance of family and ancestors in the constitution of meaning of a *poon.* In the case of the Senyor, the image of the Dead Christ invokes a strong sense of "potency" acquired through the performance of various rituals played out by members of different classes, with different interests. Indeed, the presence of the "dead lord," interred in a home throughout the year, cared for by the townspeople, must be more than just sculpted wood; it is, rather, the embodiment of a town's *still* contested, albeit unarticulated, social history.

CHAPTER 12

BODIES FOR THE GODS: IMAGE WORSHIP IN CHINESE POPULAR RELIGION

Margaret Chan[1]

THE IMAGE OF THE GODS MAGICALLY APPEARS

In mid-September 2007, hundreds of people descended upon the otherwise quiet neighborhood of Street 42, Jurong West, in Singapore. Many were Chinese. They brought bananas, oranges, and packets of peanuts and set the offerings before a tree upon which, as if by miracle, the image of two monkeys had appeared. The *Sunday Times* newspaper reported on September 16, 2007,[2] that a few days earlier an anonymous person had placed a sign on the tree. The sign told that three years ago a monkey had come to the tree in search of its father, the legendary Monkey God. A recent car accident had split open the bark of the tree, revealing the image of the simian father and son (see Figure 1, on next page). News of the magical apparition traveled quickly and the crowds came.

Visitors tied brightly colored sashes around the tree and made offerings of joss-sticks and fruit. The tree was declared miraculous. Apparently three car accidents had happened at the spot, but none was fatal owing to the protection from the tree. Some people who had asked the Monkey God image for lucky numbers won second prize in the state lottery.

The Singapore National Parks Board was asked by the newspaper to comment on the phenomenon and came up with a prosaic announcement: several minor accidents over the years had resulted in natural callusing as the tree grew new bark over the injured areas. An associate professor from the department of biological sciences at the National University of Singapore (NUS) was also interviewed, and he

[1] I thank the Office of Research, Singapore Management University, for its kind and generous support of my research through two grants, Fund No. C242/MSS7S012 and Fund No. C242/MSS8S022. I also thank Raymond Goh, Charles Goh, Chung Kwang Tong, Jave Wu, Victor Yue, Julius Bautista, and my anonymous reviewers for their generous contributions towards my research and the writing of this chapter.

[2] Adeline Chia, (2007, 16 September), "'Monkey' Tree Draws Crowds: Tree Experts say 'Monkey' Figures are Formed by Callusing but Devotees Think Otherwise", *Sunday Times Lifestyle*: L4.

concurred with that opinion. But despite the scientific explanation, the crowds still came.

Figure 1: The Monkey God's image miraculously appeared on a tree in Singapore.
Photo by Charles Goh, used with permission

Residents complained of littering, noise, and traffic jams, and a self-appointed tree custodian began a daily watch. The newspaper quoted a man who said that, with so many people worshipping it, the Monkey God in the tree would acquire even more *lingqi* (灵气, spirit power). Here a fine distinction must be made. It was the Monkey God in the tree, not the tree itself (although nature worship of trees or rocks has a place in Chinese popular religion), that was being worshipped, in the same way that a stone on the hilltop behind the Sempalung temple in the village of Sei Raya, West Kalimantan, is revered not for itself, but because it bears the footprints of Admiral Zheng He (郑和), the deified Ming (明, 1368–1644) explorer.[3]

---

[3] Johannes Widodo, "A Celebration of Diversity: Zheng He and the Origin of the Pre-Colonial Coastal Urban Pattern in Southeast Asia," in *Admiral Zheng He and Southeast Asia*, ed. Leo Suryadinata (Singapore: Institute of Southeast Asian Studies and International Zheng He Society, 2005), pp. 104–5.

MIRACULOUS MAN-MADE IMAGES

Image worship can be traced to the dawn of Chinese civilization, and the excitement caused by the magical Monkey God tree in Singapore testifies to the currency of this belief in modern times. The Monkey God image, like Zheng He's footprints set upon a stone, noted above, provide representational evidence of the sacred in nature. Image worship, on the other hand, predominantly involves man-made objects. Statues are carved out of stone or wood, or molded using bronze or clay. Nowadays, polyresin or fiberglass is the material of choice for fabricating images. People make images because image worship allows them to assert a hold on their gods.

Human agency is a tenet of Chinese popular religion; the people's will to control their own fate stemmed, as I have argued elsewhere, from a historical response to the state cult of imperial China, which disenfranchised the common people. The worship of Tian (天 Heaven) was a prerogative of the ruling elite, so the people had to create alternative avenues for communing with their gods.[4] Spirit medium worship was one such method. It was a strategy of power, since through spirit possession gods were able to rise from within the community, and ordinary people could thereby interact face-to-face with their deities. Image worship was another way through which people ensured the presence of compliant gods.

For the Chinese, the relationship between people and their gods is contractual, rather than one involving supplication. Offerings are made for favors. This position was evident to Arthur Wolf in his study of popular religion in contemporary Taiwan; people would offer to ancestors or to deities, but they expected returns.[5] The devotees who brought fruits and peanuts to the Monkey God tree in Singapore wanted to win at the lottery. The tradition of worship as bargaining extends back to the Shang era (商, 1600–1050 BCE), when gods were promised animal and human sacrifices if they brought bountiful harvests or good health.[6] But in their dealings with gods, people largely have the upper hand.

Gods are dependent on people to give their spirits materiality through the making of anthropomorphic images, and gods gain power only if their images are worshipped, so that Valerie Hansen, writing on religion in Southern Song (南宋, 1127–1279), noted: "the gods lived, even vied, for human recognition ... Without it, they languished."[7]

---

[4] C. K. Yang, *Religion in Chinese Society: A Study of Contemporary Social Functions of Religion and Some of Their Historical Factors* (Berkeley and Los Angeles, CA: University of California Press, 1961), pp. 129–37, 183–86; Stephan Feuchtwang, "School-Temple and City God," in *Studies in Chinese Society*, ed. Arthur P. Wolf (Stanford, CA: Stanford University Press, 1978), p. 117; Margaret Chan, *Ritual Is Theatre, Theatre Is Ritual: Tang-ki Chinese Spirit Medium Worship* (Singapore: Wee Kim Wee Centre, Singapore Management University and SNP Reference, 2006), pp. 20–21.

[5] Arthur. P. Wolf, "Gods, Ghosts, and Ancestors," in *Religion and Ritual in Chinese Society*, ed. Arthur P. Wolf (Stanford, CA: Stanford University Press, 1974), pp. 161–62.

[6] David N. Keightley, "The Making of the Ancestors: Late Shang Religion and its Legacy," in *Religion and Chinese Society, 1: Ancient and Medieval China*, ed. John Lagerway (Hong Kong: The Chinese University of Hong Kong and École française d'Extrême-Orient, 2006), pp. 9–11.

[7] Valerie Hansen, *Changing Gods in Medieval China, 1127–1276* (Princeton, NJ: Princeton University Press, 1990), p. 48.

CHINESE POPULAR RELIGION AS WAY OF LIFE

In the foregoing discussion, I moved from an account of a miraculous tree in modern Singapore to describe religious practices in contemporary Taiwan, beliefs of the Song era, and rituals of Shang times. It is necessary at this point to offer some justification for this broad scope, which takes knowledge from a variety of sources over a span of four thousand years of history and from countries geographically spread over China, Taiwan, and Southeast Asia. I will begin with a definition of the term "Chinese popular religion" as it is used in this text, an explanation that is necessary in view of the scholarly contestation surrounding the notion.[8] A self-reflexive note should be useful, for it will place and explain my early understanding of Chinese religion as largely shaped by the beliefs of my paternal grandmother.

In my childhood, religious notions were a part of the everyday. I knew then (as I know today) never to step on offerings found on the sidewalks. I recall the matter-of-fact attitude that governed our practices. For example, when my grandmother died, the officiating Daoist priest said we had to use well-water to wash the body. But we did not know where to find a well in urban Singapore, so the priest said we might fetch water from a tap in a public place. The Chinese popular religion I know follows C. K. Yang's description of a total diffusion of the theological into the secular.[9]

My research into Chinese popular religion, which began in earnest in 1998, continually reveals ancient ideas that echo in current observations in the field (my research has taken me to China, Taiwan, and much of Southeast Asia), and in my memories of childhood experiences, so that I see in Chinese popular religion a confirmation of Catherine Bell's description of religion as a sociocultural system that includes fundamental values, traditional practices, and attitudes that unite people across class and region.[10]

Chinese popular religion is clearly a "little tradition" in terms of Robert Redfield's concept of a great tradition of the reflective few, and a little tradition of the largely unreflective many, where the great tradition of a civilization is often an outgrowth of the little tradition.[11] Robert Weller, however, refuses the notion that there might be a unity termed Chinese religion when viewed against the reality of the wide diversity of religious practices across China.[12] More recent methods of analysis, however, reject a priori synthetic entities such as religious institutions or traditions, and instead view culture as a dynamic system for the production of

---

[8] This is not the place to enter into the debate, and I refer readers who are interested in the discussion to Yang, *Religion in Chinese Society*; Maurice Freedman, "On the Sociological Study of Chinese Religion," in *Religion and Ritual in Chinese Society*, ed. Arthur P. Wolf (Stanford, CA: Stanford University Press, 1974), pp. 19–41; Hill Gates and Robert P. Weller, "Hegemony and Chinese Folk Ideologies: An Introduction," *Modern China Symposium on Hegemony and Chinese Folk Ideologies* 13,1 (1987): Part I, pp. 3–16; Catherine Bell, "Religion and Chinese Culture: Toward an Assessment of 'Popular Religion,'" *History of Religions* 29,1 (1989): 35–57; and Stephen F. Teiser, "Popular Religion," *The Journal of Asian Studies* 54,2 (1995): 378–95, among others.

[9] Yang, *Religion in Chinese Society*, pp. 24–25, 294–300.

[10] Bell, "Religion and Chinese Culture," p. 42.

[11] Robert Redfield, *Peasant Society and Culture: An Anthropological Approach to Civilization* (Chicago, IL: The University of Chicago Press, 1956), pp. 70–72.

[12] Robert P. Weller, *Unities and Diversities in Chinese Religion* (Houndmills, Basingstoke, Hampshire, and London: Macmillan, 1987).

meanings. Under this epistemology, unity and diversity are intrinsic to the dynamics of cultural holism.[13] As Paul Steven Sangren argues:

> Chinese religion is inseparable from the entire spectrum of discourses and texts (including, in addition to written and printed texts, all kinds of rituals, shamanism, architecture, economic transactions, knowledge, even daily conversation) through which meaning is produced, reproduced, and fought for … [14]

In these terms, Chinese popular religion exists as a dynamic of ideas from Daoism, Buddhism, and Confucianism, as well as from folk beliefs and spontaneous improvisations. Stephen F. Teiser enumerates the variety of resources that scholars have mined for insight into Chinese religion, including archaeological discoveries, historical manuscripts, private commentaries on urban life, epigraphic evidence, compilations of ghost stories, poetry, popular literature, vernacular prose and drama, and hagiographies and liturgies.[15] The material spans thousands of years and covers all regions where there are communities of Chinese people. In my discussion, I, too, have relied on an eclectic range of writings and added ethnographic findings into the mix. As practices such as the carving of god images and the *kai guang* (开光, enlightening) rituals have been well documented elsewhere,[16] I will not deal with these topics. Instead, I have accumulated evidence to put together a hermeneutic theology of image worship in Chinese popular religion.

FICTION AS *LOCUS CLASSICUS*

Meir Shahar proposes vernacular fiction as the main medium for the transmission of god cults,[17] and I have argued that mythology has provided Chinese popular religion with a dramatic canon.[18] Ancient storytellers and balladeers captured the imagination of the people with their tales of valiant warriors and supernatural heroes, and continued exposure to these stories through theater and books has concretized the images of the gods in the minds of the people to form an internalized repository of religious knowledge. All characters are anthropomorphic; a monkey, a pig, even sea creatures are essentially human. This has allowed and allows for an easy relationship between people and their gods. Gods ascribed with human aspirations can be expected to behave like people and be similarly pleased with offerings of food or theatrical entertainment.

---

[13] Bell, "Religion and Chinese Culture," pp. 42–43.

[14] Paul Steven Sangren, "Orthodoxy, Heterodoxy, and the Structure of Value in Chinese Rituals," *Modern China* 13,1 (1987): 63.

[15] Teiser, "Popular Religion," pp. 379–80.

[16] See, for example, Lin Weiping, "Conceptualizing Gods through Statues: A Study of Personification and Localization in Taiwan," *Comparative Studies in Society and History* 50,2 (2008): 454–77.

[17] Meir Shahar, "Vernacular Fiction and the Transmission of Gods' Cults in Late Imperial China," in *Unruly Gods: Divinity and Society in China*, ed. Meir Shahar and Robert P. Weller (Honolulu, HI: University of Hawaii Press, 1996), pp. 184–211.

[18] Chan, *Ritual Is Theatre*, pp. 42–55.

David K. Jordan considers the Ming (明) novel *Fengshen Yanyi* (封神演义, Creation of the Gods), which he attributes to Lu Xixing (陆西星) or Xu Zhonglin (许仲琳), to have been the most important influence on popular understanding of Daoism as a religious system,[19] a view I share, so that I have used the passages from *Fengshen Yanyi* as the *locus classicus* for my discussion on image worship. *Fengshen Yanyi* is a magical telling of the defeat of the Shang dynasty and the establishment of Zhou. The last king of Shang, Zhou (纣, not to be confused with the Zhou 周 dynasty, 1046–256 BCE), was an evil man, so that the righteous had a duty to go to war to overthrow his empire. An iconic hero who came forward in this conflict was Nezha (哪吒), son of Lijing (李靖).

NEZHA'S STATUE

I begin with the part of the story that follows Nezha's suicide in atonement for his killing of the son of the Dragon King of the East Sea.

Nezha is dead, but his soul travels to Fairy Primordial, his immortal protector. Nezha is instructed to visit his mother in a dream to ask her to build a temple to her late son and set up within it a statue of Nezha. Fairy Primordial explains that if his image is worshipped for three years, Nezha will be reincarnated in human form, enabling him to fight for Zhou against the forces of Shang.

All was done according to this plan. A stream of devotees came to offer to Nezha's statue, a lifelike image seated on a pedestal in the main hall. Half a year passed, and the people's worship of his image enabled Nezha to regain part of his shape and his voice. In turn, Nezha granted the wishes of the people, bringing them peace and prosperity. But one day, Lijing, Nezha's father, learns of the temple. Thinking that his son was cheating the people, Lijing smashed the image and had the temple set on fire.

On that day, Nezha's soul was not in the temple. He returned at dusk to find it had been burnt down. Nezha was enraged against Lijing, for by smashing Nezha's image and burning down his temple, the father had left Nezha with no place to live. Nezha returns to Fairy Primordial. Anxious that Nezha should be reincarnated in time to fight the Shang armies, Fairy Primordial assembles lotus flowers and leaves in three piles to represent heaven, earth, and man. He then adds lotus stems, broken into three hundred pieces to represent the three hundred bones. Fairy Primordial mixes his own vital energies with a little golden elixir and adds this brew to the arrangement. He then grasps Nezha's soul and throws it into the center of the assemblage. There is a tremendous bang, and Nezha is reincarnated into a handsome man of white face, red lips, shining eyes, and a sturdy body sixteen feet tall.[20]

This story presents us with many insights into image worship, chiefly; 1) a spirit incarnates itself into the mortal world in order to do work for man; 2) the spirit needs an effigy in order to reincarnate; 3) worship of the image by ordinary people empowers the spirit on which the image is modeled; and 4) the spirit is not always in

---

[19] David K. Jordan, "Brief Guide to the Most Influential Chinese Novels of the Yuan, Ming, and Qing Dynasties (XIIIth to XIXth Centuries)," http://weber.ucsd.edu/~dkjordan/chin/hbnovels-u.html, last modified November 17, 2011.

[20] Gu Zhizhong., trans., *Creation of the Gods, Vol. 1* (Beijing: New World Press, 1996), pp. 155–58.

the image, so that the image is less a body that contains the spirit than it is a portal that provides spirits access to the mortal world.

IMAGES PERMIT SPIRITS TO INCARNATE THEMSELVES AND DO WORK FOR MAN

In order to learn about the role of images in worship, I spoke to two Singaporean Daoist priests, Master Jave Wu (Daoist name Xiao Huajun, 孝华君), of the Zhengyi (正 一) sect, and Master Chung Kwangtong (庄光栋, Pinyin Zhuang Guangdong, Daoist name Weiyi, 惟义), of the Quanzhen (全真) sect. Both said that the image was not the god, but was an aid to religious contemplation. Respect was accorded the image, because it was a representation of the god. "Would a person be pleased if you treated his photograph disrespectfully, as if you hit the photo with a shoe?" asked Master Chung. I propose that Master Wu and Master Chung represent an institutional view, which is at variance with the popular understanding of the function of images.

Institutional Daoism is liturgical. It has a clerical order, and the pantheon and rituals are modeled after the state bureaucracy.[21] But Chinese popular religion, as it is practiced by the ordinary people, is founded on personalized relationships between gods and people.[22] Stephan Feuchtwang, in his discussion of religion and authority, notes how commoners require an everyday responsiveness from the statues of their gods; in contrast, the state officiant "expects only the rarer, more selective, event of loyal rescue by some less concrete spiritual appearance."[23]

While the orthodox view is that statues are aids for visualization, the popular belief is that image worship is about getting gods to do work. Thus, Nezha was re-incarnated to fight in the ranks of Zhou against the Shang armies. Barend Ter Haar recounts a folklore tale of the salt lake district of Xiezhou (解州), in Shanxi (山西). During the Yuanyou era (元佑, 1086–1093), salt production declined due to problems that were held to be caused by the monster Chi You (蚩尤). The deified Guan Yu (关羽) appeared to the people in dreams to tell them that, while he would deal with Chi You, only Zhang Fei (张飞), the god's sworn brother, could defeat Chi You's wife.[24] Accordingly, the people set up an image of Zhang Fei in the local temple. That evening, there was a violent thunderstorm, and the next morning the people found the statue of Zhang Fei holding a chain wrapped about a piece of rotten wood. The wicked wife of the monster had been captured, and subsequently the yield of salt increased tenfold.

But gods were not summoned only to do grand tasks such as fighting wars. Valerie Hansen writes of a total assimilation of the gods into the everyday lives of the people during the Song era. The gods became members of the household since statues were installed on most home altars.[25] People could talk to their gods directly

---

[21] Emily Martin Ahern, *Chinese Ritual and Politics* (Cambridge: Cambridge University Press, 1981).

[22] Weller, *Unities and Diversities.*

[23] Stephan Feuchtwang, "Historical Metaphor: A Study of Religious Representation and the Recognition of Authority," *Man* 28,1 (1993): 47.

[24] Barend J. Ter Haar, "The Rise of the Guan Yu Cult: The Daoist Connection," in *Linked Faiths: Essays on Chinese Religions and Traditional Culture in Honour of Kristofer Schipper*, ed. Jan A. M. Jan De Meyer and Peter M. Engelfriet (Leiden: Brill, 1999), pp. 197–98.

[25] Yang, *Religion in Chinese Society*, p. 16.

through their images, and the gods, like people, desired paper cash and meat. Gods were also fastidious about their images being true likenesses and insisted that their statues be kept in good repair.

Hansen notes that people catered to the wishes of the gods, but, in turn, demanded a direct response from those same gods, so when bandits could not get the permission from the deities to burn down a city, they attempted to drown the god images. A local magistrate praying for rain ensured that he had secured the attention of the god by imprisoning its image; he also threatened to destroy its temple if rain was not produced in three days.[26]

The Song era saw the rise of Chinese mercantilism, and the gods were quick to learn about doing business. Hansen wrote of a god who answered people's worries about a famine not by sending good harvests, but by assuming human form in order to broker grain supply deals.[27] In modern Singapore, the prevalent obsession is to win at the lottery, and an efficacious deity is one who knows how to pick lucky numbers for the state 4D (four digits) draw.

The direct intercession of gods acting through their statues is particularly apparent in Lin Weiping's report of worship in a village in southwestern Taiwan. When there was illness, Lin reports, the villagers would take home the temple images to keep close watch on the patient.[28] In modern Singapore, there is a similar tradition. *Fushen* (副身), literally "auxiliary bodies," are small replicas of the main altar image. The portable statues are taken out in religious processions when gods tour the precinct of the temple to bless the people and exorcise evil spirits, and they are installed in homes when worshippers need the focused attention of their gods, as in times of sickness. But there are cases that demonstrate people's even more direct dealings with statues as bodies of gods.

The Imperfect Deity (十不全老爷) is worshipped for good health, for as his statue shows, this god is willing to bear bodily imperfections, such as weak eyesight, an amputated leg, or crippled hand, on behalf of his worshippers (Figure 2, on the next page). Lin writes of villagers who believed in the efficacy of the physical substance of the image, scraping the wood of the statue or taking bits of red yarn from the hair on its head to incorporate these materials into medicines.[29] Far from performing the abstract function of being an aid for religious contemplation, the very material of the image was ingested in a form of worship that was meant to demand solutions to everyday worries and afflictions. Such close, physical relationships required gods who would think and act as humans, and anthropomorphism facilitated the spread of cults. However, personalization did more than just popularize the gods; anthropomorphism took on theological import as well. A brief incursion into art history traces the development of Chinese religious imagery in popular religion.

---

[26] Hansen, *Changing Gods in Medieval China*, pp. 48–58.

[27] Ibid., pp. 75–76.

[28] Lin, "Conceptualizing Gods through Statues," pp. 470–71.

[29] Ibid., p. 471.

Figure 2: The Imperfect Deity takes on the bodily pains of worshippers,
including poor eyesight, amputated leg, and crippled hand.
Photo by Raymond Goh, used with permission

ANTHROPOMORPHISM MADE ACCESSIBLE GODS

Early institutional Daoist and Confucian beliefs posited that heavenly forces, having neither matter nor form, could not be reproduced in three dimensions.[30] This is why the fifteenth-century Tian Tan (天坛) Temple of Heaven in Beijing, where the emperors of Ming and Qing (清, 1644–1911) worshipped, contains no images.

The idea of the formless heaven can be traced to the Shang cult of the ancestor, which was designed to achieve the impersonalization of the dead.[31] The ancestors were represented by wooden tablets that were worshipped in regulated rituals that did not allow any individuation of particular personalities. This practice was elaborated upon during the Zhou dynasty; the tradition of the ancestral tablet, a

---

[30] Ann Paludan, *Chinese Sculpture: A Great Tradition* (Chicago, IL: Serinda, 2006), p. 230.

[31] Keightley, "The Making of the Ancestors," pp. 26–29.

wooden plaque bearing little more than the name of the deceased, developed from forms of worship that evolved during this time.

It has been argued that the evolution of Daoist anthropomorphic images was inspired by Buddhist statuary. Ann Paludan records that the earliest known Buddhist images found in China date to the second century, whereas the Daoists began to make votive images only from the fifth century onward.[32] Although Daoism had developed from being a philosophy to becoming a religion from the first and second centuries, early religious Daoist statuary was confined to depictions of fantastic creatures and beings. Mythical sage–heroes, legendary rulers, and immortals were sometimes shown in relief, mainly on mortuary objects, but never in independent three-dimensional forms. The Chinese did, however, make figurative sculptures—significant for my thesis—but these only depicted ordinary human beings at work: warriors, servants, farmers, and dancing girls.[33] These lifelike figurines were placed inside tombs for the utilitarian purpose of serving the dead.

Daoist temples during the late Han (汉, 206 BCE–220 CE) period were small and primitive, with designations such as "Thatched Hut" and "Peaceful Cottage."[34] In the period of the Southern and Northern dynasties, Daoist temples began to receive some royal attention, but the sponsorship of Daoist art right up to the Sui (隋, 581–618) era came mainly from citizens: clerics, farmers, merchants, generals, and nobles. The majority of Daoist sculptures of the period were stelae, so that although the gods were depicted figuratively, these figures remained essentially two-dimensional representations.[35] This situation changed during the Tang (唐, 618–906) dynasty.

The royal family of Tang proclaimed its members to be descendants of Laozi (老子),[36] and to promulgate this notion, the rulers commissioned statues of Daoist deity Laozi modeled in their own images. Thus evolved the design for sacred sculptures in the round, and where Daoist imagery hitherto was concerned with the exposition of a god's spiritual states of consciousness, Tang statues were notable for their humanistic vividness. The Tang rulers distributed these images to the people for worship, and, in the process, set the standard for religious images produced by artisans throughout the country.[37]

The anthropomorphic design was firmly established by Song, and in the twelfth and thirteenth centuries, sculptures of the gods became far more human than ever before.[38] The statues became increasingly ornate over time, and Ming and Qing temple images wore brightly colored clothes and often had gilded faces.[39] Modern god statues are rich in iconographic detail. The gods are easily identified by emblematic props; for example, Nezha is unmistakable due to the Wind–Fire Wheels on which he rides and for his Fire-Tipped Lance and Universal Ring. The faces of the gods are painted in flesh tones or with designating colors; Guan Yu, for example, is

---

[32] Paludan, *Chinese Sculpture*, pp. 174–75, 229.

[33] Ibid., p. 183.

[34] Liu Yang, "Images for the Temple: Imperial Patronage in the Development of Tang Daoist Art," *Artibus Asiae* 61,2 (2001): 193–94.

[35] Ibid., p. 195.

[36] Ibid., p. 196.

[37] Ibid., pp. 252–55.

[38] Laurence Sickman, cited in Hansen, *Changing Gods*, p. 53.

[39] Paludan, *Chinese Sculpture*, pp. 461–62.

marked by his bright red face, a detail that reflects his description in popular literature.

Figure 3: The regal but impersonal Tiangong. Photo by Margaret Chan

Art history links the development of the human-like religious image with the popularization of religion. Before the first century in India, the Buddha was represented only in aniconic forms, such as by a tree or a wheel. In order to spread the religion to the masses, the purely intellectual concepts of the Buddha gave way to the iconolatry and rituals characteristic of the popular Indian non-Aryan consciousness.[40] Liu Yang has argued that the Tang rulers had sculpted gods exuding a warm humanity in order to popularize among the common people the ideology that claimed the divine ancestry for members of the ruling house.[41]

However, this did not mean that all the gods became human and accessible. The legacy of the notion of remote supreme beings, in contrast with the more responsive personal deities, continues in Chinese popular religion today. The statues of Tiangong (天公), the Heavenly Emperor, are not seen on home altars, and people

---

[40] Amanda K. Coomaraswamy, "The Origin of the Buddha Image," *The Art Bulletin* 9,4 (1927): 287, 297–300.

[41] Liu, "Images for the Temple."

instead address the open sky when they supplicate him. Tiangong's image on temple altars shows him seated, looking impassively into a board that he holds in front of his face. Tiangong is an emperor, so mortals cannot look directly into his eyes (Figure 3, on previous page).

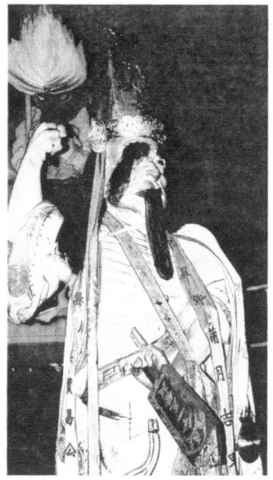

Figure 4: A vivid depiction of Da Er Ye Bo, Elder Deity of the Underworld.
Photo by Margaret Chan

In contrast, Da Er Ye Bo (大二爷伯, Elder and Second Granduncles), spirits of the underworld, are depicted as tall-and-thin, short-and-fat individuals with lolling tongues and staring eyes set beneath bushy eyebrows that grow down to their chins. Although the two are frightening to look upon, they are favorites with the people, who address them in familial terms and ply them with beer, stout, and cigarettes, and even smear opium on the mouths of the statues. Da Er Ye Bo, I am told, can always be counted on for lucky numbers. They are not so exalted as to be unaware that poor people need a little spare cash occasionally from the lottery (Figure 4, on previous page).

Ann Paludan also commented on an apparent degree of abstraction in the depiction of Chinese statuary that is in direct ratio to the rank of the subject; the lower the status of the person on which the statue was modeled, the more lifelike the representation. Thus, we see that the personalizing of the image follows a system for the establishment of social rank. For this reason, dead emperors and nobility were not depicted in statuary within their tombs, but lifelike figurines of servants and soldiers were found aplenty. The same concept apparently serves the depiction of ritual rank. The spirits that are to be served need not be manifest in a figurative image, but spirits who are to be put into service must be conjured up through the anthropomorphic image (see Figure 5, on next page).

Lin saw in the process of personification—when a block of wood is carved into a human shape—the symbolic process of objectifying a formless deity for worship.[42] I read beyond that, finding in anthropomorphism a strategy of magic that gives power to worshippers. Images are not chiefly made so that worshippers may contemplate or adore the gods; they are made to incarnate spirits that can be set to work. Nezha was incarnated to fight in the Zhou armies, and Zhang Fei's statue was set up in the temple so that he could capture Chi You's wife. My arguments consider the fact that anthropomorphism is unnecessary with regard to the notion of an object being imbued with a spirit. Stones and trees, for example, are often worshipped, but anthropomorphism is necessary to enable a spirit or divinity to enter the earthly realm to serve humans.

SPIRITS VESTED IN OBJECTS

Recalling the Nezha legend, we note that for the soul to be reincarnated, humans were obliged to make a lifelike statue that had to be worshipped for three years. When the process got truncated, the Fairy Primordial, being an immortal, could finish the job using a mystical arrangement of parts of the lotus plant. Also from the *Fengshen Yanyi*, we learn of another incident, during which an effigy is used to trap souls.

Yao Bin (姚宾) , who fought for Shang, used magic in an assassination attempt on Zhou Prime Minister Jiang Ziya (姜子牙). Yao created a Soul Snatching Trap that used a straw effigy marked with Jiang's name. At the head of the trap, Yao hung three lamps, and at its foot he placed seven lamps. Then Yao let down his hair, took up a sword, and walked in a sacred mandala pattern around the image. Yao performed this ritual three times a day, reciting charms and burning talismans in the hope that in twenty-one days he would be able to steal away the souls of Jiang, thus causing the latter's death.[43]

Yao's intention in creating a Jiang surrogate was to kill the man, not to trap his spirit to serve as a familiar. Thus, the straw effigy was not made to be as lifelike as the Nezha statue. The three lamps at the head, and the seven lamps at the foot, of the Jiang effigy, relate, respectively, to the three *hun* (魂) or *yang* (阳) elements that are contained in the bones of a person, and the seven *po* (魄) or *yin* (阴) elements that are contained in the flesh.

---

[42] Lin, "Conceptualizing Gods," pp. 464, 471.

[43] Gu, *Creation of the Gods*, pp. 475–83.

Figure 5: This nanny goddess' bare breasts and swollen belly unmistakably mark
her for duties as a wet-nurse, that is, her job is to see that babies do well.
Photo by Margaret Chan

In the grave, the *po* souls decompose together with the flesh, leaving the *hun* in
the bones. To ensure that the *po* spirits do not remain to harm the living descendants,
secondary burials of the remains may be ordered. The purpose of secondary burials
is purification, for it involves the collection of bones from the grave, which are
scraped clean of any remaining flesh before reburial.[44] Thus we note that ancestral
spirits can be both beneficent and harmful. This is probably the reason why, even as

[44] Emily Martin Ahern, *The Cult of the Dead in a Chinese Village* (Stanford, CA: Stanford
University Press, 1973), pp. 165, 175–76, 181, 203–5; James L. Watson, "Funeral Specialists in
Cantonese Society: Pollution, Performance, and Social Hierarchy," in *Death Ritual in Late
Imperial and Modern China*, ed, James Watson and Evelyn S. Rawski (Berkeley and Los Angeles,
CA, and London: University of California Press, 1988), pp. 113–14; Timothy Y. Tsu, "Toothless
Ancestors, Felicitous Descendants: The Rite of Secondary Burial in South Taiwan," *Asian
Folklore Studies* 59 (2000): 1–22.

early as the Shang era, ancestral worship was made to impersonalized spirit tablets, and Zhou rites prescribed the number of generations of ancestors that could receive worship according to the believer's social position. The royal house would offer sacrifices to no more than seven generations of ancestors, the common people only to two generations. An exception was made for the founding ancestor, for whom sacrifices continued to be made throughout all generations, for he was the symbol of the collective identity of the lineage.[45]

In order to facilitate continued worship, some families make personalized statues of their first ancestor and set these up in temples. These images keep the ancestors close to living descendants. Conversely, depersonalization in aniconic spirit tablets keeps the ancestral spirits at a distance from the mortal realm. This is why, while a photograph of the deceased is used to receive worship at the funeral, it must be replaced on the family altar in forty-nine days, at which time an impersonal plaque bearing the name of the deceased is set up in its stead.

Thus, the continuity of the spirit within the mortal realm depends on the existence of a body, and Yu argues as much, pointing to Han attempts at preserving the corpse.[46] In this light, it is interesting to note Eduard Erkes's suggestion that King Wu (武王) of Zhou might have taken the coffined body of his father, King Wen (文王), into battle against the Shang.[47] Erkes has also proposed that the personator (a living representative of the dead) or a wooden statue of the dead king, riding in a chariot, led the armies of the Zhou.[48]

THE IMAGE, AS DOES A CORPOREAL BODY, NEEDS SUSTENANCE

There is a crucial difference between the anthropomorphic image and aniconic ancestral tablet. In the tale of Ding Lan (丁兰), one of the Twenty-four Exemplars of Filial Piety, Ding Lan is said to have made an image of his dead mother (other versions say he made images of both his father and mother) and treated it as though it were the living woman. The image was no ordinary aniconic ancestral tablet, for we learn that Ding Lan's wife, jealous of her husband's attentions to the image, pricked the statue so that it bled. The reason why the statue of Ding Lan's mother had special corporeal qualities was because it was anthropomorphic, as we know from its representations in popular illustrations. A lacquer painting on a first-to-second-century basket found in Lolang shows Ding Lan with the clearly humanlike statue of his mother; art historian Dietrich Seckel judges this depiction to be the first pictorial document of a portrait statue in Chinese art.[49]

The fact that a spirit needs a body, or an image shaped like a body, in order to remain within the mortal realm is also illustrated by a ritual performed at secondary

---

[45] Yü Yingshih, "'O Soul, Come Back!' A Study in the Changing Conceptions of the Soul and Afterlife in Pre-Buddhist China," *Harvard Journal of Asiatic Studies*, 47,2 (1987): 379–80.

[46] Ibid., p. 380. For details on Han jade burial suits, see Edmund Capon and William MacQuitty, *Princes of Jade* (New York, NY: E. P. Dutton, 1973).

[47] Eduard Erkes, "Idols in Pre-Buddhist China," *Artibus Asiae* 3,1 (1928): 8.

[48] In Ssu-ma Ch'ien [Sima Qian, 司马迁], *The Grand Scribe's Record. I. The Basic Annals of Pre-Han China*, ed. William H. Nienhauser, Jr., trans. Cheng Tsaifa, Lu Zongli, William H. Nienhauser, Jr., and Robert Reynolds (Bloomington and Indianapolis, IN: Indiana University Press, 1994), p. 59, it is suggested that King Wu brought the spirit tablet of his father to war.

[49] Dietrich Seckel, "The Rise of Portraiture in Chinese Art," *Artibus Asiae* 53,1/2 (1993): 10.

burials in South Taiwan. When the remains from a primary burial are collected, the teeth are pulled from the skull and discarded without ceremony at the old grave. Timothy Tsu interprets this as an action meant to deny teeth to the spirit of the dead so that it cannot "eat up" the good fortune of the descendants: "Purification ... is thus achieved by a double denial: the ancestor is denied not just a fleshy human form but also the ability to 'eat' like a human. Not being able to eat presumably also prevents the ancestor from ever regaining the flesh he or she has lost, and so ensures his or her continual existence as a skeleton."[50] A reverse action, the feeding of a spirit through food offerings to its image, will ensure that the spirit remains tied to the mortal realm and is strong enough to be able to fulfill the wishes of devotees.

On the island of Pulau Ubin, in the northeast of the main island of Singapore, there is a temple to Dabogong (大伯公). Although Dabogong is regarded as a humble god of a locality, the Ubin community celebrates their Dabogong's feast day on Vesak day, usually reserved for celebrating the birthday of the Buddha, for they explain that their Dabogong has attained Buddhahood. When I attended the Dabogong Vesak day celebrations on May 31, 2008, I understood why the god had been promoted. His worshippers were zealous in their attentions, presenting Dabogong with much incense and paper money, a Chinese opera, and a pop concert, as well as a freshly slaughtered pig and a freshly slaughtered goat. Dabogong, although a Buddha, retained his Daoist appetite for meat.

These animal offerings are extraordinary in the Singapore context because presentations of raw meats have virtually disappeared on the mainland on account of food hygiene considerations. But this is not the only reason why these offerings deserve our attention. Symbolically, the pig and the goat served up in their elemental state constitute an offering usually reserved for Tiangong, the Heavenly Emperor. Foods served to gods follow ritual prescriptions. In China and Taiwan, Tiangong is likely to receive uncooked whole animals, always offered in an elemental state, so that if chicken is served, the bird would be raw, it would be plucked, but three feathers would be stuck into its rump. In Singapore, the higher spirits such as the San Qing (三清, Three Pure Ones), and also Tiangong, would be offered fruits and vegetarian foods. Warrior gods are served large slabs of cooked meats, such as whole roasted pigs or stewed duck and chicken, and spirit soldiers are served dishes cooked for human consumption. The offerings given to Dabogong on Pulau Ubin, which were fit for the Heavenly Emperor, proclaimed the humble god's rise to the highest rank on the divine hierarchy and added to Dabogong's *lingqi* or spirit power.

Thus, it is clear, the gods are, in fact, the souls of the dead. Statues are corporeal bodies (being literally called golden bodies, *jin shen*, 金身), through which spirits can enter the mortal realm to do work. Having bodies, the gods can move about the place. But when vested in the aniconic image of a typical ancestral tablet, spirits remain, as in the Soul Snatching Trap, locked to a spot. Philip Baity notes as much, arguing that the potential mobility of the deity being represented marks one difference between god images and ancestral tablets; while the ancestral tablet is kept only on the domestic altar of the eldest son (or in the ancestral hall), the statue may be carried about.[51] The practice of *fenshen* (分身, to have the body divided, as happens with the Singaporean *fushen* replica deities, discussed earlier), or of

---

[50] Tsu, "Toothless Ancestors," pp. 14–15.

[51] Philip C. Baity, "The Ranking of Gods in Chinese Folk Religion," *Asian Folklore Studies* 36,2 (1977): 76–78.

duplicating god images, allows the worship of the god to spread to different localities. Because replica statues allow the god to move about while, at the same time, remaining at headquarters, so to speak, this has permitted Singaporean deities to catch the travel bug. Many go on pilgrimages to the mother temple in China, flying in planes cradled in cloth slings worn about the neck of a devotee.

IMAGES AS PORTALS BETWEEN SPIRIT AND MORTAL REALMS

This notion of the mobility of gods reinforces Lin's arguments that one of the reasons for image worship is the localization of communal gods. The statues tie the gods to their temples. Lin recounts that the main god of the community he studied had, in fact, abandoned his statue in the village. However, the god remained responsive to the prayers of the community. Through his spirit medium, the god explained: "Were it not for this rotten piece of wood ... which makes my heart unable to part from you, I would simply leave."[52]

So far we have noted how the personalizations of religious statuary imbue remote gods with a humanity that helps to popularize their cults. Personification has allowed formless gods to be objectified, but, crucially, personalization is a magical process. The anthropomorphic image, as contrasted with the aniconic, gives a spirit the body it needs to exist and act in the human world, but the soul is not tied to that body. Gods appear to people in dreams, they possess and speak through spirit mediums, and, in fact, gods can be simultaneously present at different places at one time. Thus gods do not exist inside their images; remember that Nezha, for one, was away from his temple when his father smashed his image. Yet people go to temples and pray looking upon statues. The orthodox view is that the images are foci of attention; the popular reading is that statues are loci for the spirits. Both perspectives converge insofar as they recognize that gods are not confined within the physical limits of their statues, and they agree insofar as they sense the presence of gods who are close enough to listen and respond.

I have explained the situation by referring to the image of a deity as a metaphorical portal, rather than adopting the more popular suggestion, which defines the image as an abode for the god. Recalling the stories of Nezha and the Soul Snatching Trap set by Yao, we note how the image functions to enable transitions; Nezha's spirit has to become incarnate, Jiang's souls have to be snatched away from his corporeal body. In both instances, the image functions as a device that enables movements between spirit and mortal realms—hence, the notion of a portal. I have argued that it is the condition of the image as a "double-nature-being" that enables the image to serve as a magical doorway.[53] Continuing the metaphor, anthropomorphism may be regarded as the key that opens the door.

CONCLUSION: ANTHROPOMORPHISM AS A MAGICAL CONDITION

The magical condition of the "double-nature-being," is revealed when we learn that the Chinese regard the puppet—the anthropomorphic image imbued with the potential for motion—as the performing deity. This explains why the Chinese believe that puppets can self-animate. The character for puppet, *kui* 傀, is illustrative of its

---

[52] Lin, "Conceptualizing Gods," pp. 471–74.

[53] Chan, *Ritual Is Theatre*, pp. 133–49.

magical ontology as a "double-nature-being," for it combines the 亻, human radical, with that of 鬼, ghost or spirit. Even in Western linguistic terms we note a "double-nature-being" significance. First we note that 傀 is an iconic signifier, as Chinese characters are ideographs. The referent is the magical being that is both human and spirit in nature.

The power of puppets is revealed in an account in the *Shi Ji* (史记). The Shang emperor Wu Yi (武乙) committed sacrilege by fashioning idols, which he called heavenly gods. These images were clearly puppets and anthropomorphic, for Wu Yi drafted people to operate them so that he could play games of chance with them. When the heavenly gods did not win, Wu Yi humiliated them by hanging a leather pouch above them filled with blood, which he shot with an arrow, thereby drenching the images with blood. Wu Yi paid for this deed by being struck dead by lightning—a favorite revenge of the gods.[54]

Belief in the potency of puppets has not faded away completely in the present day; we note that the Chinese always store puppets with their faces covered to prevent them from self-animating. The guardian deity of Min (闽) language opera is Hai Ji (孩儿, pinyin Hai Er, Child), an articulated wooden child that many anecdotes describe coming to life, to run and play, at night. Marionette theater (as against glove puppetry or opera) is considered to be the most sacred form of theater by the Chinese. The string puppets are seen as animated god statues, and the combination of the anthropomorphic image with mobility (as if quickened by the spirit) is the reason why the puppets are the most powerfully exorcistic of ritual devices. Pregnant women do not watch marionette theater lest the spirit of the puppet enter the womb and the child be born floppy, like a marionette.

The belief in the efficacy of the puppet is not surprising, for it appears as an animated wooden deity. But the human actor wearing a mask has also been designated as *kui* (傀),[55] that is, as "double-nature-being." Poo Muchou writes that the character 鬼 appears on oracle bone inscriptions as, possibly, the graphic representation of the death mask or the mask of a shaman.[56] Thus the character 傀 is an ideograph of a person wearing an exorcistic mask. The mask enables the human actor to become the image of the character portrayed, and is therefore a device of sacral transmogrification. *Nuo* (傩) drama traces its origins to the performances of ancient shamans wearing masks. Till today, *Nuo* masks are revered as the very gods themselves and are kept in temples. Before a performance, the masks are paraded through the village, and people make offerings of food and incense to them. Actors pray to the gods to possess them, and when they don the masks, they are transmogrified into *xi shen* (戏神), the gods of performances themselves.[57]

The tradition of the mask acting as a sacral device of transmogrification continues in modern Min theater rituals, when the god of fortune himself opens the show. He is an actor who becomes the anthropomorphic image of the god by the

---

[54] S. Ch'ien, *The Grand Scribe's Record*, p. 49.

[55] William Dolby, "The Origins of Chinese Puppetry," *Bulletin of the School of Oriental and African Studies* 41,1 (1978): 98.

[56] Poo Muchou, "The Concept of Ghost in Ancient Chinese Religion," in *Religion and Chinese Society, 1: Ancient and Medieval China*, ed. J. Lagerway (Hong Kong: The Chinese University of Hong Kong and École française d'Extrême-Orient, 2006), p. 175.

[57] Yu Qiuyu, "Some Observations on the Aesthetics of Primitive Chinese Theatre," trans. Hu Dongsheng, Elizabeth Wichmann, and Gregg Richardson, *Asian Theatre Journal* 6,1 (1989): 17.

wearing of a mask. After the ritual, the mask is wrapped in a red cloth and stored away, both to keep the mask out of the gaze of common folk, as well as to contain the power of the mask. The tradition of the masked actor is perpetuated in the painted faces of Chinese opera performers.[58] Daoist priest Jave Wu told me how, in the past, sacred characters would be written on the face of the actor before it was painted in order to protect the actors from possession by the spirits. Then, opera garments would often have the phrase *jie yong* (借用), "borrowed for use," written on the inner hem, to reflect the belief that the costumes rightfully belonged to spirits.

On the opera stage today, the mystical tradition of the painted mask is now largely lost, and only the makeup for Guan Yu (who we met in the tale of the salt lake monster) is believed to be transformative. However, the painted mask as a ritual device that allows a spirit to enter into a mortal being is employed in contemporary spirit-possession ceremonies by *jiajiang* exorcists (家将, infernal generals). *Jiajiang* are Taiwanese exorcists who, when possessed, are held to be somewhere between being humans and gods or ghosts.[59] They are dressed in costumes and wear distinctive painted masks that transform them into the image of the possessing demigods. The statue of a god, the puppet, the masked *Nuo* actor, the painted and costumed *jiajiang* exorcist; all are images, "double-nature-beings," and, as such, are magical portals that allow the spirit to enter into the earthly realm to serve man.

---

[58] Rinnie Tang, David Harris, and Bernard Schmidt, "From the Funeral Mask to the Painted Face of the Chinese Theatre," *TDR: The Drama Review—Masks* 26,4 (Winter 1982): 60–63.

[59] Donald S. Sutton, "Transmission in Popular Religion: The Jiajiang Festival Troupe of Southern Taiwan," in *Unruly Gods: Divinity and Society in China*, ed. Meir Shahar and Robert P. Weller (Honolulu, HI: University of Hawaii Press, 1996), pp. 212–13. See also Donald S. Sutton, *Steps of Perfection: Exorcistic Performers and Chinese Religion in Twentieth-Century Taiwan* (Cambridge, MA and London: Harvard University Asia Center, 2003).

CONTRIBUTORS

Julius BAUTISTA (Editor) is Senior Lecturer at the Department of Southeast Asian Studies of the National University of Singapore (NUS). He received his PhD in anthropology and cultural history at the Australian National University, and has subsequently published on religious practice in Southeast Asia, with a focus on Christian iconography, religious piety, and the relationship between religion and the state. He is author of *Figuring Catholicism: An Ethnohistory of the Santo Niño de Cebu* (Ateneo, 2010) and co-editor (with Francis Lim) of *Christianity and the State in Asia: Complicity and Conflict* (Routledge, 2009). Dr. Bautista is also an associate of the NUS Asia Research Institute (ARI) "Religion and Globalisation in Asian Contexts" Cluster.

Sandra CATE is an anthropologist and folklorist at San Jose State University in California. She explores art, expressive and material culture, religion, tourism, and concepts of heritage in Southeast Asia and in the diaspora. She has written about Buddhist temple architecture and murals, narrative festival scrolls, silk tourism, Mien/Yao embroidery, and Bangkok traffic jams. Her recent work focuses on contemporary art practices in Southeast Asia. Cate wrote *Making Merit, Making Art: A Thai Temple in Wimbledon* (University of Hawaii Press, 2003) and, with H. Leedom Lefferts, is working on a book entitled *Buddhist Storytelling in Thailand and Laos,* which will be published by the Asian Civilisations Museum, Singapore.

Margaret CHAN is Associate Professor of Theatre/Performance Studies (Practice) in the School of Social Sciences, Singapore Management University. She received a doctorate in performance studies from the University of London in 2002, after distinguished careers in acting and journalism in Singapore. Her revised dissertation, *Ritual is Theatre, Theatre is Ritual: Tang-ki Chinese Spirit Medium Worship*, was published in 2006. Her research focuses on Chinese popular religion in the Southeast Asian Chinese diaspora, with a special focus on Indonesia.

Liana CHUA is Lecturer in Anthropology at Brunel University, London. She works on conversion to Christianity, ethnic citizenship, landscape, resettlement and conservation in Malaysian Borneo, and on artefact-oriented theory and museology more broadly. She was formerly a Research Fellow in Social Anthropology at Gonville and Caius College, University of Cambridge, where she taught courses on artefact-oriented theory, performance, and museology, and has worked on nineteenth-century Bornean collections and photographs at the University Museum of Archaeology and Anthropology. She is the author of *The Christianity of Culture: Conversion, Ethnic Citizenship, and the Matter of Religion in Malaysian Borneo* (Palgrave-

McMillan, 2012), and co-editor (with Mark Elliott) of *Distributed Objects: Meaning and Mattering after Alfred Gell* (forthcoming in 2013).

Cecilia S. DE LA PAZ is an Associate Professor at the Department of Art Studies, College of Arts and Letters, University of the Philippines (Diliman), where she serves as Department Chair since 2009. She holds a MA in Art History (1993) and PhD in Philippine Studies (2011) from UP. She is an independent curator and recipient of fellowships from the Asian Public Intellectuals (2001) of the Nippon Foundation and the Salzburg Global Seminar (2011). She has published articles for academic journals dealing with cultural studies, focusing on the relationship of museums and local communities, as well as performativity and religious sculptures.

Alexandra DE MERSAN holds a PhD in Social Anthropology from the Ecole des Hautes Etudes en Sciences Sociales (EHESS, Paris). Her research in Burma has covered such subjects as material religion, ritual, territory, migration and socio-religious dynamics, ethnicity, and nation-building. She is an associate member of the Centre Asie du Sud-Est (Paris), and is currently working as a researcher within a Franco-German team on a program entitled "Local Traditions and World Religions: The Appropriation of 'Religion' in Southeast Asia and Beyond." She is also a Lecturer in Anthropology at the Institut National des Langues et Civilisations Orientales (INALCO).

Johan FISCHER is an Associate Professor in the Department of Society and Globalisation, Roskilde University, Denmark. He has conducted research on modern Islam and consumer culture in Southeast Asia and Europe, with a central focus on the proliferation of *halal* commodities on a global scale. His publications include the monograph "Proper Islamic Consumption: Shopping among the Malays in Modern Malaysia" (2008) and the monograph "On the Halal Frontier: A Global Religious Market in London," which forms part of Palgrave Macmillan's book series "Contemporary Anthropology of Religion."

Janet HOSKINS is Professor of Anthropology at the University of Southern California. She is the author of *The Play of Time* (University of California Press, 1994, winner of the 1996 Benda Prize in Southeast Asian Studies), and *Biographical Objects: How Things Tell the Stories of People's Lives* (Routledge, 1998), and is the contributing editor of *Headhunting and the Social Imagination in Southeast Asia* (Stanford, 1998), and editor of *Fragments from Forests and Libraries* (Carolina Academic Press, 2001). She has published several articles on Caodaism in Vietnam and California, and has also researched and produced an ethnographic documentary titled "The Left Eye of God: Caodaism Travels from Vietnam to California." She teaches in the Visual Studies program at USC and is on the advisory board of USC's Center for Religion and Civic Culture.

Klemens KARLSSON received his PhD from Uppsala University in 2000. His research has focused on religion and visual art in South and Southeast Asia. His special interest has been in the so-called aniconic Buddhist art in early India and, more recently, in Buddhist visual culture and ethnicity in the borderlands of Myanmar/Burma, Thailand, Laos, and China, especially concerning the Shan/Tai Khun people. He is today Head of the Department of Publication Infrastructure,

School of Education and Communication in Engineering Science at KTH Royal Institute of Technology, Stockholm, and has a special interest in scholarly communication, peer review, open access, and bibliometrics.

Laurel KENDALL holds a PhD with distinction from Columbia University, is Curator of Asian Ethnographic Collections at the American Museum of Natural History, and Adjunct Professor at Columbia University. Dr. Kendall is a specialist on Korea who also does comparative work in Vietnam, and her many works include *Shamans, Housewives, and Other Restless Spirits* (University of Hawaii Press, 1985), and (co-edited with Charles F. Keyes and Helen Hardacre), *Asian Visions Authority: Religion and the Modern States of East and Southeast Asia* (University of Hawaii Press, 1994). Dr. Kendall is currently editor of the "Contemporary Anthropology of Religion" series (Palgrave) sponsored by the Society for the Anthropology of Religion, American Anthropological Association, and President of the Society for East Asian Anthropology of the American Anthropological Association.

H. Leedom LEFFERTS is Professor of Anthropology, Emeritus, at Drew University. Madison, New Jersey. He has been a Fulbright scholar in Thailand and Laos and conducted cultural anthropological fieldwork in mainland Southeast Asia and southern China since 1970. In 2011–12, he held a Senior Research Fellowship at the Asian Civilisations Museum, Singapore, for work on Vessantara scrolls. He co-authored *Textiles and the Tai Experience in Southeast Asia* (Textile Museum, 1994), and has written numerous articles on Tai textiles and textile technology as symbols of women's place in Buddhism. More recently, with Louise Allison Cort, he has conducted fieldwork on the technology of indigenous Southeast Asian ceramic production.

NGUYỄN Thị Thu Hương is secretary of the Academic Council of the National Museum of History, Hanoi, and a researcher in the Department of Cultural Heritage of Vietnam. During her time at the Vietnam Museum of Ethnology, she contributed her skills as curator, interpreter, fund-raiser, and project manager. She is the author of "Museums and Universities: Should there be a collaboration?" in *Proceedings of the Conference on "Renovating Approaches to Ethnographic Museums and Collections"* (Vietnam Museum of Ethnology, 2002), and co-editor of *Tai Textiles in the Mekong Region: Continuity and Change* (Vietnam Museum of Ethnology, 2006). She holds an MA in Museum Anthropology from Columbia University, in New York.

Anthony REID is Emeritus Professor of History at the Australian National University's (ANU) College of Asia and the Pacific, and a Visiting Fellow in its Department of Political and Social Change. His work over many years has focused on the early modern history of Southeast Asia, nationalism, minorities, and social, economic, and religious history, with particular interest in Indonesia and Malaysia. He was a member of ANU's former Department of Pacific and Asian History for many years until 1999, before moving offshore as founding director, successively, of the Center for Southeast Asian Studies at the University of California, Los Angeles, and of the Asia Research Institute of the National University of Singapore.

Richard A. RUTH is an Assistant Professor of Southeast Asian History at the United States Naval Academy in Annapolis, Maryland. A cultural historian of Thailand and

Vietnam, he earned his doctorate from the Department of History at Cornell University, Ithaca, NY, where he was active in the Southeast Asian Program. Previously, he worked as research assistant at Yale University's Cambodian Genocide Project, and as field agent for nongovernmental aid organizations in Thailand, Vietnam, Cambodia, and India. He is the author of *In Buddha's Company: Thai Soldiers in the Vietnam War* (University of Hawaii Press, 2011).

Kenneth SILLANDER is Senior Lecturer in Sociology at the Swedish School of Social Science, University of Helsinki. He received his PhD in social anthropology from the University of Helsinki in 2004. He has done fieldwork among the Bentian of Indonesian Borneo since 1993 and published articles on Bentian social organization, rituals, naming practices, and ethnicity. He is co-editor, with Thomas Gibson, of *Anarchic Solidarity: Autonomy, Egalitarianism, and Fellowship in Southeast Asia* (Yale University Southeast Asia Studies, 2011), and co-editor, with Pascal Couderc, of *Ancestors in Borneo Societies: Death, Transformation, and Social Immortality* (NIAS, 2012).

VŨ Thị Thanh Tâm is a researcher in the Department of Delta and Sea at the Vietnam Museum of Ethnology. Her research concerns wood-carving and religious statue production in contemporary Vietnam. Her publications include "Painting in Ngo Trang Hamlet," in *Researches of the Vietnam Museum of Ethnology* 5, 2005; "Wood Carving in Long Dinh Hamlet," in *The South* (Land and Humanity Press, 2006); and "Carving Statues in Son Dong Village," in *Review of Ethnology* (Vietnam, 2008).

YEOH Seng Guan holds a PhD from the University of Edinburgh. He is Senior Lecturer at the School of Arts and Social Sciences, Monash University (Sunway Campus, Malaysia). With a research focus in urban anthropology in the Southeast Asian region, he has conducted fieldwork in various localities in Malaysia, the Philippines, and Indonesia. Recent publications include book chapters in Joshua Barker et al., eds., *Figures of Southeast Asian Modernity* (University of Hawaii Press, forthcoming), and Francis Loh K. W., ed., *Building Bridges, Crossing Boundaries: Everyday Forms of Inter-ethnic Peace Building in Malaysia* (2010). Seng Guan also produces ethnographic documentaries.

SOUTHEAST ASIA PROGRAM PUBLICATIONS

Cornell University

Studies on Southeast Asia

Number 58   *The Spirit of Things: Materiality and Religious Diversity in Southeast Asia*, ed. Julius Bautista. 2012. ISBN 970-0-87727-758-3 (pb.)

Number 57   *Demographic Change in Southeast Asia: Recent Histories and Future Directions*, ed. Lindy Williams and Michael Philip Guest. 2012. ISBN 978-0-87727-757-6 (pb.)

Number 56   *Modern and Contemporary Southeast Asian Art: An Anthology*, ed. Nora A. Taylor and Boreth Ly. 2012. ISBN 978-0-87727-756-9 (pb.)

Number 55   *Glimpses of Freedom: Independent Cinema in Southeast Asia*, ed. May Adadol Ingawanij and Benjamin McKay. 2012. ISBN 978-0-87727-755-2 (pb.)

Number 54   *Student Activism in Malaysia: Crucible, Mirror, Sideshow*, Meredith L. Weiss. 2011. ISBN 978-0-87727-754-5 (pb.)

Number 53   *Political Authority and Provincial Identity in Thailand: The Making of Banharn-buri*, Yoshinori Nishizaki. 2011. ISBN 978-0-87727-753-8 (pb.)

Number 52   *Vietnam and the West: New Approaches*, ed. Wynn Wilcox. 2010. ISBN 978-0-87727-752-1 (pb.)

Number 51   *Cultures at War: The Cold War and Cultural Expression in Southeast Asia*, ed. Tony Day and Maya H. T. Liem. 2010. ISBN 978-0-87727-751-4 (pb.)

Number 50   *State of Authority: The State in Society in Indonesia*, ed. Gerry van Klinken and Joshua Barker. 2009. ISBN 978-0-87727-750-7 (pb.)

Number 49   *Phan Châu Trinh and His Political Writings*, Phan Châu Trinh, ed. and trans. Vinh Sinh. 2009. ISBN 978-0-87727-749-1 (pb.)

Number 48   *Dependent Communities: Aid and Politics in Cambodia and East Timor*, Caroline Hughes. 2009. ISBN 978-0-87727-748-4 (pb.)

Number 47   *A Man Like Him: Portrait of the Burmese Journalist, Journal Kyaw U Chit Maung*, Journal Kyaw Ma Ma Lay, trans. Ma Thanegi, 2008. ISBN 978-0-87727-747-7 (pb.)

Number 46   *At the Edge of the Forest: Essays on Cambodia, History, and Narrative in Honor of David Chandler*, ed. Anne Ruth Hansen and Judy Ledgerwood. 2008. ISBN 978-0-87727-746-0 (pb)

Number 45   *Conflict, Violence, and Displacement in Indonesia*, ed. Eva-Lotta E. Hedman. 2008. ISBN 978-0-87727-745-3 (pb.)

Number 44   *Friends and Exiles: A Memoir of the Nutmeg Isles and the Indonesian Nationalist Movement*, Des Alwi, ed. Barbara S. Harvey. 2008. ISBN 978-0-877277-44-6 (pb.)

Number 43   *Early Southeast Asia: Selected Essays*, O. W. Wolters, ed. Craig J. Reynolds. 2008. 255 pp. ISBN 978-0-877277-43-9 (pb.)

Number 42   *Thailand: The Politics of Despotic Paternalism* (revised edition), Thak Chaloemtiarana. 2007. 284 pp. ISBN 0-8772-7742-7 (pb.)

Number 41   *Views of Seventeenth-Century Vietnam: Christoforo Borri on Cochinchina and Samuel Baron on Tonkin*, ed. Olga Dror and K. W. Taylor. 2006. 290 pp. ISBN 0-8772-7741-9 (pb.)

Number 23   *Nguyễn Cochinchina: Southern Vietnam in the Seventeenth and Eighteenth Centuries*, Li Tana. 1998. Second printing, 2002. 194 pp. ISBN 0-87727-722-2.

Number 22   *Young Heroes: The Indonesian Family in Politics*, Saya S. Shiraishi. 1997. 183 pp. ISBN 0-87727-721-4.

Number 21   *Interpreting Development: Capitalism, Democracy, and the Middle Class in Thailand*, John Girling. 1996. 95 pp. ISBN 0-87727-720-6.

Number 20   *Making Indonesia*, ed. Daniel S. Lev, Ruth McVey. 1996. 201 pp. ISBN 0-87727-719-2.

Number 19   *Essays into Vietnamese Pasts*, ed. K. W. Taylor, John K. Whitmore. 1995. 288 pp. ISBN 0-87727-718-4.

Number 18   *In the Land of Lady White Blood: Southern Thailand and the Meaning of History*, Lorraine M. Gesick. 1995. 106 pp. ISBN 0-87727-717-6.

Number 17   *The Vernacular Press and the Emergence of Modern Indonesian Consciousness*, Ahmat Adam. 1995. 220 pp. ISBN 0-87727-716-8.

Number 16   *The Nan Chronicle*, trans., ed. David K. Wyatt. 1994. 158 pp. ISBN 0-87727-715-X.

Number 15   *Selective Judicial Competence: The Cirebon-Priangan Legal Administration, 1680–1792*, Mason C. Hoadley. 1994. 185 pp. ISBN 0-87727-714-1.

Number 14   *Sjahrir: Politics and Exile in Indonesia*, Rudolf Mrázek. 1994. 536 pp. ISBN 0-87727-713-3.

Number 13   *Fair Land Sarawak: Some Recollections of an Expatriate Officer*, Alastair Morrison. 1993. 196 pp. ISBN 0-87727-712-5.

Number 12   *Fields from the Sea: Chinese Junk Trade with Siam during the Late Eighteenth and Early Nineteenth Centuries*, Jennifer Cushman. 1993. 206 pp. ISBN 0-87727-711-7.

Number 11   *Money, Markets, and Trade in Early Southeast Asia: The Development of Indigenous Monetary Systems to AD 1400*, Robert S. Wicks. 1992. 2nd printing 1996. 354 pp., 78 tables, illus., maps. ISBN 0-87727-710-9.

Number 10   *Tai Ahoms and the Stars: Three Ritual Texts to Ward Off Danger*, trans., ed. B. J. Terwiel, Ranoo Wichasin. 1992. 170 pp. ISBN 0-87727-709-5.

Number 9   *Southeast Asian Capitalists*, ed. Ruth McVey. 1992. 2nd printing 1993. 220 pp. ISBN 0-87727-708-7.

Number 8   *The Politics of Colonial Exploitation: Java, the Dutch, and the Cultivation System*, Cornelis Fasseur, ed. R. E. Elson, trans. R. E. Elson, Ary Kraal. 1992. 2nd printing 1994. 266 pp. ISBN 0-87727-707-9.

Number 7   *A Malay Frontier: Unity and Duality in a Sumatran Kingdom*, Jane Drakard. 1990. 2nd printing 2003. 215 pp. ISBN 0-87727-706-0.

Number 6   *Trends in Khmer Art*, Jean Boisselier, ed. Natasha Eilenberg, trans. Natasha Eilenberg, Melvin Elliott. 1989. 124 pp., 24 plates. ISBN 0-87727-705-2.

Number 5   *Southeast Asian Ephemeris: Solar and Planetary Positions, A.D. 638–2000*, J. C. Eade. 1989. 175 pp. ISBN 0-87727-704-4.

Number 3   *Thai Radical Discourse: The Real Face of Thai Feudalism Today*, Craig J. Reynolds. 1987. 2nd printing 1994. 186 pp. ISBN 0-87727-702-8.

Number 1   *The Symbolism of the Stupa,* Adrian Snodgrass. 1985. Revised with index, 1988. 3rd printing 1998. 469 pp. ISBN 0-87727-700-1.

SEAP Series

Number 23   *Possessed by the Spirits: Mediumship in Contemporary Vietnamese Communities.* 2006. 186 pp. ISBN 0-877271-41-0 (pb).

Number 22   *The Industry of Marrying Europeans,* Vũ Trọng Phụng, trans. Thúy Tranviet. 2006. 66 pp. ISBN 0-877271-40-2 (pb).

Number 21   *Securing a Place: Small-Scale Artisans in Modern Indonesia,* Elizabeth Morrell. 2005. 220 pp. ISBN 0-877271-39-9.

Number 20   *Southern Vietnam under the Reign of Minh Mạng (1820-1841): Central Policies and Local Response,* Choi Byung Wook. 2004. 226pp. ISBN 0-0-877271-40-2.

Number 19   *Gender, Household, State: Đổi Mới in Việt Nam,* ed. Jayne Werner and Danièle Bélanger. 2002. 151 pp. ISBN 0-87727-137-2.

Number 18   *Culture and Power in Traditional Siamese Government,* Neil A. Englehart. 2001. 130 pp. ISBN 0-87727-135-6.

Number 17   *Gangsters, Democracy, and the State,* ed. Carl A. Trocki. 1998. Second printing, 2002. 94 pp. ISBN 0-87727-134-8.

Number 16   *Cutting across the Lands: An Annotated Bibliography on Natural Resource Management and Community Development in Indonesia, the Philippines, and Malaysia,* ed. Eveline Ferretti. 1997. 329 pp. ISBN 0-87727-133-X.

Number 15   *The Revolution Falters: The Left in Philippine Politics after 1986,* ed. Patricio N. Abinales. 1996. Second printing, 2002. 182 pp. ISBN 0-87727-132-1.

Number 14   *Being Kammu: My Village, My Life,* Damrong Tayanin. 1994. 138 pp., 22 tables, illus., maps. ISBN 0-87727-130-5.

Number 13   *The American War in Vietnam,* ed. Jayne Werner, David Hunt. 1993. 132 pp. ISBN 0-87727-131-3.

Number 12   *The Voice of Young Burma,* Aye Kyaw. 1993. 92 pp. ISBN 0-87727-129-1.

Number 11   *The Political Legacy of Aung San,* ed. Josef Silverstein. Revised edition 1993. 169 pp. ISBN 0-87727-128-3.

Number 10   *Studies on Vietnamese Language and Literature: A Preliminary Bibliography,* Nguyen Dinh Tham. 1992. 227 pp. ISBN 0-87727-127-5.

Number 8   *From PKI to the Comintern, 1924–1941: The Apprenticeship of the Malayan Communist Party,* Cheah Boon Kheng. 1992. 147 pp. ISBN 0-87727-125-9.

Number 7   *Intellectual Property and US Relations with Indonesia, Malaysia, Singapore, and Thailand,* Elisabeth Uphoff. 1991. 67 pp. ISBN 0-87727-124-0.

Number 6   *The Rise and Fall of the Communist Party of Burma (CPB),* Bertil Lintner. 1990. 124 pp. 26 illus., 14 maps. ISBN 0-87727-123-2.

Number 5   *Japanese Relations with Vietnam: 1951–1987,* Masaya Shiraishi. 1990. 174 pp. ISBN 0-87727-122-4.

Number 3   *Postwar Vietnam: Dilemmas in Socialist Development,* ed. Christine White, David Marr. 1988. 2nd printing 1993. 260 pp. ISBN 0-87727-120-8.

Number 2   *The Dobama Movement in Burma (1930–1938)*, Khin Yi. 1988. 160 pp.
            ISBN 0-87727-118-6.

Cornell Modern Indonesia Project Publications

All CMIP titles available at http://cmip.library.cornell.edu

Number 75   *A Tour of Duty: Changing Patterns of Military Politics in Indonesia in the
            1990s.* Douglas Kammen and Siddharth Chandra. 1999. 99 pp.
            ISBN 0-87763-049-6.

Number 74   *The Roots of Acehnese Rebellion 1989–1992*, Tim Kell. 1995. 103 pp.
            ISBN 0-87763-040-2.

Number 72   *Popular Indonesian Literature of the Qur'an*, Howard M. Federspiel. 1994.
            170 pp. ISBN 0-87763-038-0.

Number 71   *A Javanese Memoir of Sumatra, 1945–1946: Love and Hatred in the
            Liberation War*, Takao Fusayama. 1993. 150 pp. ISBN 0-87763-037-2.

Number 69   *The Road to Madiun: The Indonesian Communist Uprising of 1948*,
            Elizabeth Ann Swift. 1989. 120 pp. ISBN 0-87763-035-6.

Number 68   *Intellectuals and Nationalism in Indonesia: A Study of the Following
            Recruited by Sutan Sjahrir in Occupation Jakarta*, J. D. Legge. 1988.
            159 pp. ISBN 0-87763-034-8.

Number 67   *Indonesia Free: A Biography of Mohammad Hatta*, Mavis Rose. 1987.
            252 pp. ISBN 0-87763-033-X.

Number 66   *Prisoners at Kota Cane*, Leon Salim, trans. Audrey Kahin. 1986. 112 pp.
            ISBN 0-87763-032-1.

Number 64   *Suharto and His Generals: Indonesia's Military Politics, 1975–1983*, David
            Jenkins. 1984. 4th printing 1997. 300 pp. ISBN 0-87763-030-5.

Number 62   *Interpreting Indonesian Politics: Thirteen Contributions to the Debate, 1964–
            1981*, ed. Benedict Anderson, Audrey Kahin, intro. Daniel S. Lev. 1982.
            3rd printing 1991. 172 pp. ISBN 0-87763-028-3.

Number 60   *The Minangkabau Response to Dutch Colonial Rule in the Nineteenth
            Century*, Elizabeth E. Graves. 1981. 157 pp. ISBN 0-87763-000-3.

Number 57   *Permesta: Half a Rebellion*, Barbara S. Harvey. 1977. 174 pp.
            ISBN 0-87763-003-8.

Number 52   *A Preliminary Analysis of the October 1 1965, Coup in Indonesia (Prepared
            in January 1966)*, Benedict R. Anderson, Ruth T. McVey, assist.
            Frederick P. Bunnell. 1971. 3rd printing 1990. 174 pp.
            ISBN 0-87763-008-9.

Number 48   *Nationalism, Islam and Marxism*, Soekarno, intro. Ruth T. McVey. 1970.

Number 37   *Mythology and the Tolerance of the Javanese*, Benedict R. O'G. Anderson.
            2nd edition, 1996. Reprinted 2004. 104 pp., 65 illus. ISBN 0-87763-041-0.

Copublished Titles

The Ambiguous Allure of the West: Traces of the Colonial in Thailand, ed. Rachel V. Harrison and Peter A. Jackson. Copublished with Hong Kong University Press. 2010. ISBN 978-0-87727-608-1 (pb.)

The Many Ways of Being Muslim: Fiction by Muslim Filipinos, ed. Coeli Barry. Copublished with Anvil Publishing, Inc., the Philippines. 2008. ISBN 978-0-87727-605-0 (pb.)

Language Texts

INDONESIAN

Beginning Indonesian through Self-Instruction, John U. Wolff, Dédé Oetomo, Daniel Fietkiewicz. 3rd revised edition 1992. Vol. 1. 115 pp. ISBN 0-87727-529-7. Vol. 2. 434 pp. ISBN 0-87727-530-0. Vol. 3. 473 pp. ISBN 0-87727-531-9.

Indonesian Readings, John U. Wolff. 1978. 4th printing 1992. 480 pp. ISBN 0-87727-517-3

Indonesian Conversations, John U. Wolff. 1978. 3rd printing 1991. 297 pp. ISBN 0-87727-516-5

Formal Indonesian, John U. Wolff. 2nd revised edition 1986. 446 pp. ISBN 0-87727-515-7

TAGALOG

Pilipino through Self-Instruction, John U. Wolff, Maria Theresa C. Centeno, Der-Hwa V. Rau. 1991. Vol. 1. 342 pp. ISBN 0-87727—525-4. Vol. 2., revised 2005, 378 pp. ISBN 0-87727-526-2. Vol 3., revised 2005, 431 pp. ISBN 0-87727-527-0. Vol. 4. 306 pp. ISBN 0-87727-528-9.

THAI

A. U. A. Language Center Thai Course, J. Marvin Brown. Originally published by the American University Alumni Association Language Center, 1974. Reissued by Cornell Southeast Asia Program, 1991, 1992. Book 1. 267 pp. ISBN 0-87727-506-8. Book 2. 288 pp. ISBN 0-87727-507-6. Book 3. 247 pp. ISBN 0-87727-508-4.

A. U. A. Language Center Thai Course, Reading and Writing Text (mostly reading), 1979. Reissued 1997. 164 pp. ISBN 0-87727-511-4.

A. U. A. Language Center Thai Course, Reading and Writing Workbook (mostly writing), 1979. Reissued 1997. 99 pp. ISBN 0-87727-512-2.

KHMER

Cambodian System of Writing and Beginning Reader, Franklin E. Huffman. Originally published by Yale University Press, 1970. Reissued by Cornell Southeast Asia Program, 4th printing 2002. 365 pp. ISBN 0-300-01314-0.

Modern Spoken Cambodian, Franklin E. Huffman, assist. Charan Promchan, Chhom-Rak Thong Lambert. Originally published by Yale University Press, 1970. Reissued by Cornell Southeast Asia Program, 3rd printing 1991. 451 pp. ISBN 0-300-01316-7.

Intermediate Cambodian Reader, ed. Franklin E. Huffman, assist. Im Proum. Originally published by Yale University Press, 1972. Reissued by Cornell Southeast Asia Program, 1988. 499 pp. ISBN 0-300-01552-6.

Cambodian Literary Reader and Glossary, Franklin E. Huffman, Im Proum. Originally published by Yale University Press, 1977. Reissued by Cornell Southeast Asia Program, 1988. 494 pp. ISBN 0-300-02069-4.

HMONG

White Hmong-English Dictionary, Ernest E. Heimbach. 1969. 8th printing, 2002. 523 pp. ISBN 0-87727-075-9.

VIETNAMESE

Intermediate Spoken Vietnamese, Franklin E. Huffman, Tran Trong Hai. 1980. 3rd printing 1994. ISBN 0-87727-500-9.

Proto-Austronesian Phonology with Glossary, John U. Wolff, 2 volumes, 2011. ISBN vol. I, 978-0-87727-532-9. ISBN vol. II, 978-0-87727-533-6.

To order, please contact:
Mail:
Cornell University Press Services
750 Cascadilla Street
PO Box 6525
Ithaca, NY 14851 USA

E-mail: orderbook@cupserv.org

Phone/Fax, Monday–Friday, 8 am – 5 pm (Eastern US):
Phone: 607 277 2211 or 800 666 2211 (US, Canada)
Fax: 607 277 6292 or 800 688 2877 (US, Canada)

Order through our online bookstore at:
www.einaudi.cornell.edu / southeastasia / publications /